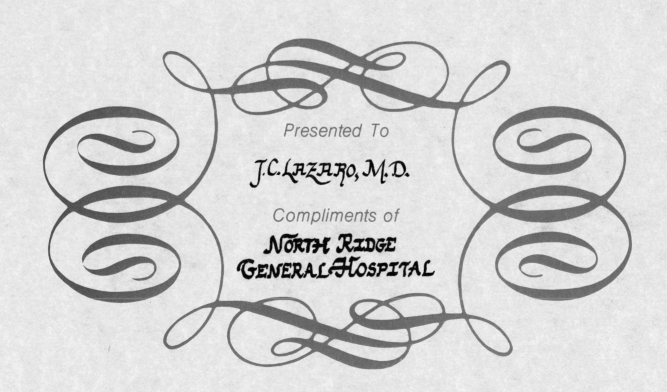

Presented To

J.C. Lazaro, M.D.

Compliments of

**North Ridge
General Hospital**

FORT LAUDERDALE
AND BROWARD COUNTY

FORT LAUDERDALE
AND BROWARD COUNTY

AN ILLUSTRATED HISTORY BY STUART B. McIVER

Picture Research
by Rodney E. Dillon, Jr., and Daniel T. Hobby
"Partners in Progress"
by Bill Luening
Produced in cooperation with
the Fort Lauderdale Historical Society, Inc.

Windsor Publications, Inc.
Woodland Hills, California

Windsor Publications, Inc.
History Books Division
Publisher: John M. Phillips
Editorial Director: Lissa Sanders
Production Supervisor: Katherine Cooper
Senior Picture Editor: Teri Davis Greenberg
Senior Corporate History Editor: Karen Story
Corporate History Editor: Phyllis Gray
Marketing Director: Ellen Kettenbeil
Production Manager: James Burke
Design Director: Alexander D'Anca
Art Production Manager: Dee Cooper
Typesetting Manager: E. Beryl Myers
Proofreading Manager: Doris R. Malkin

Staff for *Fort Lauderdale and Broward County*
Editor: Annette Igra
Picture Editor: Susan Wells
Editorial Assistants: Susan Block, Patricia Buzard, Judith
    Hunter, Patricia Morris, Pat Pittman
Sales Managers: Ernie Fredette, Susan Ritchie
Layout Artists: John Fish, Don Gould
Production Artists: Beth Bowman, Ellen Hazeltine, Julie Sloto
Typographers: Cheryl Holland, Barbara Neiman, Cynthia B. Pinter
Proofreaders: Jeff Leckrone, Kaylene Ohman

Frontispiece: The moods and vistas of Broward County are captured in this array of postcards representative of those that have been popular with tourists for the past 60 years. Photographs courtesy, Fort Lauderdale Historical Society. Background illustration by Mike Swift

Library of Congress Cataloging in Publication Data

McIver, Stuart B.
    Fort Lauderdale and Broward County.

    "Produced in cooperation with the Fort Lauderdale
Historical Society, Inc."
    Bibliography: p.
    Includes index.
    1. Fort Lauderdale (Fla.)—History. 2. Broward County
(Fla.)—History. 3. Fort Lauderdale (Fla.)—Description.
4. Broward County (Fla.)—Description and travel. 5. Fort
Lauderdale (Fla.)—Industries. 6. Broward County (Fla.)—
Industries. I. Title.
F319.F7M35   1983   975.9'35   83-16970
ISBN 0-89781-081-3

TO MY UNCLE, BOB BETTS,
A LIBRARIAN WHO KNOWS MORE ABOUT BOOKS
THAN ANYONE I EVER KNEW

The beautiful Hollywood Beach Hotel, the largest in Broward County when it was built in 1925, was the centerpiece of the city. A product of the 1920s land boom, Hollywood grew up from the wilderness to become the county's largest city within five years. Courtesy, Fort Lauderdale Historical Society

CONTENTS

Graceful palms, quiet water, and the gentle curves of a bridge bring to mind the peaceful landscape of tropical Fort Lauderdale in the early years of its development. This watercolor by Mary Thayer Todd is titled Bridge in Rio Vista. *Courtesy, Fort Lauderdale Historical Society*

Fort Lauderdale's prime importance during the Second Seminole War was as a base for expeditions into the Everglades. Such expeditions resulted in the capture and death of relatively few Seminoles, but they effected important psychological victories by demonstrating that even the wetlands were vulnerable to white incursions. Courtesy, National Archives

Chapter I

FROM INDIAN LEGEND TO INDIAN WARS

The mighty Chief Al-la-pa-taw, "Alligator Man," had seen storm clouds many times in the past, recounts an Indian legend of uncertain origin, but these held a strange color that disturbed him. He gazed at the sky with growing uneasiness. Cutting short his hunting foray, he hurried home to his tribe. For the chief and his people, a night of terror lay ahead, a night of violent, frightening electrical storms and then, in the depths of the darkness, a giant earthquake.

When morning came, their world was calm again, but it was no longer the same world. In place of solid, dry land, they saw now a crystal-clear river flowing to the sea.

Al-la-pa-taw named it Himmarshee, which some say means "the New River."

No one knows whether such an event ever occurred. Perhaps the legend lives because South Floridians like to promote their land with colorful, dramatic tales or because geologists say it could have happened that way, that an earthquake could have freed an underground river. What is known is that the New River contains meanders, or ox-bows. These are characteristic of a mature river system, not one that has sprung into being only recently.

There are other theories as to how the river got its name. Some think an early explorer or mapmaker observed a river that he or earlier explorers had previously simply overlooked. Hence, to him, it was a "new" river.

Perhaps the river owes its name to an inlet that has moved at least three times since the days of the early explorers; in other words, it was a "new river inlet," which became "New River Inlet." For instance, the

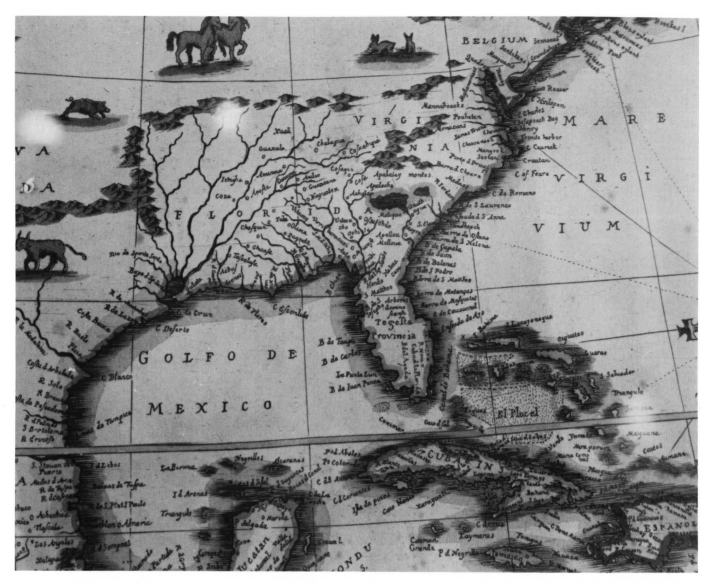

Above: Probably of Flemish origin, the 1631 "American Septemtrionalis" map is the earliest known document identifying the New River, "R. Novo," by its present name. The map's notations are in Latin. "Florida" is the name given to the entire southeast, while the peninsula proper bears the name "Tegesta Province." Courtesy, Deerfield Beach Historical Society

Facing page, bottom: Sixteenth-century engravings by Flemish artist Theodore De Bry provide a rare, if fanciful, view of life among Florida's original inhabitants. De Bry copied the scenes from paintings by Frenchman Jacques Le Moyne de Morgues, whose paintings depicted the Timucuan Indians of northeast Florida between 1564 and 1565. Courtesy, Fort Lauderdale Historical Society

1773 account by William Gerard De Brahm, official surveyor for King George III of England, says:

The great Rains in May 1765 filled this River and its Marshes with so much water that its weight within and the Sea without by Force of the N.E. gales demolished the Bank and made this Inlet between 25th and 30th May 1765.

The New River would eventually become the focal point around which a world-famous resort and later a diversified metropolitan area of a million people would develop. A clear, blue stream, the river flowed through a coastal ridge, a large freshwater marsh, a coastal sound, and then out into the ocean through an inlet that has occupied a number of different locations over the years. All the major streams in the area, Hillsboro River, Middle River, and Cypress Creek, arose no more than 20 miles to the west from a wide, shallow, slow-moving body of water, which the Indians called Pa-hay-o-kee, or Grassy Waters. It would later be called the Everglades.

Florida was discovered in 1513 by the Spanish explorer Juan Ponce de León, and the principal mark left by subsequent European explorations in the southeast Florida region came from ships that wrecked offshore.

The oldest discovered so far dates back to 1715, the year the Spanish Plate Fleet was demolished by a July hurricane. At least one of these treasure galleons wrecked near Hillsboro Inlet, to the north of the New River.

Some two decades later, a British ship went to the bottom south of New River, possibly a casualty in the obscure English-Spanish hostility known as the War of Jenkins' Ear. (A smuggler named Jenkins told the House of Commons that a Spanish commander had boarded his boat, sliced off his ear, and then insulted the Crown. When Jenkins produced the ear, an already angry Parliament decided it was time for another war with Spain—the War of Jenkins' Ear—part of which was fought on Florida soil and waters.)

Spain maintained Florida as a colony for two-and-a-half centuries, until 1763, when the Spanish government ceded Florida to England in exchange for the city of Havana. Long before Europeans settled on the New River, the Tequesta Indians had lived along its banks. Their settle-

Above: Juan Ponce de León made the first documented European landing in Florida near St. Augustine on April 2, 1513. Sailing down the east coast after claiming the new land for Spain, he was probably the first to sight the shores of today's Broward County. From the Florida Photographic Collection, Florida State Archives

ments on the river have been traced back to the time of Christ and in the surrounding area to 1450 B.C. When the Spanish left Florida for Havana in 1763, the remnant of the Tequestas, less than 200, left with them, in fear of the agressive Creek Indians moving down into South Florida.

Twenty years later Spain regained Florida following the War of American Independence. For Spain, governing La Florida the second time around proved to be a difficult task. In west Florida the nefarious adventurer William Augustus Bowles harassed the Spanish unrelentingly, leading and inciting Indian raids. In the course of his swashbuckling career, he called himself "director general" of the State of Muskogee, a sovereign nation of Creeks and Cherokees he sought to establish. Others called him "desperado," "vagabond," and "Captain Liar." In 1788 he landed at the Miami River, moved north with a small band of Indians, and attacked John Hambly's trading post near Lake George in central Florida.

Juan Nepomuceno de Quesada, since 1790 governor of Spanish east Florida, knew that followers of Bowles, including one Charles Lewis, had settled illegally somewhere along the southeast coast of Florida, possibly on the banks of Rio Nuevo. As governor, Juan Nepomuceno was hardly reassured by a 1790 economic report, which said of the southeast coast: "... no people settled in those localities, no one ventures to risk his negroes and property to the inroad of Indians, pirates and rogues from the Bahamas who infest all these coasts." Bowles was threatening the Spanish again, this time from the Bahamas. And now word came that his followers numbered among the "pirates and rogues" on the south coast.

Tension between France and Spain convinced the governor it would be imprudent to commit his meager military force to a venture some 300 miles south of his capital, St. Augustine. To investigate the Bowles rumors, he decided instead on a spy mission.

On February 23, 1793, the schooner *Juan Nepomuceno* set sail from St. Augustine. On board were three covert agents, carefully briefed for the mission. Ten days later they reached the mouth of Rio Nuevo, or as the interlopers they were seeking called it, the New River.

After sailing up New River Sound and then up the river itself, a total distance of eight miles, they came to a palmetto-thatched house. A man armed with a rifle came out. They told him they were looking for water; actually, they had emptied their water kegs to give themselves a cover story.

The man, an Englishman about 40 years of age, had come to the New River about five or six months earlier. His name was Captain Joseph Robbins, and he had been one of Bowles' right-hand men on the 1788 expedition into Florida. Robbins lived now on the river with his mulatto wife, Rachel, their daughter, Susannah, and an American named Joel Radcliff.

Robbins told the agents that the house and a plantation some two miles west belonged to Charles Lewis, who apparently had stayed on in the area following the 1788 raids. Robbins also said that Lewis owned five horses, a gift from none other than Bowles. Lewis, his wife Frankee, and their children had sailed to Nassau about a month earlier to deliver a load of fish oil and venison hams and were expected back soon.

In his journal of the trip, the mission's interpreter, John Hambly, whose family trading post had been attacked by Bowles, wrote:

The house stands on a pine bluff on the south side of the river, about 10 yards distant—A small fowl house opposite—About thirty yards from the dwelling house up the river stands a small house which we found to be a blacksmith's shop . . . This shop, tools, and ec. it is said belong to Lewis and that when here he makes harpoons.

By March 16, the spies were back in St. Augustine. Captain Sebastian Verezaluze, the head of the mission, recommended to the governor that a reward be offered to a band of Indians "to seize Lewis secretly and convey him and his family as prisoners to Apalachee or whatever place seems best to Your Excellency."

Quesada agreed and passed the recommendation on to Havana. But the authorities in Havana, facing the more serious threat of attack by the French, disregarded the governor's letter. Although the spy mission accomplished little else, it did leave for posterity the first documented account of the first known white settlers on New River.

By the end of the 18th century, the pressures exerted by a young and vigorous United States of America were driving new groups of Indians southward into Florida. These Indians were called Seminoles, a loose designation that included both Creeks and Mikasukis. When, exactly, the Seminoles first reached the New River area is not known.

Along the New River, white settlement continued at a slow pace. In 1796, just three years after the Lewis family had been marked for expulsion, the Spanish government reportedly approved a claim to the Lewis land by Frankee Lewis. In 1810 Spanish nobleman Juan Arrambide acquired a large land grant extending from New River to Biscayne Bay. Arrambide introduced black slavery to the New River, using slaves and Cuban laborers to cut timber.

A weakened power by this time, Spain was finding the new nation to the north of Florida an energetic and troublesome neighbor. In 1818 an army led by General Andrew Jackson had stormed into Spanish Florida to punish Indians for attacks along the Georgia border. This would be known later as the First Seminole War. Unable to control either the Indians or the Americans, who freely ventured across the border, Spain

Above: Andrew Jackson led American troops into Florida in 1818 to punish Creek and Seminole Indians who had been raiding the Georgia border settlements. In what became known as the First Seminole War, Jackson not only attacked the Indians, but seized St. Marks and Pensacola, deposing the Spanish governor of west Florida. In 1819, when this engraving was produced, Spain ceded Florida to the United States. Two years later, Jackson became the first American governor of the new territory. Courtesy, National Portrait Gallery, Smithsonian Institution, Washington, D.C.

Above right: British adventurer William Augustus Bowles, who had lived among the Creeks in northern Florida, is seen here in Indian costume. Bowles' schemes to establish an Indian empire threatened Spain's precarious hold on Florida in the late 18th century. His plans failed, however, and he died in a Havana prison in 1808. Some of his Bahamian followers were the first recorded white settlers on the New River. From the Florida Photographic Collection, Florida State Archives

agreed to sell Florida to the United States in 1819. Three years later Congress officially established the Territory of Florida.

Americans began pouring in, seeking land and recovery of black slaves, many of whom had fled into the area during Spanish rule and allied themselves with the Seminoles, who moved south ahead of the Americans in increasing numbers. Quiescent in Spanish days, New River began to blossom after the United States acquired Florida. By 1824 a group of settlers, mostly transient Bahamians who subsisted through turtling, fishing, and salvaging shipwrecks, lived on the river. The following year Frankee Lewis received confirmation of her right to the land the Spanish had granted her in a document called the Frankee Lewis Donation.

A resident who claimed to be both a doctor and a French nobleman arrived in 1828. Count Odet Philippe, allegedly appointed a surgeon in the Royal Navy of France by his friend Napoleon, migrated to Charleston, South Carolina, and then to the New River, where he tried his hand at salt-making. The Count's slaves scooped out large holes on the beach, which were allowed to fill with seawater. After initial evaporation, the residue was transferred to boilers. Ideally, this process produces layers of commercial salt, saltpeter, and alum, but Philippe's venture failed—too much saltpeter, too much alum, too little salt.

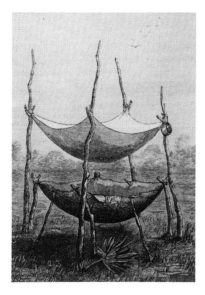

Despite the noble status he claimed, the Count was by no means the leader of the New River Settlement. That honor went to William Cooley, a native of Maryland who settled first in North Florida in 1813. There he learned the language of the Seminoles and cultivated their friendship.

In 1824 Cooley arrived at New River, where he became the area's first manufacturer. Cooley processed and shipped arrowroot, a commercial starch made from the coontie, or compte, plant, which grew in such profusion in the area that Indians called the New River the Cooti-hatchee. In the wet season the river provided the waterpower for Cooley's starch mill. Operated by three men, his equipment could produce 450 pounds of finished arrowroot a day, for which he received 8 to 16 cents per pound. Cooley's coontie mill was housed in a 27-by-14-foot building. The mill was attached to his 50-foot wharf, where processed arrowroot was loaded onto schooners for shipment to Key West. From there it was shipped to Northern and European ports.

Beyond his factory stood two storage houses, a kitchen, and slave quarters. His 29-acre farm produced sugarcane, corn, potatoes, pumpkins, and other vegetables. Coconut palms and lime and orange trees were scattered through his farm, along with a number of domesticated animals, among them 80 hogs.

His real pride, however, was his house. In 1835 Cooley felt the time had come to build a proper home for himself, his wife, and their three children. Now in his early fifties, he held a position of considerable power and respect in South Florida. Since 1831 he had been justice of the peace for the New River Settlement. In addition, he was an official appraiser of wrecked vessels and their cargoes, a licensed master pilot, and a guide and explorer of note. He was a confidante of Richard Fitzpatrick, territorial representative from Key West, who owned land in the New River area, and a close friend of young Stephen Mallory, also of Key West. Mallory, assistant to the overseer of Fitzpatrick's New River plantation, would later become Secretary of the Navy in the Confederate government.

Cooley's substantial frontier home measured 20 feet by 50 feet. It was built of cypress logs and was sealed and floored with 1.5-inch planks. The one-story house was well-furnished and comfortable. Madeira wine, cigars, and good food made his home a haven for any visitors of consequence, for his fellow settlers, and for Indians camped near the river.

For Cooley there would be little opportunity to enjoy his home. It would, in fact, become the scene of heart-breaking tragedy for him. A terrible conflict was already building in Florida. As the Americans pressed Florida's Indians to give up their lands and move to reservations in the West, the Indians concluded they had no choice but to resist. In June 1835, following a fruitless parley, their great leader, Osceola, had been seized by Indian agent General Wiley Thompson and placed in chains.

Thompson's impulsive act proved a blunder of enormous magnitude—as well as his own death warrant. The following day Osceola was released, but the seeds of war had been planted.

In September difficulty of a different kind struck the South Florida coast. A hurricane, the fiercest Frankee Lewis could remember in her half-century in Florida, lashed out, destroying ships all along the coast. Near Hillsboro Inlet, a 200-ton Spanish brigantine, *Gil Blas*, was blown ashore. Cooley, as appraiser for the area, removed what goods could be salvaged. Later that fall a Key West merchant bought what remained of the wreck and hired Cooley to complete the salvage operation—a task Cooley was never to finish.

Throughout the state the Indians were becoming restive, and among the New River Indians animosity toward Cooley was growing. During a dispute with the Creeks, a group of white men had killed their old chief, Alibama, and burnt his hut. Cooley, as justice of the peace, took the men into custody. Later, however, in Key West, the charges were dropped due to lack of evidence. This increased the Indians' resentment against the white man, much of which was directed at Cooley, whom they accused of withholding vital evidence.

On December 28 Central Florida Seminoles struck Fort King, near today's Ocala, and General Thompson was shot dead by Osceola. The same day Major Francis L. Dade and his contingent of more than a hundred men were on their way from Tampa to Fort King when Indians ambushed them and slaughtered all but a handful of the troops.

On January 6, 1836, Cooley and his crew left home early in the morning to return to the *Gil Blas* wreck. At noon the Indians, covered with war paint, slipped toward the Cooley home. The two older children were reciting their lessons to their tutor, Joseph Flinton. Mrs. Cooley was taking care of her infant son.

Suddenly, blood-curdling war whoops shattered the quiet of the river settlement. Flinton leaped to his feet and tried too late to bar the door. A group of 15 to 20 Indians forced their way into the house. They killed the tutor first, mangling his body with an ax and then scalping him. Horrified, Mrs. Cooley grabbed her son and fled with the two older children toward the river. About 150 yards from the house the Indians shot her. The ball entered between her shoulders, passed through her breast, and entered the tiny body of her baby. Cooley's nine-year-old son was clubbed to death, probably with a piece of firewood, and the 11-year-old Cooley girl, who was shot, died with her recitation book in her hand.

A neighbor, young William Rigby, was aroused by the screaming from across the river. Gathering his aged widowed mother and two younger sisters, he led the family to the safety of the Cape Florida Lighthouse, some 25 miles to the south on Key Biscayne.

The artist who rendered this drawing, The Horrid Massacre of the Whites in Florida, in December 1835, and January, February, March and April 1836, *probably had the attack on the Cooley family, among others, in mind. Five people were killed in the Cooley Massacre, and the shock and fear it generated decimated the entire New River settlement. Courtesy, Library of Congress*

The Indians plundered Cooley's property, carrying away $7,000 worth of cargo from the *Gil Blas* and his livestock, but they took no more lives.

Word reached Cooley at the wreck. He returned home to find the bodies of his beloved wife, his three children, and the tutor. His house was burned to the ground, and his two black slaves had disappeared. Cooley buried the victims, then joined the other New River settlers who had fled to Cape Florida. There he found one of his slaves who had overheard a conversation that indicated the motive for the massacre was Cooley's failure to convict the killers of Chief Alibama. But the Cooley Massacre, occurring less than 10 days after the Dade Massacre and the murder of the Indian agents could have been part of a greater conflict. The Second Seminole War would soon reach the once peaceful banks of the New River.

The Cooley Massacre signaled the end of the community called New River Settlement. More than half a century would pass before white settlers in any number would return to the river. But the area was by no means deserted. The Indians increased in number, and in the summer of 1836 the river saw the brief emergence of the Andros Island Camp.

Negroes, many of them former slaves who had joined the Seminoles, saw themselves facing certain slavery as the white man moved down the peninsula. A large group of Indian Negroes, as they were called, assembled at New River, where an armed Spanish schooner picked them up in early July and carried them to Indian Key. The ship acquired provisions there and then sailed on to the Bahamas.

Apparently a sizable number of Negroes left Florida to proceed to Andros Island, some of them attempting to cross the swiftly flowing Gulf Stream in canoes. How many died on these escape efforts will never be known. Enough reached the island to form a colony of 90 to 150 Seminole Negroes at Red Bay. The largest group was led by the medicine man, Scipio Bowlegs, a black who had taken the surname of the famous chief, Billy Bowlegs.

Meanwhile, the Second Seminole War was heating up. All over the peninsula the Indians were rising to resist the white man's efforts to remove them to Western reservations.

An old, snowy-haired Indian named Arpeika who sold fish to officers at Fort King was nicknamed Sam Jones by a soldier from New York after a Sandy Hook fishseller. The lighthearted name suggests that the soldier probably liked the ancient Indian, but failed to take him seriously. Two wars later the army of the United States was taking him very seriously, still trying and still failing to subdue the old man. Offers of large amounts of money to resettle in the West brought this eloquent answer: "In Florida I was born. In Florida I will die. In Florida my bones shall bleach."

Sam Jones was a Mikasuki medicine man, not a chief. Yet he commanded fighting units the U.S. Army could not subdue. His influence reached out far beyond the Mikasukis that made up his small band. When the war started, he was already in his seventies. Of all the Indians, he would prove to be the most implacable, resourceful, and ruthless. He was, above all, simply unconquerable.

As the war drove the Indians southward, Sam Jones left his town at the headwaters of the St. Johns River. On Christmas Day, 1837, he fought at Lake Okeechobee against a man who would later be President, Colonel Zachary Taylor. By 1838 Sam Jones and his Mikasukis were living in the Everglades, west of New River, on high hammock land called the Seven Islands of Sam Jones. He was the most dangerous Indian in the area when Major William Lauderdale, who commanded the heralded Tennessee Volunteers, arrived in South Florida. Although already in his fifties and in poor health, Lauderdale responded to his country's call for military service. It was hoped that duty in a warm land would restore his strength. The trip into Florida, however, proved arduous for Lauderdale's men and their horses. Heat, humidity, insects, and sharp-edged Florida plants took a heavy toll of the volunteers' mounts. (Sam Jones claimed that his spells caused the deaths of the horses.)

From Fort Jupiter, Lauderdale's men hacked their way south through hammocks and palmettoes, following the three-to-five mile wide pine ridge that provided the only high ground between the coastal marshes

General Andrew Jackson is shown addressing the Tennessee Volunteers in this engraving from the War of 1812. A detachment of Tennessee Volunteers, led by Major William Lauderdale, established the first fort on the New River in March 1838. That fort, as well as two successive outposts, took its name from Major Lauderdale. Courtesy, Tennessee State Library

Navy Lieutenant Levin M. Powell commanded a joint army-navy expedition which reinforced Lauderdale's command on March 8, 1838. This force occupied Camp Powell, across the New River from Fort Lauderdale, and participated in the advance on Pine Island, a Seminole refuge in the Everglades. Powell, seen here in a Civil War-era photograph, later rose to the rank of rear admiral. Courtesy, Fort Lauderdale Historical Society

and the watery Everglades. They had previously found a large, freshly-made Indian trail along the Hillsboro River. The trail headed toward New River. During a heavy rain Lauderdale's command arrived at New River on March 5. The trail they made became known as Lauderdale's Route and later as Military Trail.

The next day the major and two of his lieutenants picked a site for a fort, selecting a spot where the stream divided into north and south forks, about an eighth of a mile above "Cooley's patch." The troops began construction of a 30-foot square, two-tiered blockhouse. It was completed on March 10. The 50-by-60-foot picket with which Lauderdale planned to enclose the blockhouse was not finished until early April, shortly after he had left New River. General Thomas S. Jesup, commander-in-chief for Florida, decreed: "The new post established on New River by the Tennessee Battalion of Volunteers and Company 'D,' 3rd Artillery, will be called Fort Lauderdale."

General Jesup had already enlarged the major's command by sending Lieutenant Levin Powell, with 152 soldiers and sailors, to New River. Across the river, directly south of Fort Lauderdale, the lieutenant established Camp Powell.

The most important reason for maintaining the fort on the river, Major Lauderdale felt, was its location in the heart of the coontie country. He believed it would isolate a major source of food for the Indians. In scouting the area around the fort, the major found a deserted Indian village in the forks of the New River directly across from the new fort.

To the west, in the Everglades, Major Lauderdale found high ground which became islands during the wet season. These were the Seven Islands of Sam Jones; the largest was Pine Island. South of the Seven Islands, Lauderdale's expedition encountered a large hammock where Indians assembled to socialize and to plan strategy; the military designated it Council Island.

On March 18 Lieutenant Colonel James Bankhead assumed control of the fort. Four days later he mounted a large-scale operation against Pine Island. Major Lauderdale led 100 mounted volunteers as more than 500 American military men moved against 50 to 100 braves under the Mikasuki leader, Sam Jones.

Night fell before the Americans could encircle the Indians. In the morning they were gone. The Americans once again had failed to capture the old medicine man, or defeat his warriors. But in a sense they had scored important gains. To the boast of the Indians that white troops could never follow them into the Sea of Grass, they had proved they could move effectively into the waters of the Everglades. And in forcing the Indians from Pine Island, they had captured valuable coontie-processing equipment, canoes, and weapons. The Indians were still free, but they were also still on the run.

On April 2 Fort Lauderdale acquired its third commander in its short history. Lieutenant Colonel William Selby Harney assumed command of all military operations south and west of New River.

Two days later Major Lauderdale and his volunteers left the fort that bore his name. Their enlistment period was nearly over. The major had spent just 29 days in the area before starting the long trip back to Tennessee, to his wife, his six children, and the plantation that awaited him. He never made it back to his beloved Cumberland Valley. On May 11 Major William Lauderdale died at the U.S. Army Barracks in Baton Rouge, Louisiana.

Even before the major's death, Fort Lauderdale had been abandoned. The military, believing most of the Indians had left the New River area, departed from the fort on May 7. The Indians returned and burned the fort. New River was again their home, and shipwrecks off the coast were theirs alone to salvage. Any American survivors were slaughtered by Sam Jones' warriors, according to a contemporary account.

The following winter the American military came back to the river. This time a new fort was built nearer to the coast to ease supply and communication problems. The second Fort Lauderdale, occupied on February 14, 1839, was built on the north side of New River, close to the bank on a slight elevation. A log stockade about 8 to 10 feet high surrounded the post. The southeast corner of the fort contained a log blockhouse two stories high. At the southwest corner stood a watchtower with an observation platform reached by a long, slender ladder.

The new encampment proved to be temporary. By summer it was clear that the best location would be at the beach. From a fort on the ocean the military could protect shipwreck victims along the south coast. A substantial fort, the third Fort Lauderdale garrisoned well over a hundred men. Soldiers occupied the third fort in September 1839.

An uneasy lull in hostilities prevailed briefly after a peace parley in May 1839 at Fort King. Sam Jones had selected Chitto-Tustenuggee (Snake Chief) as his successor and chief negotiator at the conference. An agreement was reached calling for the Indians to remain in Florida on land south of the Caloosahatchee River on the west coast.

"I shall never again raise my hand against the white man," said Sam Jones, "for I am old now, and what can an old man like me do."

Many believed the Florida War was over. An attack on a trading post on the Caloosahatchee in early July shattered this hope. Then on September 27 Chitto-Tustenuggee invited Lieutenant Christopher Tompkins, commander of the Fort Lauderdale, to bring his men to the old fort, about two miles to the west, to watch an Indian ball game. Tompkins became wary as the Indians grew increasingly insistent. Instead of all of his men,

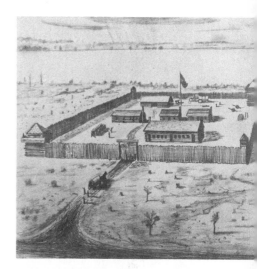

This artist's conception of a Seminole War fort may represent the third Fort Lauderdale. United States artillerymen manned the seaside outpost from mid-May 1839 until February 1842. According to a contemporary account, the soldiers constructed the rectangular stockade and three corner blockhouses, each containing one cannon, in September 1839. Captain E. D. Keyes, who assumed command of the fort in November 1841, was not impressed, calling it "a cluster of cane-built huts and a few Indian wigwams." Courtesy, Fort Lauderdale Historical Society

Above: As a young artillery lieutenant, Robert Anderson accompanied William Lauderdale to the New River in 1838, and helped construct the first Fort Lauderdale. In 1861, as a major, he earned a place in American history as the Union commander of Fort Sumter. Courtesy, Fort Lauderdale Historical Society

Facing page: Two maps, drawn by Captain Abner Doubleday, trace the route of the Arch Creek-New River road, a major transportation artery along the southeast coast of Florida during and immediately after the Third Seminole War. Doubleday never carried out his original plans to bridge the New River, probably because of the river's depth and the low military priority of the area. Courtesy, National Archives

he decided to send two privates with the Negro interpreter, George. They were to size up the situation and return promptly.

When they did not return as planned, Lieutenant Tompkins grew uneasy. In late afternoon he and a fellow officer proceeded quietly upriver. At the old fort they saw no signs of Indians or of their own people.

"Here . . . here I am," moaned a voice from the dark, shaded bank. Lying in the water, Private Edward Hopkins was crying for help. "I am wounded and they have killed George and Boyce." Hopkins told them the Indians had as many as 300 warriors. He lingered for six hours before dying from a gunshot wound in the abdomen, the first Fort Lauderdale casualty of the war.

The next day they found the body of Private Thomas Boyce floating in the river. As they sought to recover him, one of the men saw a black man in a thick mangrove swamp. "George is alive," he called out. The interpreter told them the three men, arriving at the old fort, had been asked, "Have the officers come?" When another Indian called out, "Yes," a third voice cried, "Now for it."

George turned to see Sam Jones' son, Sponge, and Chitto-Tustenuggee's brother, Ochee Hadjo, with their rifles aimed at Tompkins' men. George pulled at Hopkins and fell sideways into the river just as gunfire rang out. Pretending to be dead, George lay quietly in the river. In the distance he could hear the voice of Sam Jones.

The Indians had sought a major victory, a massacre on the same scale that destroyed the forces of Major Dade. They had failed, and the Americans at Fort Lauderdale had learned that Sam Jones was still not ready for peace.

From Fort Lauderdale, the U.S. military launched many forays into the vast watery world that lay to the west—the Florida Everglades. Two U.S. Navy lieutenants, Levin Powell and John T. McLaughlin, helped create a new concept of naval strategy as they found themselves pursuing Indians in canoes through marshes, sloughs, and shallow streams. What emerged was riverine warfare, a strategy that demanded smaller boats, joint action by army and navy, and specialized combat groups organized for sustained land and sea operations. The techniques developed would be used again by the American military 125 years later in southeast Asia.

The casualty figures from Fort Lauderdale revealed all too well the horror of fighting in a wet, hot, humid, hostile, subtropical world. Of the 14 men who died, only five were killed by the Indians. Two men drowned while on duty, the other seven were victims of various ailments, principally diarrhea and fever.

Eventually, it ended, the longest war the young American nation had ever fought. It had cost the United States $40 million and the lives of more than 1,500 men. Nearly 4,000 Indians remained in hiding when the unpopular war wound down in 1842. Of these, roughly 40 were Sam Jones' Mikasukis.

The New River was quiet again. White settlers did not return, and only a handful of Indians remained when Florida became the 27th state in 1845. The Americans, however, had not forsaken their policy of Indian removal. The army's new tactic called for an extensive surveying program to locate the Indians, isolate them, and cut off their trade with white men. Thus weakened, the army felt the remnants would be easier to handle.

In 1855 the survey produced the Ives Map, the first really reliable map of South Florida, and in short order it ignited the Third Seminole War. In the Big Cypress Swamp an 11-man survey team, for no apparent reason, destroyed the prize banana patch of the Seminole leader, Billy Bowlegs. The Seminoles struck back and another war was on.

Fought principally in southwestern Florida, the Third Seminole War brought little activity to Fort Lauderdale, used primarily as a camp, not as a fully-activated fort. No white settlers were living on the New River, and only one, a man named Cobb, was living near Hillsboro Inlet. Three friendly Indians told him there would be war and urged him to leave. He moved south to Fort Dallas on the Miami River in 1856.

The army's most notable achievement on the lower east coast was the construction in 1857 of a road from Fort Dallas north to the Fort Lauderdale area. Captain Abner Doubleday, the father of the great American game, baseball, headed the road-building project. His soldiers built a corduroy road through the swamp and constructed bridges over rivers and creeks, reaching the south bank of the New River. Doubleday's troops were withdrawn from the area before a planned bridge over New River could be built.

In the Seminole Wars several military figures who would gain fame in the Civil War visited or served at Fort Lauderdale, among them such future generals as William Tecumseh Sherman, George Thomas, the "Rock of Chickamauga," and Robert Anderson, William Lauderdale's second-in-command who later commanded Fort Sumter during the attack that precipitated the Civil War. The Confederates were represented at Fort Lauderdale by Joseph Johnston and by Robert E. Lee, who visited the fort in 1849 on a coastal survey trip between the Second and Third Seminole Wars.

When the third war ended, there were less than a hundred Indians still in South Florida. Among these was a man who had been written off as senile in the Second Seminole War. When the final Seminole War ended in 1858, Sam Jones, the scourge of the New River country, was blind, too weak to walk, but at age 108 still unconquered.

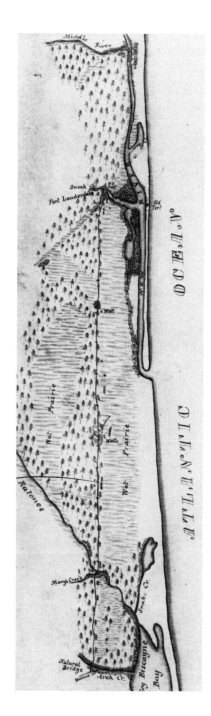

The frontispiece of James A. Henshall's book, Camping and
Cruising in Florida, is a typical late 19th century scene of a
Florida "wonderland," complete with water, palm trees, and a
glowing moon. The book, which contains excellent descriptions of
the Hillsboro and New River regions and the Everglades, was
compiled from Henshall's articles in the popular sporting
magazines Forest and Stream and American Field. Courtesy,
Fort Lauderdale Historical Society

Chapter 2

QUIET YEARS ON THE RIVER

The sloop *Enterprise* left Mosquito Inlet above Cape Canaveral for Nassau in the Bahamas, its cargo a typical load for a blockade runner, four bales of cotton. But the small sloop failed to reach its destination—on March 8, 1863, a boat dispatched by the Union gunboat *Sagamore* captured the *Enterprise* off Hillsboro Inlet. Captain and crew were taken aboard the *Sagamore*, and the sloop was towed to the Miami River.

Hardly a major naval battle, the capture of the *Enterprise* nonetheless emerged as the closest thing to Civil War action in the Hillsboro-New River area. Florida's lower east coast was still so sparsely settled that the Federal blockade board, meeting in Washington, D.C., in July 1861, took no action at first against southeast Florida, dismissing it with the observation that the area "can hardly be said to be inhabited and is of no great consequence except as a convenient place of resort for pirates." The following year, after Confederate sympathizers had extinguished the lights in both the Jupiter and Cape Florida lighthouses, the United States Navy mounted an active blockade of the southeast Florida coast.

In addition to capturing 13 blockade runners between Jupiter and Biscayne Bay, the Union Navy also launched attacks on the mainland. In July 1863 an expedition from the *Sagamore* landed at the settlement on the Miami River, roughly 30 miles south of New River, and burned a starch mill belonging to a blockade runner, George Lewis, grandson of the first white settlers on the New River, Charles and Frankee Lewis.

Confederate sympathizers on the Miami River created a problem for the Isaiah Hall family. Hall's pro-South neighbors were angry at him for serving as pilot for the *Sagamore*. When they attempted to send Hall's Georgia-born wife, Lavinia Booth, to a North Florida camp to make clothes for Confederate soldiers, the Halls fled in a small boat. Luckily

Former U.S. Vice-President and Confederate Secretary of War John C. Breckinridge passed through present-day Broward in his flight down the coast and on to Cuba at the end of the Civil War. Accounts of the journey written by Breckinridge and one of his companions provide a vivid picture of southeast Florida during this period. From Cirker, Dictionary of American Portraits, Dover, 1967

they were picked up at sea by the *Sagamore.* The crew of the gunboat took up a collection for them, raising $50, and then dropped them off at the relatively deserted New River. The Halls stayed there for the duration of the war before returning to Miami to find their home gone.

When the war drew to a close in 1865, Union officials feared high-ranking Confederate officials might try to flee first to Florida and then escape by sea. One who succeeded was John C. Breckinridge, who had been Vice-President under President James Buchanan, a candidate for President in 1860, and Secretary of War for the Confederate States of America. Breckinridge and five companions traveled overland to the Indian River. He must have felt he was in friendly country: in the election of 1860, running as a candidate of the Southern Democrats against Abraham Lincoln, he had received every vote cast between the Upper Keys and Cape Canaveral, a total of 24.

Continuing south in a small lifeboat, the Breckinridge party was accosted by a U.S. transport but avoided detection by posing as wreckers, hunters, and fishermen. Then, at a location some observers believe to have been New River Inlet, they encountered a sailboat manned by three armed men who were probably deserters. At gunpoint Breckinridge's group forced the strangers to swap boats. At the Miami River they actually engaged in gunfire in obtaining provisions. Two days later, on June 10, 1865, Breckinridge was in Cuba.

Five years passed and the New River remained a virtually deserted part of Florida. Only a handful of white settlers and Indians were living on the river at the start of the new decade.

In 1870 a survey was conducted by Marcellus A. Williams, Deputy Surveyor for the State of Florida. In surveying and platting the state, Williams produced an extremely useful set of section charts. Williams' survey map shows "old settlement, cocoa-nut trees" on the beach just north of Fort Lauderdale as well as an Indian camp on the river's south fork. Williams often took his 13-year-old son, Arthur, on his survey trips. Young Arthur must have liked New River. By the time he was 30, he would return to launch the area's first real-estate venture.

The census of 1870 was taken by William S. Allen, assistant marshall from Biscayne, Florida. In all of Dade County, which stretched from St. Lucie Inlet to Jewfish Creek in the Upper Keys, he turned up only 85 white people. In his census he did not count Indians, not even the Seminoles who obligingly rowed the boat that transported him around the county.

Among the small group on New River, Allen found a pig farmer, one John J. "Pig" Brown, who would prove to be the downfall of a tough and resourceful political boss, William Gleason. A native of Virginia, the 48-year-old Brown had come to the river in 1868. He lived with his wife,

Lavinia, their five children, and their daughter-in-law, Josephine, and in 1870 had a net worth of $500.

In the chaotic years of the early postwar era the most powerful political figure in South Florida was William H. Gleason, a New York carpetbagger who rode the tide of Reconstruction politics to a share of the Florida governorship. In 1866 Gleason was elected lieutenant governor on the Republican ticket headed by Harrison Reed. Two years later Gleason allied himself with a group of "Radical" Republicans, started impeachment proceedings against Reed, and declared himself governor. Gleason took the state seal and played at running the government from a hotel across the street from the Capitol. When the infighting finally ended, Reed was cleared and Gleason was the one who was impeached.

On his return to Dade County, Gleason suffered one more indignity. He had to cross New River in a boat so unseaworthy that passengers tried to keep their clothes dry by removing them and carrying them on their heads. Even so, Gleason got thoroughly wet when the boat sank.

The resourceful Gleason bounced back quickly. He took over the offices of county clerk, tax assessor, and school board member, using his authority shamelessly to further enrich himself. Gleason was clearly "the boss" of South Florida.

In 1872 Gleason decided he wanted to return to Tallahassee, this time as a representative. To run against him, the Democrats picked the pig farmer, John Brown. Some say Brown had not even been informed of his candidacy. Even so, when the votes were counted, Brown had won, 16 to 14.

Gleason promptly had a henchman invalidate three pro-Brown votes, producing a 14-to-13 edge for the former "governor." A review panel headed by the same henchman certified the results, and Pig Brown had to continue his idyllic life on New River, far from the halls of Tallahassee.

Four years later Gleason stood for reelection, and again Pig Brown opposed him. Once more the count showed Pig ahead by three votes, 27 to 24. Gleason challenged the results, citing irregularities at a polling place on property he owned. When the votes at that precinct were thrown out, Gleason had the edge again, 7 to 4.

But the battle wasn't over. Election returns in Florida and two other Southern states were being contested in a Presidential election so close that Republican Rutherford B. Hayes was not declared President until one day before inauguration. For a time the Democratic candidate, Samuel Tilden, appeared to have won, but he dropped his challenges at the end in return for Hayes' pledge to return home rule to the South.

For Florida, Reconstruction was over and with it Gleason's power to manipulate election results. The patient Pig Brown, who had twice drawn more votes than South Florida's political boss, was now ready for

New York native William H. Gleason, who came to the Miami area from Wisconsin in 1866, was South Florida's most notorious carpetbagger. A leader of the state's Radical Republican political faction, he served as lieutenant governor and self-proclaimed governor in the late 1860s. He represented Dade County in the Florida House of Representatives from 1873 to 1877, when he was unseated by New River's John J. "Pig" Brown. Although Gleason never again held state office, he remained a prominent figure in Florida throughout the late 19th century. Courtesy, Historical Association of Southern Florida

Washington H. Jenkins served as keeper of the House of Refuge between 1876 and 1883. This tintype, taken shortly after he and his family moved out of the house, shows Jenkins with his wife Mary and their four children. Jenkins divorced his wife in the mid-1880s, remaining in South Florida until his death in 1906. Courtesy, Fort Lauderdale Historical Society

Tallahassee. He sold his farm and his pigs, headed north to the state capital, and was never seen again on the New River.

Very few were on hand on the New River in 1876 to observe the final victory of Pig Brown, the nation's centennial, or the establishment of Life Saving Station Number 4, the Fort Lauderdale House of Refuge. The United States Life Saving Service built five Houses of Refuge along the lower east coast of Florida, from Indian River Inlet to Biscayne Bay. Charlie Pierce, who lived on Hypoluxo Island in Lake Worth, wrote:

Why did the Government build these houses of refuge for shipwrecked sailors? At the time these houses were built, the entire East Coast was what one might term a howling wilderness . . . the sailors wrecked along this unsettled coast had little chance to leave it except by passing vessels on the sea; and in many parts of the coast were in danger of starvation . . . A case of this kind happened in a hurricane of October, 1873, a vessel was wrecked halfway between Biscayne Bay and New River . . . A few days later when found by a man that had walked up the beach from Biscayne Bay, the half-starved crew were existing on spoiled fish.

The story of the crew's hardships published in New York newspapers drew the attention of government officials. The superintendent of the Life Saving Service ordered immediate construction of the five houses.

The Fort Lauderdale House of Refuge was completed on April 24, 1876. It was to have been built on part of the Fort Lauderdale property owned by the government. Lumber for the house was floated ashore from an offshore schooner, but because of a miscalculation the wood came ashore farther north than planned. The house was built where the lumber beached, at a site near what would later become Hugh Taylor Birch State Park.

All the houses were built from the same basic design, a 54-foot by 25-foot rectangle, constructed sturdily to withstand gales and hurricanes, even though they faced the ocean. Downstairs was divided into four comfortable rooms for the keeper and his family. Upstairs was a stuffy, windowless, but clearly welcome loft for shipwrecked sailors.

Washington Jenkins, a young farmer born in South Carolina 31 years earlier, became the first keeper. Although they were employees of the Life Saving Service, keepers were not expected to perform actual life saving but rather to provide food, water, and a dry bed—in short, a refuge. Keepers were paid $400 annually.

Jenkins was required to fill out an information form on such subjects as the rise and fall of the tide, depth of the offshore waters at high and low tide, and population density:

"What is the number of male inhabitants between the ages of fifteen and fifty two years within three miles of your station?"

His answer: "None."

For the keepers, life was a lonely and monotonous existence. Ship-wrecks were rare and so were visitors to the house. A particularly welcome one was James Henshall, a physician and author from Cincinnati who wrote about South Florida for the publications *Forest and Stream* and *American Field,* and in 1884 wrote a book, *Camping and Cruising in Florida.* Dr. Henshall wrote of his 1879 visit:

We arrived at Station No. 4, nine miles from the Hillsboro River... Mr. Jenkins has charge of this station, which is on a strip of beach separating New River from the sea... Two miles below is the site of old Fort Lauderdale, where there is a flourishing grove of cocoa palms. New River is a fine stream, which divides into several branches opposite to the station... Mr. Jenkins sailed us in his canoe a few miles up the main branch of the river... we landed and walked a few miles to some fine hamaks [hammocks or tree islands] between New River and Snake Creek... On our return I shot a number of ducks with Jenkins' gun, and had a shot at a bear on the shore but he got away.

In 1882 Henshall returned and wrote: "New River, for six miles above its mouth, is the straightest, deepest and finest river I have seen in Florida, although a narrow one. It is famous for its sharks (regular man-eaters, some of them), and for the immense number and variety of its fishes... Rushing in and out with the tide, at New River, fishes can be seen by thousands."

That year Henshall's party traveled the New River to the Everglades in an Indian cypress canoe borrowed from Jenkins. They proceeded up the river past hammocks of water-oak, swamp-maple, bay, Spanish ash, and palmettoes, through a belt of "tall cypresses, with pale and grizzled trunks... ornamented in a fantastic fashion with the scarlet plumes of air-plants... draped in heavy folds and festoons of gray Spanish moss."

Henshall called the Everglades "unique, there is nothing like it anywhere else. As far as the eye can reach stretches a broad, level expanse, clothed in verdure of a peculiarly fresh and vivid green, a rich and intense color seen nowhere but here. The surface is dotted and diversified by thousands of islets and islands, of all shapes and sizes, from a few yards to many acres in extent, clothed with a tropical luxuriance of trees, shrubs and vines."

In the distance the travelers saw smoke rising. As they moved closer, several canoes darted out from behind the islands. One canoe came directly toward them, carrying a tall, young Indian clad in a light-colored shirt, red belt, and red turban, and an elderly Indian sitting amidships. The older Indian, Chief Little Tiger, invited them to visit his village. The

Top: The New River Seminole village James A. Henshall visited in 1882 consisted of a cluster of open huts or "chickees," such as the one seen in this illustration from an 1884 government survey. By the 1880s, memories of Seminole-white hostilities were rapidly fading into the past, and positive public interest in Florida's Indians revived. Courtesy, Fort Lauderdale Historical Society

Bottom: Commodore Ralph Middleton Munroe, an early Miami settler, took the earliest known photographs of the New River area in 1885 or 1886. Munroe's photographs depict a narrow, deep, fast-flowing stream, lined with moss-draped cypress trees. Courtesy, Historical Association of Southern Florida

In 1883, thirteen-year-old Guy M. Bradley lived at the Fort Lauderdale House of Refuge, where his father served as keeper. Two years later, Bradley, then residing at Lantana, explored Cypress Creek and Lettuce Lake with two companions. Serving as Audubon warden beginning in 1902, Bradley was killed by plume hunters near Flamingo in 1905, the first warden to die in the line of duty. Courtesy, Historical Association of Southern Florida

village consisted of a cluster of 25 to 30 huts on the edge of the pine woods. It was governed by Little Tommy and Little Tiger, the son of old Tiger Tail, a principal chief of the Seminoles during the Indian wars. Tiger Tail was said to have passed the age of 100 when he was killed by lightning at Pine Island.

The Indians, observed Dr. Henshall, led a quiet, peaceable, and semi-pastoral life, cultivating fields of corn, pumpkins, sweet potatoes, beans, and bananas in the rich hammocks of the Everglades. They continued to make coontie and in the winter hunted for deer and bear. Henshall's dog, Cuff, made friends with the Indians' dogs and disappeared on the trip. Tiger promised to find the dog and return him. One day after Henshall returned to the House of Refuge, Tiger was seen poling a small canoe across New River Sound. Seated in the bow was the dog Cuff.

The monotonous tranquility that engulfed the House of Refuge was disrupted in the fall of 1882. The appointment of a new superintendent of the U.S. Life Saving Service brought wholesale firings, including that of Wash Jenkins, who was replaced on January 2, 1883, by Edwin R. Bradley of Hypoluxo Island.

When the Bradley family, which included three children, Lou, Guy, and Flora, arrived, they found Jenkins deathly sick, too weak even to walk. The condition of Jenkins indicated trouble ahead for the Bradleys. Their eldest son, Lou, aged 13, soon developed health problems. "His face was puffed and colorless and his fingernails were blue," wrote his friend, Charles Pierce. "He wanted to sleep all the time."

Later that spring Pierce visited the Fort Lauderdale House of Refuge. He observed: "When I arrived . . . I was distressed to hear that Guy and his sister were very sick from the mysterious malady that afflicted Wash Jenkins . . . Flora, who was about 10 years old, died that afternoon . . . The workmen engaged in repairing the station made a coffin and she was buried the next day under a wide-spreading sea grape tree. Guy swelled up so badly he could not walk. I carried him to the graveside."

In late summer of 1883 Edwin Bradley resigned his post as keeper of the House of Refuge and returned to the shores of Lake Worth. What had caused the strange sickness that had afflicted so many at the House of Refuge—an infection, a poison, a vitamin deficiency disease, or possibly a contaminated water supply? No one has ever solved the mystery.

Two years later Lou and Guy Bradley and their friend Charlie Pierce returned to the area to hunt plume birds on Cypress Creek, to the south of Hillsboro River. They explored the area around a body of water called Lettuce Lake, named for its heavy infestation by an aquatic plant called water lettuce.

In the 1880s ladies' hats decorated with plumes became so fashionable that many species of birds were virtually exterminated. When the boys went plume hunting in 1885, the sport was still legal. Twenty years later Guy, a plume hunter turned conservation officer, would become the first Audubon warden to die in the line of duty, gunned down near Flamingo by a man trying to stop the arrest of his sons for killing protected birds.

The Bradley boys left Cypress Creek and returned home to find their father had a new job, that of carrying mail from Lake Worth to the Biscayne Bay settlements via the "barefoot route." In the 1880s the standard U.S. Post Office route for a letter from Lake Worth to Biscayne Bay called for the item to be sent first to Jupiter, 22 miles north of the Lake Worth settlements. From Jupiter the letter went by Indian River steamboat to the railhead at Titusville and then by train to New York. Next it was carried by steamer to Havana, and from Cuba it was transported by a trading schooner to Biscayne Bay. A letter would travel 3,000 miles in a period of six weeks to two months to reach a settlement 68 miles away.

The barefoot route devised by the Bradleys required the mailman to sail or row from Palm Beach to the foot of Lake Worth, walk down the beach to the Hillsboro Inlet, row across, and then walk to the New River Inlet, which also had to be crossed by rowboat. Then came a 10-mile walk to Baker's Haulover at the head of Biscayne Bay, where a small boat fitted with oars and a sail waited to carry the mailman to the post office on the Miami River 12 miles away. The round trip took six days, the mailman returning home on Saturday following his Monday departure. Both the Orange Grove and Fort Lauderdale Houses of Refuge were used to provide shelter.

The trickiest part of the route was positioning boats at inlets and rivers so they would be available for the barefoot mailman at all times. For

Mail carriers walked the beaches between remote settlements at various times in Florida's history. The "barefoot route," established between the Lake Worth and Biscayne Bay regions in 1885, has become part of the folklore of the lower east coast even though the "barefoot mailmen" were only active for seven years. The completion of a road between the Palm Beach and Miami areas in 1892 rendered the colorful beachwalkers obsolete. Courtesy, Fort Lauderdale Historical Society

Left: This monument, erected in 1936 at Hillsboro Inlet, marks the area where barefoot mailman Ed Hamilton disappeared on October 11, 1887, while attempting to cross the inlet. Various contemporaries attributed Hamilton's death to drowning, sharks, and alligators, but his actual fate remains unknown. Courtesy, Fort Lauderdale Historical Society

Philadelphia promoter Hamilton Disston's 1881 agreement to pay the state one million dollars for four million acres of overflowed lands rescued Florida from post-Civil War financial difficulties and made Disston the nation's largest landowner. Disston centered his attention on the Kissimmee and Lake Okeechobee regions, where he initiated drainage projects, but part of his purchase lay within the boundaries of present-day Broward County. Unfortunately, Disston overextended himself financially, and his dreams of opening Central and South Florida to settlement ended in bankruptcy and eventual suicide. Courtesy, Florida Photographic Collection, Florida State Archives

example, at Hillsboro Inlet a boat had to be waiting for the southbound carrier. Then, having crossed the inlet, the mailman would need a spot on the south side where the boat would be ready for his return. Concealing the boat was essential, because if anyone else used it to cross the inlet, the boat would be on the wrong side of the water for the mail carrier. In the dry season he could wade across Hillsboro Inlet at low tide, but when the rainy season arrived, it was too deep and swift for safe swimming. Furthermore, sharks moved in and out of the inlets, and at high water alligators and snakes were washed down to the inlets.

Walking the barefoot route was a hard, tiring task and, like the job of the House of Refuge keeper, a lonely and monotonous one. In the fall of 1886 an event occurred that shattered the monotony of life on the southeast coast. Settlers called it, fondly, the "Great Wine Wreck." Offshore a Spanish ship broke up, discharging a huge cargo of wine and brandy. Casks floated ashore from Palm Beach all the way to the Keys. Jack Peacock, keeper of the Fort Lauderdale House of Refuge, bathed in the wine, hoping it might cure his arthritis. Indians rushed to the beaches and tried to tow casks of wine back up the river to their villages. Edwin Bradley came up with the most ingenious scheme of all. Where casks had surfaced along the barefoot route, he hid them away so the barefoot mailman might have a little liquid refreshment as he walked his rounds under the blazing Florida sun.

In the early summer of 1887 Bradley relinquished the route, turning it over to George Charter, a former Vermonter, and Ed Hamilton, who had come to the Lake Worth country from a small rural county in western Kentucky. It would be a tragic move for the young Kentuckian.

In the fall of 1887 squalls and gales pounded the coast and drenched the area with torrential rains. Rivers overflowed along the entire lower east coast. It was a difficult, even dangerous, time to travel.

On Sunday, October 9, Hamilton set out from Palm Beach. He complained to Charlie Pierce of not feeling well but felt he could make the trip with the aid of his trusty bottle of Perry Davis Pain-killer. He spent the night at the Orange Grove House of Refuge and set out the next morning for Hillsboro Inlet, a half-day's walk.

Hamilton was due back at the Hypoluxo post office at noon on Saturday. Noontime came and then sunset and sunrise the next morning and still no trace of the barefoot mailman. The next day Charter led a search party. That night as they reviewed the meager scraps of information on Hamilton with the keeper of the Orange Grove House of Refuge, they heard a faint call from the beach. At the water's edge they saw the dark form of a boat and a man struggling to pull the boat up out of the reach of the waves. They ran to the boat calling for Ed.

But it was not Hamilton. The man in the darkness was Charles Coman, keeper of the Fort Lauderdale House of Refuge. Alarmed that Hamilton had not reached the station on his trip south, he too had set out to look for the mailman.

On Monday, the day Hamilton was due at Fort Lauderdale, a stranger had appeared, walking down the beach from the north. The man had told Coman that a party of hunters with a portable boat had carried him across Hillsboro Inlet. Coman did not believe this story—he believed the man had used Ed's boat.

The next morning Charter and Coman walked down the beach, following the path Hamilton would have taken. At the inlet they discovered Hamilton's knapsack hanging on the limb of a sea grape tree. In the bag were the mail pouch, his trousers and shirt, a spoon, and his bottle of Perry Davis Pain-killer. Near the water's edge lay his underclothes. "Sharks got him," posited Charter. "Sharks ate him. He tried to swim the inlet and sharks got him."

The man whom Coman had suspected of taking Hamilton's boat was later charged with tampering with government property and tried in federal court in Jacksonville. He was acquitted and his name can no longer be found in court records.

The same year Hamilton died, 1887, Arthur T. Williams returned to the New River, the area he had visited with his surveyor-father as a 13-year-old boy. Now at 30 he was about to become the first in a long line of real-estate developers.

In 1881 the Board of Trustees of the Internal Improvement Fund of Florida had agreed to sell four million acres of land to Hamilton Disston, heir to the Disston saw fortune. He planned a massive drainage program near Lake Okeechobee, which promised to open up vast tracts of Florida land. Associated with Disston was Sir Edward Reed, of Hextable, Kent County, England. He headed a group of British investors who formed the Florida Land and Mortgage Company in 1883 and purchased more than two million acres from Disston, including acreage on New River. Sir Edward was a poet, a magazine editor, a pioneering designer of armored ships, a member of Parliament, and an author of books on ship design and travel.

Williams, who also owned beachfront property, had bought roughly 1,000 acres extending about two miles along the south side of the river from Sir Edward Reed's Florida Land and Mortgage Company. Williams called his development Palm City. An ad in the Jacksonville *Florida Times-Union* declared:

We are now selling lots in Palm City for $10 each, 50x100 and pay cost of recording and taxes for two years. If you are looking for an opportunity to secure a good home where a good living can be reasonably earned, where land is high

Arthur T. Williams, son of surveyor Marcellus Williams, accompanied his father to South Florida in 1870. Sixteen years later, as a prosperous young Fernandina businessman, he bought from Sir Edward Reed two sections of land on the south side of the New River. Advertised as Palm City, this property was the first in the New River area to be platted for sale. Only 26 lots were sold, however, and apparently no buildings were ever constructed in Palm City. Courtesy, Mrs. John P. Hines

Top: Jacksonville attorney Duncan U. Fletcher was the president of the Florida Fiber Company, which grew sisal hemp on 1,310 acres along the Middle River in the early 1890s. Elected to the United States Senate in 1909, Fletcher served for 27 years. Courtesy, Florida Photographic Collection, Florida State Archives

Bottom: As president of Henry Plant's South Florida Railroad Company, James E. Ingraham explored the Everglades from Fort Myers to Miami and then followed the Atlantic coast north to Fort Lauderdale in the spring of 1892. Plant never pursued his idea of draining and developing the Everglades, but the knowledge gained about the lower east coast won Ingraham a new job as general agent for Henry Flagler. Courtesy, Historical Association of Southern Florida

and choice, where climate is invigorating and delightful, and a point where land is valuable and sure to rapidly enhance in value, we suggest to you with confidence an investment in Palm City lots.

When Williams platted Palm City, the area had only one white resident, Charles Coman. In 1887 Williams sold 26 lots at $10 each, but by 1890 buyers were already forfeiting the land for taxes. That year five blocks of land were sold at $1.20 at a tax sale in Juno, which had been declared the Dade County seat in the 1888 election. Four years later the company was selling land, when it could, as acreage, ignoring the plat.

In 1890 William and Mary Brickell of Miami bought approximately 895 acres of the Florida Land and Mortgage Company's vast holdings at $1.35 an acre. The Brickells, who already owned the old Frankee Lewis Donation, were the New River's largest landholders.

By this time the area's population had grown enough for Dade County to tackle the problem of inadequate transportation in South Florida. Boats were commissioned by the county for use in crossing the rivers, and the route that Abner Doubleday had built was established as a public road. In addition, the county authorized the construction of a road from Lantana to Lemon City on Biscayne Bay. Guy Metcalf of Juno, a man of many interests and connections, was awarded the contract to build the new road.

The year 1890 also saw the establishment of the area's first large commercial venture. Duncan U. Fletcher of Jacksonville, later a U.S. Senator, headed the Florida Fiber Company, which bought 1,310 acres on Middle River. The company's mission was to grow sisal hemp for use in rope and other textiles. In an 1890 circular Fletcher stated:

Our plantation is all high and dry . . . with a river front of over two miles . . . However, with our present means, we are able to work a comparatively small force which unless a good portion of our treasury stock is sold, will not enable us to fully accomplish our purpose, i.e., to have 1,000 acres growing within a year, in order to put up machinery and commence cutting within three years.

In 1892 James E. Ingraham, who conducted an exploration of the Everglades for the West Coast railroad baron, Henry Plant, visited the farm. In his report he wrote: ". . . we met Mr. C.G. Phillips, a young man at present in charge of the property of the Florida Fiber Company of Jacksonville on Middle River . . . The Florida Fiber Company owns about 2 miles north, south of the Middle River, have 7 acres set out in Sisal hemp with perhaps an acre in nursery of the same plant. Their buildings consist of two small houses of one room each; frame buildings but unfinished inside."

The enterprise never really thrived. In December 1891 Fletcher petitioned Dade County for tax relief for his troubled firm. He asked that taxes be reduced from $32.41 down to some nominal figure. Lack of a labor force, leaf wilt, and frost apparently plagued the firm, which abandoned the venture but retained the land, platted it, and later sold lots in a development called Progresso.

By 1890 the House of Refuge was in need of repair. The Life Saving Service concluded too that it should be moved onto government-owned land, as was originally intended. While moving the house south to the Fort Lauderdale military reservation, the service received a letter from P.E. Cunningham, a Jacksonville attorney associated with the Florida Fiber Company. Cunningham claimed he owned the land where the house was located and ordered them not to move any buildings or even to set foot on his land. The superintendent wrote back that the request was "rather late." By November 1891 the move had been completed.

In 1891 the mobile House of Refuge gained another function. On August 18 it was designated the Fort Lauderdale Post Office. The area's first postmaster was William C. "Cap" Valentine. Valentine, a civil engineer, surveyor, farmer, and justice of the peace, was born in Virginia around 1840. In the Civil War he fought for the South. The new postmaster, who lived at the station with keeper Captain Dennis O'Neill, kept the mail in a cigar box. O'Neill was a boat-builder, deep-sea diver, and a sea captain. He had once sailed aboard a schooner bound from Central America with a load of mahogany. In 1871 the schooner wrecked near Hillsboro Inlet, and the captain made his way to Florida shores by riding a mahogany log through a school of sharks.

Close friends, the two men shared a common employer, the U.S. government, which paid them every three months. Both men were whiskey enthusiasts, so payday signaled a quarterly drinking spree at the House of Refuge.

In late 1892 the road from Lantana to Lemon City was completed at a cost of $24.50 a mile. The Bay Biscayne Stage Line went into operation, ending the era of the barefoot mailman. The stage's fare was $6 to New River from either Lantana or Lemon City, $10 round trip. Board and overnight lodging at a tent hotel at New River cost $2.

Nine of the ten streams the road crossed were provided with bridges. The tenth, New River, was the widest and deepest. It was served by a ferry near Tarpon Bend. Edward Moffatt ran the tent camp on the north side of the river and operated the ferry. Then Guy Metcalf, who had built the road and was now managing the stage line and the ferry, decided to replace Moffatt with his cousin from Melbourne. On January 31, 1893, the cousin, a man who would later be regarded as the founder of modern Fort Lauderdale, arrived at New River. His name was Frank Stranahan.

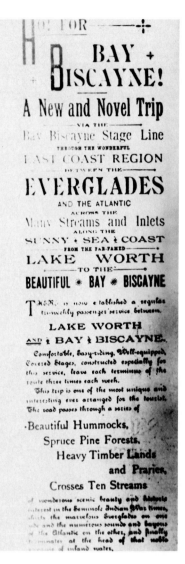

This 1893 timetable for the Bay Biscayne Stage Line's route between Lantana and Lemon City promised "Comfortable, Easy-riding, Well-equipped Covered Stages." The "stagecoach" was actually a mule-drawn, springless wagon with a canvas cover. It could accommodate five or six people with baggage, but since as many as eight often made the trip, the passengers took turns walking alongside. A night's rest at the Adirondack Camp on New River must have been a welcome relief. Courtesy, Fort Lauderdale Historical Society

Frank Stranahan's trading post building, which stood on the New River for six years, was replaced by a two-story pine structure in 1901. This larger building, constructed by E.T. King, served first as a new trading post and ultimately as Frank and Ivy Stranahan's home. Today it is Broward County's oldest building. This view from the south side of the river shows the house as it appeared between 1913 and 1915. Courtesy, Fort Lauderdale Historical Society

Chapter 3

STRANAHAN AND FLAGLER

Frank Stranahan spent his first night at New River Camp under a grove of live oaks. When he awoke in the morning, he found about 30 Seminoles sleeping on the ground all around him. "I think I will get along with them all right," he wrote his brother, a remarkably prophetic statement from a man who would become the best white friend the New River Indians had ever known.

A native of Vienna, Ohio, Stranahan had come to Florida for his health, impaired while working in the Youngstown steel mills. He arrived in Melbourne in the late 1880s, then moved on down to New River when his cousin Guy Metcalf offered him the job of running the camp, the ferry, and the post office, which had been moved to New River Camp from the House of Refuge.

When he arrived at New River, his only neighbors were Captain Denny O'Neill, Cap Valentine, a Negro cook who worked at the camp, and the Indians, a sizeable number of whom lived on a large hammock near the camp. Farther to the north lived William C. Collier, who planted an orange grove on the North Fork of the Middle River. The Seminoles, who loved his oranges, called him "Colo" and named the river "Colo-hatchee" in his honor.

Stranahan's introduction to the facts of Fort Lauderdale life came quickly. Without delay he encountered the Indians, the largest population group, and the Brickells, the biggest landholders. Then he found himself in the middle of a dispute over the peculiar tendency of early pioneers to build on land whether they owned it or not.

The Brickells owned the real estate on which Guy Metcalf had built the camp and a portion of the road. Since they wanted to develop their choice Cooley Hammock land themselves, they agreed to relocate the road at their own expense provided the camp and ferry were moved farther west. On May 1, 1893, the Dade County Commissioners received a curt note from Mary and William B. Brickell, declaring: "You are hereby notified that I have had a Road cut and grubbed on the Section Line at New River. Please have the Ferry moved and use the new road within thirty days."

In the new alignment Stranahan acquired 10.7 riverfront acres from the Brickells, the first of many land purchases that would eventually make him one of the wealthiest men in the area. On this land he built his trading post, Stranahan & Company, a one-story frame building set back from a wooden bulkhead and dock on the river.

With the sharp eye of a talented entrepreneur, Stranahan saw the potential in establishing an Indian trading post. Soon after his arrival he began to buy pelts and hides from the Seminoles for resale through a trading post in Lantana. His rapport with the Indians, built firmly on a reputation for fairness and honesty, soon led to the development of a prosperous trade with the Seminoles. From the west a flotilla of dugout canoes, manned by 100-150 Seminoles who had hunted for weeks in the Everglades and the Big Cypress Swamp, would converge on the trading post.

Above: Seminole Indians from throughout South Florida traded at Frank Stranahan's trading post. This Indian father and daughter were photographed there in the late 1890s. Their clothing—longshirt and vest, patchwork dress and beads— illustrates the unique combination of traditional items and trade goods adopted by the Seminoles in the late 19th century. Courtesy, Fort Lauderdale Historical Society

Right: By 1897 Frank Stranahan's business had prospered sufficiently to allow the addition of a porch around the trading post and the replacement of the camp's tents with more permanent cottages. The open structure with a rounded roof pictured behind the trading post was a chickee built in about 1896 to shelter the Indians who traded with Stranahan. In the foreground is a boat slip where the Seminoles docked their canoes. Courtesy, Fort Lauderdale Historical Society

The Indians usually arrived in the afternoon and remained in camp from four days to a week. When the Indians were at Stranahan's post, they slept on his porch or under a canvas roof he built as a dormitory for visiting Seminoles. Stranahan paid them in cash for skins and pelts, which he then resold to a trading house in Jacksonville. The Indians then used their money to buy food, calico, traps, ammunition, and other supplies. Some Seminole groups received as much as $1,500 for their skins and pelts. Stranahan refused to sell the Indians intoxicants. Some, however, would go north to Whiskey Street in West Palm Beach. Stranahan would usually persuade them to leave their guns behind.

In addition to his income from the trading post, Stranahan received a steady $25 per month from the county for operating the ferry. A frame structure 20 feet wide and 30 feet long, the cable-operated ferry carried wagons and large loads across the river at no charge. Individuals were simply rowed across by Stranahan.

For a while Stranahan, a shy, reserved man, lived a quiet but busy life on the river, trading with the Indians and operating the ferry and camp. He had no inkling that the isolation of New River was about to end. The moving force in the massive changes that lay ahead was a man who had two things in common with Stranahan. Both were sons of Presbyterian ministers, and both had lived in Ohio. There the similarity ends. Stranahan was essentially a small-town businessman, deeply involved and concerned with day-to-day happenings in his rather small corner of the world.

Henry Morrison Flagler, on the other hand, was nothing less than a captain of industry, a tycoon, a dreamer of great dreams, and a "doer" on an enormous scale. With John D. Rockefeller, he had founded Standard Oil of Ohio in 1870. Then, at 56, an age when many men would have retired, Flagler set about building a second empire, the Flagler System, which included a railroad, hotels, huge land-development companies, a canal company, a finance company, and newspapers in Palm Beach and Miami. The east coast of Florida, from St. Augustine to Key West—this was the domain of Henry Flagler.

But in the severe winter of 1894-1895 Flagler's empire reached only as far south as Palm Beach. He had no immediate plans to go farther south until a series of hard freezes destroyed the state's citrus crop, winter vegetables, and coconut palms throughout North and Central Florida. Confidence waned sharply in Florida's potential as a major agricultural state.

But citrus crops south of New River were undamaged. In Miami Mrs. Julia Tuttle dramatized the glory of South Florida's tropical winters by sending orange blossoms wrapped in damp cotton to Flagler in St. Augustine. Flagler decided to see for himself. His own Florida East Coast

Frank Stranahan, seen relaxing at his New River camp in this circa 1896 photograph, is often referred to as Fort Lauderdale's first permanent white settler. Although this designation is open to debate since postmaster "Cap" Valentine had settled at the beach in 1891, Stranahan was the first in an unbroken chain of settlers who made their homes in the New River area where the new village would grow. Courtesy, Fort Lauderdale Historical Society

Henry Morrison Flagler had already made his fortune with the Standard Oil Company when he turned his attention to Florida's east coast in the late 1880s. From that time until his death in 1913, his name was synonymous with the state's development. His many enterprises included hotels, land development companies, steamship lines, and the Florida East Coast Railway. This 1890s portrait shows Flagler at the time he was extending his railroad south to Palm Beach and Miami. Courtesy, Henry Morrison Flagler Museum

Railway carried him as far as West Palm Beach, where he boarded a launch to Fort Lauderdale. The rest of the way he rode in a cart drawn by a mule.

To encourage him to extend his railroad to Miami, both Mrs. Tuttle and the Brickells agreed to give him land in Miami. In addition, Mrs. Brickell offered him land on New River. Sizing up the situation quickly, Flagler decided that night that his railroad would continue on to Fort Lauderdale and then to the shores of Biscayne Bay.

In a letter to Mrs. Tuttle dated April 22, 1895, Flagler wrote: "Included in Mr. Brickell's proposition was 100 acres at New River . . . not that I expect to build up a town at New River, but I think it is good farming land, and I should hope to recoup myself to some extent by the sale of property given to me in that Neighborhood."

Flagler's letter indicates he was under the mistaken belief that he was dealing with Mr. Brickell. He was to learn rather quickly that the Brickell who ran the show was Mary, not William.

Born in Yorkshire, England, Mary Bulmer met and married William Brickell in Australia. A picturesque past followed the Brickells into Miami, highly embellished by William's colorful narrative style. He claimed to have been a world traveler who had amassed a vast fortune. Along the way he suffered huge losses in the wholesale grocery business in Cleveland. After that, Mary reportedly took over the family business. After the Civil War the Brickells established a trading post on the Miami River. In 1868 they bought the old Frankee Lewis Donation from Harriet English and in 1890 bought 895 acres from Sir Edward Reed.

Mary Brickell has been described as steely-eyed, imperious, cool, and aloof, yet she was well known for her kindness to the Seminoles and Negroes in the area. Although some called her a penny-pincher, she made unsecured loans to many, both black and white. However, no one could say Mary Brickell wasn't a good businesswoman—at her death she left an estate of $5 million.

In the summer of 1895 a New Smyrna farmer named Philemon N. Bryan, aided by his 17-year-old son Tom, supervised a crew of 400 black laborers in clearing the right-of-way for Flagler's railroad from the Cypress Creek area to New River, a distance of about 10 miles. Two days before the railroad was due to reach the river, the Brickells filed a plat for a town of one square mile with the Dade County Circuit Court.

Flagler's surveyors had hoped to run the railroad along the coastal ridge, adjacent to the county road. This would have taken the railroad through the original Frankee Lewis Donation, now owned by the Brickells. And just as they had moved Guy Metcalf's camp to the west, now they set about nudging the mighty Flagler away from their choicest property.

The Brickells, however, were willing to bargain. They gave the tycoon the right-of-way and they agreed to give him half of the lots in a proposed new plat. In return Flagler agreed to reroute his railroad farther to the west, to plat a new town called Fort Lauderdale, to promote the town in his advertising and publicity, and to build a railroad station that would make the town a regular stop between West Palm Beach and Miami.

In later years it was said that because of his battles with Mary Brickell, Fort Lauderdale was not one of Flagler's favorite towns. But the old man kept his word, and work proceeded on a plat for "Town of Fort Lauderdale, Dade Co., Fl." This was completed by civil engineer A.L. Knowlton in 1895.

February 22, 1896, was a good deal more than George Washington's birthday in Fort Lauderdale. For the settlement something important was happening and apparently everybody was on hand to celebrate. In West Palm Beach, Sue King and three of her children climbed aboard the train

Philemon N. Bryan, one of Florida's leading citrus growers, faced financial ruin after the "Big Freeze" of 1894 to 1895 destroyed his New Smyrna groves. Fortunately for Bryan, his fruit-shipping activities had acquainted him with Henry Flagler, and the railroad tycoon subsequently gave him the contract to build the Florida East Coast Railway 10 miles north from New River. He and his wife Lucy are in the center of this circa 1921 family photograph. To the left is Tom M. Bryan and at right is Reed A. Bryan. Courtesy, Reed A. Bryan III

for the first trip to Fort Lauderdale, where Ed King was waiting for his wife and children. The Kings were in good company. On board the train were Flagler himself; James R. Parrott, president of the railway; the famous American actor, Joseph Jefferson; and Charles B. Cory, naturalist, scientist, sportsman, and millionaire.

As the train thundered through the South Florida countryside, small groups gathered along the way to cheer the locomotive on to Fort Lauderdale. Greeting the train at New River were Frank Stranahan, Ed and Byrd King, Captain Denny O'Neill, Cap Valentine, and Louis Marshall, who had hauled a shipment of tomatoes by barge to the tracks. When the train headed back, Marshall would become the first local farmer to ship winter vegetables north via the railroad. From the back country the Seminoles sent a delegation, Doctor Tommie, Johnny Jumper, Cropeared Charlie, and Charlie Willie.

For 20 minutes the settlers offered congratulations to the Flagler party. Then the train headed back to West Palm Beach It had been a momentous occasion for the little settlement and would in fact qualify as one of the most important days in the town's history. To the railroad the day was less significant. Years later when a question arose about the date of the train's arrival, the railroad's librarian reported that Fort Lauderdale was

In February 1896 Louis H. Marshall became the first Fort Lauderdale area farmer to ship vegetables north on the Florida East Coast Railway. In subsequent years, such shipments contributed greatly to the economic growth of the region. This packing-house, which Marshall built on the south fork of the New River about 1902, was a popular gathering place for early residents. Courtesy, Fort Lauderdale Historical Society

Left: The first train to reach Fort Lauderdale arrived February 22, 1896, greeted by four Seminole Indians and a handful of settlers. For two months, until the bridge over the New River was completed, the tiny settlement was the Florida East Coast Railway's southern terminus. The first railroad station, seen in the center of this Austin Smith drawing, was a boxcar. Courtesy, Fort Lauderdale Historical Society

so inconsequential in 1896 that the company didn't even bother to make a notation of the event.

When the railroad reached Fort Lauderdale, the town's white population had not yet climbed back to the level it reached prior to the Cooley Massacre, but other groupings of settlers could now be found in the area. For example, a number of German farmers living near Lettuce Lake had named their settlement Dresden. This designation was changed in 1896 when Frank Sheene, working with George O. Butler as a surveyor for the Florida Coast Line Canal and Transportation Company, gave the area the name Pompano, a tribute to the tasty fish that abounded nearby. Sheene and Butler stayed on and settled in the area. Butler became Pompano's first postmaster and in 1899 Mrs. Butler started the area's first school, a one-room structure on the northeast shore of Lettuce Lake. (The school would be blown away by the 1903 hurricane.)

Above: According to tradition, both Henry Flagler (left) and Joseph Jefferson (right) were aboard the first train to Fort Lauderdale. Jefferson, probably the most renowned American actor of the late 19th century, visited Fort Lauderdale frequently in the 1890s and early 1900s. Courtesy, Henry Morrison Flagler Museum

Along his railroad Flagler established small towns, which could serve as home for his railroad workers and later as farm towns where settlers could grow fruits and vegetables, the freight he needed for his trains. These settlements were not called developments but rather colonies. The Flagler colonization program spun off a town called Deerfield near the Hillsboro River (1897) and to the south of Fort Lauderdale the towns of Modello (1898) and Hallandale (1898).

One of the beneficiaries of Flagler's expanding empire was Cap Valentine, whose civil engineering skills were again in demand. Cap surveyed and platted Modello, named after Flagler's Model Land Company. In 1898 twelve Danish families from Chicago journeyed to Modello to take advantage of discounted train fares, rebates on shipments of furniture and household goods, and enticing land deals.

After the Danish immigrants arrived, James E. Ingraham, now president of the Model Land Company, remarked to his Swedish brother-in-law, Luther Halland: "Why don't you go down there and start a Swedish settlement?" Again, Cap was called on to survey and plat a town to be called Hallandale.

The railroad sparked new settlement and brought in new settlers. Not long after they rode into Fort Lauderdale on the train, actor Joe Jefferson

Heir to a silk and wine fortune, Charles B. Cory of Boston began studying natural history as a hobby and eventually became one of America's most noted ornithologists. He first came to Florida in 1877 and found the wilderness conditions perfect for his studies and for his favorite pastimes—hunting and fishing. In 1906 Cory went bankrupt and turned to natural history as a full-time profession, serving as curator of ornithology at Chicago's Field Columbian Museum until his death in 1921. From Cirker, Dictionary of American Portraits, *Dover, 1967*

persuaded the millionaire sportsman, Charles Cory, to move his $100,000 floating palace, the *Wanderer*, from Palm Beach down to Stranahan's trading post. Ninety feet in length, the white houseboat contained 12 bedrooms, a magnificently appointed lounge, recreation rooms, the area's only piano, and a gun room, which housed an elaborate collection of fishing tackle and a virtual arsenal of firearms. As an old-timer commented, "There were sufficient weapons on board to have reopened the Seminole War at a moment's notice."

War with the Seminoles, however, would not have appealed to Cory. He was on excellent terms with the Indians and was fascinated by their culture and language, which he studied and described in detail in his book *Hunting and Fishing in Florida* in 1896. Stranahan owned a copy of the book, the sixth that Cory had written up to that time.

Cory, a burly man who sported a handlebar mustache, brought to the little community of primitive shacks a touch of spectacular luxury; celebrity visitors included former President Grover Cleveland and Admiral George Dewey, hero of the Spanish-American War, and Cory held the wildest parties the river had ever seen. From the American stage Jefferson brought in young women described by observers as "wild actresses." One of those who observed was young Tom Bryan. He would row his boat over to the *Wanderer* and peer through the darkness at the goings-on aboard the houseboat.

When they weren't enjoying wild life on the river, Cory and Jefferson were enjoying it in the back country. When they went hunting, they hunted in style, equipped with tents, cots, the latest in camp stoves, and an experienced chef to prepare meals for them on the trail. Cory hunted wild turkeys near Cypress Creek and organized a panther hunt in the Deerfield area. Dick King, brother of Ed King, described a Cory panther hunt:

Several of Charlie Willie's boys who were experienced hunters went with them. And those Indian lads were smart fellows. They could have gotten that panther the first day out, but they strung things out as long as they could and kept the party on the trail 10 days before they got their cat, and a big one, too, measuring nine feet from tip to tip. Cory didn't mind, though, as he loved the sport and would probably have been disappointed if they'd rushed things for him.

While Cory hunted panther in South Florida, an adventurer of great future significance to the area was becoming involved in an international contest. On the island of Cuba, just 90 miles south of Florida, a storm was building, not a West Indian hurricane but a war for independence that would in time involve the United States. Cuban patriots seeking an end to Spanish rule needed guns, and sympathetic Americans, called "filibusters," were eager to oblige them, even though gunrunning was illegal. The most famous of the filibusters was Napoleon Bonaparte Broward, one of three owners of the speedy, oceangoing tug, *The Three Friends*. The tug's fearless captain, "Dynamite" Johnny O'Brien, gained his nickname from a voyage in which he transported 60 tons of dynamite to Colombia, prevailing against a hurricane, a severe electrical storm, generally rough seas, and a crew that became hysterical upon learning the nature of the cargo.

Reports persist that Broward on occasion tied up his famous tug at Stranahan's docks, but little is known of this matter, perhaps because gunrunners prefer to operate in secrecy. What is known is that in May 1897 a sternwheeler, *Biscayne*, somewhere on New River, was loaded with two carloads of arms and ammunition, along with 30 Cubans under the command of a Colonel Mendez. The cargo was to be transferred to the tug *Dauntless*, captained at that time by Dynamite Johnny himself.

A special Treasury Department agent named Benjamin F. Hambleton, vacationing in Fort Lauderdale, was cruising on a sloop near New River Inlet when he observed the *Biscayne* in waters that would usually be considered too rough for a sternwheeler. When the seas became calmer, the *Biscayne* joined the *Dauntless* for the transfer. Hambleton, armed with a double-barreled shotgun, bore down on them in a rowboat, shouting, "In the name of the law, I command you to stop putting those arms on this vessel! You are all under arrest!"

Hambleton scrambled aboard but was quickly disarmed and pitched back rudely into his rowboat. Unfortunately for the *Dauntless*, May 31 was just not a lucky day. Before the loading of arms could be completed, the *Marblehead*, one of the few U.S. ships that could outdistance the filibuster's boat, arrived on the scene. After a six-hour chase the *Marblehead* caught the gunrunners.

Since the transaction had been interrupted, the deck was still cluttered with boxes marked ".43 caliber" and bundles of rifles wrapped in burlap. A lieutenant from the *Marblehead* indicated a box of cartridges and asked Jim Floyd, a Negro sea captain, "What are these, sardines?" Captain Floyd gladly agreed with him. The remark revealed how little interest the government really had in prosecuting the gunrunners. At Key West the case was suspended, due to lack of evidence. In less than two weeks the *Dauntless* was back in business.

American sympathies were clearly with the Cuban cause and with the filibusters who had achieved the status of heroes, a perception that would aid Broward later in his campaign for the governorship. In 1898 those sympathies would draw the United States officially into the clash that would become the Spanish-American War.

A man who joined the army as a medic during the Spanish-American

Filibusterer and New York harbor pilot "Dynamite Johnny" O'Brien commanded the Three Friends *on its last gunrunning voyage in December 1896. In May of the following year, he attempted to sail the tug* Dauntless *to Cuba from New River Inlet, but was intercepted by a United States cruiser. Courtesy, Fort Lauderdale Historical Society*

Ivy Julia Cromartie, Fort Lauderdale's first schoolteacher, came to the New River village from Lemon City in October 1899. She taught school for less than one year before marrying Frank Stranahan on August 17, 1900. During her long life, Ivy Stranahan was active in a number of civic and charitable ventures, and was perhaps the most well-known of Fort Lauderdale's "pioneer" citizens. This photograph was taken when she was 17, a year before she came to Fort Lauderdale. Courtesy, Fort Lauderdale Historical Society

War played an heroic role in the young community of Fort Lauderdale. He was known affectionately as the "Little Doctor." When he first practiced medicine in Fort Lauderdale, he was not officially a doctor, but he certainly was little, just five feet five.

As a child in Goldsboro, North Carolina, Tom Kennedy had seen the family home burned to the ground by General Sherman. By the time he arrived in Palm Beach in the late 1890s, he had developed a working knowledge of medicine. He was employed briefly at the Flagler residence to watch over the empire builder's hopelessly insane second wife. Kennedy later wrote:

Mr. Bill Lainhart hired me then for a couple of weeks to watch the Flagler residence . . . so if Mrs. Flagler became violent or got away from the nurses, I could assist them. I had nothing to do but keep in calling distance of the house, so I almost memorized Flint's Practice of Medicine. *I studied it the whole time I was on that job.*

Kennedy came to Fort Lauderdale in 1899, planning to raise tomatoes. Since there was no doctor in the area, he was consulted on occasion by the pioneers. Then in November 1899 Walter Marshall returned from Miami with a severe illness. From his days as an army medic, Kennedy recognized the symptoms: jaundice, vomiting, and a high fever. He diagnosed yellow fever, the dreaded "yellow jack."

Virtually everyone in the community caught the disease. Kennedy had no choice but to do everything in his power to save as many lives as he could. He started the day working his tomato fields, then traveled to the cypress and palmetto huts to check temperature and pulse. He prescribed doses of calomel, epsom salts, and quinine. When the disease had run its course, Fort Lauderdale was the only settlement in South Florida that had escaped without a fatality.

Kennedy went back to his tomato farm west of the tracks. Then one day two doctors arrived from the federal Bureau of Health. After questioning him, they charged him with practicing medicine without a license. At his hearing Kennedy explained that he was the only person available to help with the medical emergency. The doctors not only cleared him of all charges, they told him to submit a bill for his services. Tom Kennedy used the money the government paid him to enroll in the University of the South (Suwanee), where he earned his medical degree. At last he was a bona fide doctor.

In 1901 he returned to Fort Lauderdale, married Mollie Dent, and established himself as a doctor whose services were available to all, whether they could pay the bill or not. Once, after treating a patient in Delray Beach, Dr. Kennedy started to walk back home, only to pass out from the heat near the FEC tracks. When Flagler heard of the incident, he told employees: "When the Little Doctor needs to go anywhere, take him."

In 1899 the settlers at Fort Lauderdale learned what they needed to qualify for a county school—a schoolhouse and a minimun of nine pupils. Ed King built a one-room schoolhouse south of the river, and the rest of the community located 12 children of school age. Fort Lauderdale was ready for its first school.

The job as the town's first schoolteacher went to 18-year-old Ivy Julia Cromartie from nearby Lemon City. A native of North Florida, she had moved with her family to Biscayne Bay country. Later she described her introduction to her new job:

At the Fort Lauderdale station, I was greeted by Mr. Ed King, a local school trustee. He led the way to the railroad dock on New River where his "pop-boat" was moored. A pop-boat was a small craft, much like a row boat, with a gasoline engine installed in the center. With no mufflers on these boats, the rapid loud explosions were the only sounds to break the silence on New River in those early days. Mr. King steered down the river and up Tarpon Creek to his home. . . . Greeted by Mrs. King, a charming hostess, I was to live with the King family during the ensuing months.

The opulent stern-wheel houseboat Wanderer, *built in Titusville in 1896 by wealthy naturalist and sportsman Charles B. Cory, brought rich and famous guests on hunting and fishing expeditions along southeast Florida waterways. Joseph Jefferson was Cory's annual guest on the* Wanderer *for several years, and former president Grover Cleveland and Admiral George Dewey stayed aboard the vessel while visiting Fort Lauderdale. Courtesy, Henry Morrison Flagler Museum*

W. H. "Harry" McNab worked as a painter on Henry Flagler's Palm Beach hotels before coming to Pompano in 1898, his family joining him the following year. The McNabs, like many early South Florida residents, became prominent landowners and businessmen as the area grew in the early 20th century. In the 1920s Harry McNab helped found Pompano's first bank and served on the city commission. Courtesy, Miami Herald

Within a few days school was ready to begin in a small room, 20 by 30 feet, with a dozen used chairs and desks. For a monthly salary of $40, Ivy taught grades one to eight. Set in scrub pine and palmetto, the school was about a mile and a half from the King home. The settlers had cleared a footpath for the new schoolmarm. On her walks to and from school she might encounter quail, wild turkeys, raccoons, wildcats, squirrels, turtles, and snakes. She was particularly fond of the numerous birds and would in time become a dedicated and active member of the Florida Audubon Society.

She met Frank Stranahan when he delivered her mail one day. Later she wrote: "If I thought I had mail, I would ring the 'ferry bell' and someone would come in a rowboat or canoe to take me to the post office. If I did have mail and did not call for it, Mr. Stranahan would come across in his pop boat with his lantern to deliver it; this set everyone to wondering."

Frank would also call for her when school was out. Together they would go freshwater fishing up the New River. "This ride was beautiful," she recalled. ". . . The crystal clear water was like an aquarium. We could see trout and snapper or bream hidden under the ferns and lillies."

When Ivy returned home to Lemon City, Frank wrote her regularly. On May 4, 1900: ". . . remember be brave and true to me and I think I can say you will not forget or regret the many pleasant days we have passed together lately especially on last Sunday on the beach. I forward by mail . . . the Kodak views."

And on May 15: "There is going to be an ice cream party at Mrs. King's Thursday night. From rumors you will have several invitations from men. Kindly accept this as one."

By August his letter to her refers to their impending marriage: ". . . Time is short, wish to ask you question that I should have done several days ago. In getting the License how do you wish your name to appear on it and age . . ."

On August 16, 1900, Frank and Ivy were married at Lemon City. Their honeymoon took them to Asheville, North Carolina, to Niagara Falls, to his former home in Ohio, and finally to her grandparents in Garland, North Carolina.

Stranahan commissioned Ed King to build for him and his young bride a trading post to replace the original and to serve as their home. The interior was sealed with Dade County pine, and broad porches were built for both the first and second floors. The Indians quickly stamped their approval on the spacious covered porches by using them as sleeping quarters on their trips to the post. Neither Frank nor Ivy seemed to mind.

"Reared in a large family amidst accompanying social events, my young married life might have been a little lonely had it not been for the

Indians who came to my husband's trading post," she recalled. Just as her husband had before her, she had made friends with the Indians.

In 1890 the census taker had reported zero population at Fort Lauderdale, a rank injustice since it is known that the population at the time was actually one. Captain Denny O'Neill, keeper of the House of Refuge, was the sole inhabitant. The census of 1900 showed a dizzying increase, rising to 91. The town had finally caught up with and passed the population it had attained before the Cooley Massacre. The town was ready now for a new century.

In Pompano more and more settlers were moving in to establish farms. Emil Ehmann began the cultivation of pineapples, later switching to tomatoes, and still later to beans and peppers, crops that yielded higher profits.

Isaac Hardy moved his family of four boys and three girls from Hypoluxo Island to Pompano, a distance of 22 miles, on a raft which he floated down the Florida East Coast Canal. On the north bank of Cypress Creek, he built a house sturdy enough to serve as the town's hurricane shelter when the autumn storms swept into South Florida. The same year, 1899, L.R. Smoak, his son Oliver and daughter Lillian, and Harry McNab came to Pompano. Liking what he saw, McNab sent for his brother, Robert, and their mother and sister. The family became a major landowner in the area.

In 1902 the bucolic serenity of Pompano was interrupted by an exciting event, the wreck of the ship *Copenhagen*. Members of the crew brought articles ashore to sell, and Isaac Hardy bought the ship's bell, which he used to call his sons in from the field.

As the 20th century began, 12 families were living in Hallandale— seven Swedish, three English, and two black. Purchase of an outlying tract for farming entitled a settler to a free lot in an area to the east, called the "town section." Luther Halland enlisted the aid of a Swedish immigrant, Olof Zetterlund, to help promote the settlement. Halland, whose company was based in New York, came to Florida to set up a small trading post and to serve as the community's first postmaster.

As was the case in Pompano, pineapples proved an important early crop, but the settlers soon switched over to tomatoes. These would become the dominant crop in Hallandale. At one time 13 packinghouses lined the east side of the railroad.

The Danes in Modello also cultivated tomatoes, in the East Marsh section between the railroad and the coastal canal. In 1902 the little Danish colony at Modello was joined by a Dane named Andrew Christian Frost. At age 26 he had come to the United States and settled in Wisconsin, where he served in the state house of representatives. James Ingraham, touring the Midwest, met Frost and persuaded him to come to South

Tomatoes were the major crop in farmlands surrounding Pompano, Fort Lauderdale, Modello, and Hallandale at the turn of the century. Henry Flagler's Model Land Company encouraged tomato farming and developed much of the agricultural land in present Broward County. The Florida East Coast Railway, which shipped South Florida produce north, also promoted tomato growing in the area as a great profit-maker. Courtesy, Broward County Historical Commission

Prominent Chicago lawyer Hugh Taylor Birch, shown here with his wife, came to Florida in 1893 to escape the hustle and bustle of the forthcoming Columbian Exposition. Sailing down the Atlantic coast in a rented sloop, he was forced to seek refuge in New River Inlet during a storm. Instantly attracted to the beauty of Fort Lauderdale's undeveloped beachfront, he soon bought property there. Courtesy, Fort Lauderdale Historical Society

Florida. In 1902 he became an agent for the Model Land Company and moved to Modello. A warm, outgoing man, Frost was effective in attracting settlers to the area.

Frost initiated a petition to incorporate the community of Modello as Dania, and on November 30, 1904, twenty-eight of the community's thirty-five registered freeholders gathered in Seminole Hall to sign a charter calling for Dania's incorporation. The town's first mayor was John Millikan.

In the community's early days Frost proved to be an active builder. He erected a general store, which housed the post office, and in 1905 constructed Dania's first school. After a second story was added, the building also became the town's first hotel. The year 1903 saw the founding of the Dania Methodist Church. That same year a group of Methodists began holding meetings with a circuit preacher in the Fort Lauderdale schoolhouse.

One of the most important events of the early 1900s was the appearance of a new inlet near the House of Refuge. One account, published in Guy Metcalf's paper, *The Tropical Sun*, stated that high water "tore out" the inlet, which had a depth of nine feet at the bar at mean low tide. *The Sun* later called it one of the best inlets on the east coast of Florida.

Another version said that Nature was aided by Ed King and 15 men who helped the sea by digging to create a more convenient access. Cap Valentine opposed the project, perhaps fearing it might spoil the privacy of his nearby Burnham's Point home. With his assistant, Warren Smith, he rowed out to the scene, armed with two guns. The excavators, anticipating his opposition, were armed even more effectively. They presented Cap and Smith each with a quart of Hayner's Dry Whiskey. In no time at all, Cap was digging with the rest.

In 1902 Valentine played a key role in another landmark event, the first wedding in Fort Lauderdale. Frank Oliver, who had helped Cap survey Dania, called on his former employer to perform the ceremony as the town's justice of the peace. *The Tropical Sun* published a rather fanciful account of the wedding of Oliver and Eva Bryan:

Last Monday one of the most important events of the season occurred when Mr. F.R. Oliver and Miss Eva Bryan were married ... Late in the afternoon the yacht Trenton *called at the Oliver residence, taking on the bride and groom to be ... The party proceeded down river to the residence of Col. W.C. Valentine, where the ceremony was performed with the yacht swinging in midstream.*

The account was written by Will Marshall, whose ability to embellish the facts foretold a successful career in politics. In 1911 he would become

Fort Lauderdale's first mayor. The actual ceremony, according to Mrs. Eva Oliver, was less elaborate. Cap, from the dock at his home, had bound the two in holy matrimony while they struggled to keep their balance standing in the yacht *Trenton*, which turned out to be a rowboat.

The performance of the marriage proved to be Cap's final contribution to Fort Lauderdale. On a Saturday evening, March 29, 1903, Cap and two of his workers set out for Stranahan's store for supplies. Returning to his farm upriver, Valentine, who had been drinking, stood up in the small boat and fell overboard. His companions fished him out, but he stood up again, and again he fell into the water. This time, his friends were unable to save him. Around noon the following day his body was recovered in 27 feet of water.

At a time when most settlers and visitors preferred the sheltered waters of the river, Hugh Taylor Birch gazed upon the beach at Fort Lauderdale and called it "the most beautiful spot upon which I had laid eyes in all my travels."

Hugh Taylor Birch has been called a civilized man, an authority on astronomy, entomology, botany, ornithology, geology, and law. He was also a wealthy and successful attorney, serving at one time as general counsel to Standard Oil. To escape Chicago's corporate pressures, he sought release in the enjoyment of nature. Over a period of time he and John McGregor Adams bought three miles of oceanfront, plus other properties in separate parcels from Mary MacDonald and Arthur T. Williams, the Palm City promoter, for $3,500.

After a disagreement in 1902, Birch and Adams divided the property. Adams took the land near the House of Refuge, Birch the northernmost half. For Ed King, their falling-out meant extra business: the construction of a hunting lodge in the shape of a gun for Adams, and a winter home on the beach for Birch. Adams died shortly thereafter, but Birch remained for a good four decades, the first of many to enjoy the beach at Fort Lauderdale.

In 1904 Napoleon Bonaparte Broward, the filibuster, ran for governor. Already a hero, the tall, handsome Broward proved to be an effective campaigner. In championing the cause of Everglades drainage, he proposed a reclamation program to perserve public lands for the people rather than for the railroads and large corporate interests. In the November election Broward, the Democratic candidate, received 75 percent of the vote.

In January of 1905 he assumed the governorship and began an administration that would later be called the Broward Era. His impact on the entire state would prove to be enormous, and nowhere would this impact be greater than on the New River and the Everglades to the west.

Former gunrunner Napoleon Bonaparte Broward was elected governor of Florida in 1904. His progressive platform called for regulation of railroads and large corporations, educational reform, and drainage of the Everglades. The strong support that Broward received from the Fort Lauderdale area was one reason the region was chosen as the launching point for the Everglades drainage project. Courtesy, Miami Herald

Built as an intermediate beacon between the older lights at Jupiter and Fowey Rocks, the Hillsboro Lighthouse warns sailors of the dangerous shoals off the coast of northern Broward County. The skeletal iron tower was built in Detroit between 1905 and 1906, and erected at Hillsboro Inlet in 1907. Since that time, the light has remained one of the most powerful on the Atlantic coast. Courtesy, Fort Lauderdale Historical Society

Chapter 4

THE DAY OF THE DREDGE

In 1892 Captain John H. Newman, a civil engineer, crossed the Everglades as leader of the James Ingraham expedition. He crossed the Glades again in 1905 when the Broward Administration hired him to make a detailed survey of a possible canal route from New River to Lake Okeechobee. From Newman's survey and two others, the trustees of the Internal Improvement Fund (IIF) would select the pathway for the construction of the first drainage canal into the Everglades.

Governor Broward favored the St. Lucie River, the east coast river closest to Lake Okeechobee. The IIF trustees, who had the final decision, picked New River, apparently for political reasons. Stuart and Fort Pierce, the towns that would benefit from a St. Lucie canal, were anti-Broward strongholds. Fort Lauderdale and the surrounding towns, however, had given the governor strong support in the primaries and elections. On December 12, 1905, the trustees adopted Newman's recommendations for the Broward Administration's first drainage canal, which would start where Sabate Creek flowed into the south fork of the New River and follow the open Glades to the south shore of Lake Okeechobee.

For many decades Floridians had believed that the Everglades could be drained simply by cutting a few channels through the coral ridge that formed the eastern boundary of the river of grass. Millions of acres would then become available for farmlands, orange groves, and new settlements. It seemed so simple, particularly in light of Broward's campaign slogan, "Water will run downhill."

Reed Bryan was hired to supervise the construction of two dredges near Sailboat Bend. It would be a busy year for Bryan, his father, P.N. Bryan, and his brother, Tom, who would in 1906 build the Bryan Hotel, later renamed the New River Inn. A handsome structure on the

When this portrait of Reed A. Bryan appeared in the May 1908 issue of Watson's Jeffersonian Magazine, *the Everglades drainage program was well under way. In addition to supervising dredge operations for the state during the early 1900s, Bryan was one of Fort Lauderdale's major vegetable growers, raising tomatoes on newly drained Everglades land west of the settlement. Courtesy, Fort Lauderdale Historical Society*

river that boasted 40 rooms, broad porches, a large dining room, and a spacious lawn, it was the first inn built as a hotel. Fort Lauderdale's first hotel, the Osceola, was converted from a packinghouse.

Even as a boy Reed Bryan acquired a reputation for fearlessness, based in part on his delight in riding untamed farm horses that older men avoided. Thus the task of building dredges was hardly one to awe the ambitious young man. Working with machinery the state bought from a Chicago firm, he completed the first dredge in the spring.

Governor Broward and his family came down from Tallahassee for the christening of *The Everglades* on April 2, 1906. Reed Bryan's sister, Constance, smashed a bottle of champagne across the bow. "The largest and finest dredge south of Philadelphia," the *St. Augustine Record* called it. In October the second dredge, *Okeechobee*, was completed.

Drainage began on the Fourth of July, as work crews began digging what would become known as the North New River Canal. Anxious to get the project moving, Broward had ruled out a new, more precise survey. Instead, the surveying parties worked just ahead of the dredge, hammering in stakes for the giant machine to follow.

On April Fool's Day, 1907, the second dredge, *Okeechobee*, began to dig the South New River Canal, using the same survey technique. A legislative committee reviewing the program reported in August that the dredges had dug more than a mile of canals and drained some 750 acres on which farmers were already growing tomatoes. But by the end of the year, the dredges had dug only about 4.5 miles of canal and had reclaimed only about 12,000 acres. At the rate they were moving, one of Broward's opponents charged, the dredges would need a century to reclaim a million acres.

While the dredges were cutting canals, the Broward Administration was busy with court battles. The big land companies, whose claims conflicted with the state, wanted no competition from newly-reclaimed lands. Lawsuits blocked a state attempt to levy taxes to finance the work. Draining the Everglades was proving to be far from simple.

Nearer to the coast events were proceeding more smoothly. At Hillsboro Inlet, scene of the barefoot mailman's tragic death, the Champion Bridge Company was completing the area's first lighthouse. The all-steel skeleton tower rose 136 feet in the air and took two years to build.

The lighthouse was called the Big Diamond because of its unusual lens. Purchased from a Parisian firm for $7,250, the lens consisted of a series of triangular glass prisms arranged in circular fashion. Light generated by a large kerosene burning lamp first shone from the Hillsboro Lighthouse in March 1907. The lighthouse was built to warn seafarers of rocky shoals some 200 to 300 feet out from the beach, marking the northern limit of the Florida reef. At the time it was built, the light was the strongest in the

United States.

At Pompano a young man from Georgia, George Blount, arrived in 1906 to work for the Florida East Coast Canal survey team. After the survey, he knew the location of the choicest land. Blount bought five acres of coastal muckland and seven acres of drier land to the west. His two brothers joined him, and the Blounts became major landholders.

Eight or ten miles west of Pompano, H.F. Hammon, the first man to settle at Palm Beach, began to buy large tracts. The small farming settlement that developed was named Hammondville.

By 1908 the farmlands around Pompano had attracted enough settlers to raise the question of incorporation. On June 6, 1908, thirty-one registered voters gathered at the Florida East Coast Railway depot and passed a resolution calling for the creation of the Town of Pompano. Judge John R. Mizell, a former customs collector from Pensacola, was selected as mayor and police judge. J.K. Peacock, proprietor of a general store, was named council president, and George Blount was named town clerk. Members of the council included E. Rogers and Aden Waterman Turner, who would later become mayor of Pompano and still later the first county sheriff.

The record book of the council's first eight years has been lost, but a review of some of the ordinances passed gives insight into the concerns of

Although Governor Napoleon Bonaparte Broward did not originate the idea of draining the Everglades, his energy and decisiveness were instrumental in setting reclamation plans in motion. Broward's frequent visits to the dredge construction site at Fort Lauderdale's Sailboat Bend indicated his personal interest in the project. In this 1906 photograph, he stands in the foreground with hand in pocket, inspecting work on the dredge Okeechobee. Courtesy, Fort Lauderdale Historical Society

Georgian George L. Blount was on his way to Miami in 1906 when a railroad porter at Starke told him of the agricultural opportunities available at the new settlement of Pompano. Impressed with the small farming community, Blount settled at Pompano and went to work as a surveyor for the Florida Coast Line Canal and Transportation Company. From his initial investment in 12 acres, Blount soon became one of Pompano's most prosperous farmers, as well as a banker and real estate agent. He was the first city clerk in 1908, a Broward County commissioner from 1916 to 1917, and a state legislator from 1929 to 1931. Courtesy, Miami Herald

the citizens. One ordinance prohibited owners from allowing livestock to roam at large in the streets. Another established "blue laws," which called for a fine of up to $50 for working on Sunday. Still another spelled out fines and short jail sentences for a variety of undesirables, including "rogues and vagabonds, common pipers and fiddlers, stubborn children, common night walkers and all other idle and disorderly persons, boarding incoming and outgoing trains while in motion."

Less than a year after Pompano's incorporation, Pompano and Deerfield briefly became a part of Palm Beach County, a new county created by slicing off a large section of Dade.

With talk of Pompano's incorporation in the air, Dania cast a covetous eye on the settlement on New River. In 1908 Andrew Christian Frost published a letter in the *Miami News-Record* that stated:

Dania has five stores, one hotel, a stone church, the LaBree boot works, a blacksmith shop, Mrs. Palmer's bakery, Coulter's Jewelry, two lumber yards, one lawyer, a new cement block school, and a jail of the same . . . The citizens of Dania now contemplate taking in more territory next summer as far as New River. If the Fort Lauderdale citizens on the north side of the river wish to be incorporated in Dania, Dania will have no objection.

That same year the Broward drainage program was running into money problems. Selling off Everglades land seemed the best answer. In July R.P. Davie of Colorado Springs agreed to buy about 27,500 acres at two dollars an acre. Then in December the Broward Administration completed a huge land sale to Richard J. Bolles, a New Yorker who had made a fortune in Colorado gold mines and Oregon farmland. He contracted to pay one million dollars for 500,000 acres of Everglades land.

During the year Broward had run unsuccessfully for the U.S. Senate, losing to Duncan U. Fletcher, who had tried to raise sisal on Middle River. On January 5, 1909, Broward relinquished the governorship to Albert W. Gilchrist. During the Broward years only 15 miles of canal had been completed, but the program was now irreversibly in motion.

The first settlement on land reclaimed through drainage was called Zona. Many of the early settlers had worked on the Panama Canal and decided to name their canal town after the canal zone they had just left. By 1909 settlers who had bought land from the Everglades Land Sales Company were beginning to arrive in the area where the drainage program had started. The first permanent settlers were Dean and Emil Cross and the four Hill brothers from Michigan. They were soon joined by two families who would prove important to the future of the area, the Griffins from Kentucky and the family of Hamilton M. Forman, from Illinois.

In Fort Lauderdale on September 10, 1901, the state granted a charter for the town's first bank, the Fort Lauderdale State Bank. Capitalized at $15,000, the bank opened in a small building near Stranahan's store. Before the bank opened, virtually all financial transactions had taken place in his store, since he was in effect the village banker.

That same year Fort Lauderdale acquired its first newspaper, the *Fort Lauderdale Herald,* a weekly edited by Professor William Heine. The paper was printed in DeLand and shipped to New River. The first to be printed locally was Colonel George Mathews' weekly, the *Fort Lauderdale Sentinel,* which began publication in March 1911.

The year 1911 proved to be a memorable one for Fort Lauderdale, marked by the town's incorporation and by the first land boom. On January 6, members of the newly formed Board of Trade discussed incorporation as a way of overcoming sanitation problems. The board voted to move ahead with incorporation plans. At that same meeting it voted to ask "all energetic ladies of the town to meet with the board to form a civic organization." First called the Women's Civic Improvement Association, it soon became the Woman's Club of Fort Lauderdale.

On March 27, 1911, forty-five of the town's qualified voters assembled at the new schoolhouse, built the year before. The building would later become the first county courthouse. Chairman for the meeting was a Mr. Myers. The first issue to be decided was the size of the town. The citizens picked one-and-a-half miles square as the dimensions, feeling that two miles square would be too large.

When the chairman asked if anyone had any objections to incorporation, Dr. Kennedy came forward. Reported the *Sentinel:* "He said that the whole thing had been done wrong, that he did not believe in the secret Sunday morning meetings held without giving due notice to the people interested. That is all I have to say and walked out."

The rising vote for incorporation was carried without further opposition. Reed Bryan proposed Fort Lauderdale as the name of the town and then nominated William H. Marshall as mayor. Marshall won easily, gathering 30 votes to 6 for Joe Farrow. A Mr. Ivery had nominated himself but was unable to garner a second.

Elected to the City Council were William C. Kyle, William O. Berryhill, Ed King, Tom Bryan, and Willie H. Covington. Frank Bryan was named city clerk and Kossie Goodbread city marshall at $40 per month, plus a dollar for every arrest.

At its first meeting the council turned its attention promptly to the problem that had brought it into being. Its first action was a vote to buy or rent a mule or horse and wagon for emptying privies and disposing of refuse. For $230 the town bought from Vivian W. Craig a wagon and a draft animal, henceforth referred to in city minutes as "the sanitary mule." The honor of operating the department went to Goodbread.

James Hill, pictured here with his wife Eva and three sons, came from Michigan with his three brothers in 1909 to farm the newly-drained land along the South New River Canal. At the time, the Hills' only neighbors were Dean and Emil Cross. Two years later, a group of workmen returning from the Panama Canal Zone joined them, formed the Zona Glades Company, and named their little settlement Zona. Courtesy, Broward County Historical Commission

Businessman and farmer William H. Marshall became Fort Lauderdale's first mayor when the town was incorporated in 1911. When Broward County was created four years later, Marshall became its first state representative. A Georgia native, Marshall first came to Fort Lauderdale to spend time with some relatives in 1899 when he returned from Cuba following service in the Spanish-American War. Courtesy, Fort Lauderdale Historical Society

While the city fathers were pushing through incorporation, Richard Bolles was hard at work selling land from his vast South Florida holdings. His Florida Fruit Lands Company introduced the contract method of land sales, tied in with a lottery, which he tried to mask as an auction. In addition to the company's land in the Glades, much of it under water, Bolles also had bought high and dry land just north of Fort Lauderdale, at a place platted as Progresso by Duncan U. Fletcher's Florida Fiber Company after its sisal hemp venture failed. For $240, to be paid off at $10 a month, a purchaser of a Bolles lot received a contract entitling him to a lot in Progresso and a farm in the Everglades. The size and location of the farm would depend on luck of the draw in a future auction/lottery.

Bolles' salesmen toured the Midwest, motivating rural purchasers with descriptions of the Everglades as "Tropical Paradise," "Promised Land," "Land of Destiny," and the "Magnet Whose Climate and Agriculture would bring the Human Flood." The *New York World* called these eager salesmen "swamp boomers."

During a one-week period in March 1911, more than 3,000 people alighted from Florida East Coast Railway trains, overwhelming the town of Fort Lauderdale, which had turned up only 143 residents in the census of 1910.

Tom Watson, candidate for President on the 1904 Populist ticket and new owner of the gun-shaped hunting lodge on the beach, described the scene in his *Jeffersonian Magazine:*

I was there when these bargain seekers (or, I might say suckers) began coming to Fort Lauderdale. One day . . . I saw three long, heavily loaded trains come to the place; at one time they simply filled the woods, as there was not house room for one-fourth of the crowd in town. More than a thousand tents were put through the piney woods between March 15 and 20. Fort Lauderdale two years ago had nearly 150 inhabitants, counting men, women and children and dogs . . . The Everglades is the best country in the whole world to raise alligators, rattlesnakes, mosquitoes and malaria.

After two weeks the auction/lottery was over. Tents were removed, temporary offices were closed, the woods were deserted again, and the *Fort Lauderdale Herald*, which in its moments of glory had become a daily for a few days, closed its operation. Bolles continued to sell lots but trouble was beginning to surface. For one thing, many buyers were finding that their land was under water. The *Washington Times* called it "one of the biggest land swindles in history," and a Congressman from Missouri, where the Bolles Company was headquartered, declared in the House of Representatives that the promotion scheme of Bolles' agents constituted "one of the meanest swindles ever devised or conducted in this country, resulting in the victimization of about 25,000 people."

Meanwhile, the U.S. Post Office was building a case against Bolles for fraudulent use of the mails. The indictment against him and his top aides contained 22 counts and filled 122 pages, the longest indictment ever returned in the Kansas City Federal Court. Bolles and his lawyer, J.L. Billingsley, the Fort Lauderdale town attorney, were arrested on December 18, 1913.

Bolles' defense was that he had acted in good faith, based on glowing promises from state officials that drainage would convert the Glades into vast and fertile farmland. After a month of hearings, the case was dismissed. Many felt he had been persecuted unfairly, since he gave good title to all lands he sold. A tiny, dapper, and courteous man, Bolles was well liked in Fort Lauderdale.

The government, however, kept after the persuasive Bolles, and in time his health began to deteriorate. On March 25, 1917, he boarded the Florida East Coast Railway in West Palm Beach and died shortly thereafter in his berth.

Ironically, in later years the Glades farmland sold by Bolles generally turned out to be worthless, while the Progresso lots, thrown in as a sales gimmick, rose steadily in value.

To F.W. DeCroix, a stalwart booster of Dade County, Fort Lauderdale was "The Coming Queen City of the Everglades," which is the title he gave to a chapter in a 1911 book he wrote about the area. Elsewhere he called Fort Lauderdale the "Gateway to the Everglades." He wrote glowingly about its "fine beach, good drinking water ... [and] merchants." He characterized the citizens of Fort Lauderdale as "one large happy family, each doing their share in a clean, manly and honorable way for the health and welfare of the city."

DeCroix wrote about the thriving business community that had now developed in Fort Lauderdale. Hiram G. Wheeler had opened a general merchandise store in competition with the Stranahan store. Berryhill and Cromartie and the Everglades Grocery Company, owned by W.H. Andrews, William C. Kyle, and John T. Kelly, gave the town two active groceries. DeWitt G. TenBrook and I.K. Gordon operated a real-estate office on Brickell Avenue.

Despite DeCroix's enthusiastic views on Fort Lauderdale and the Everglades, the drainage program was proving a frustrating venture. It was, however, proceeding. By the end of 1911 the North New River Canal was nearing completion. Meanwhile, work was continuing on the South New River Canal, which would extend 25 miles west to connect with the 79-mile Miami River Canal. By the end of the year 16.5 miles had been dug on the northern end of the Hillsboro Canal and 1.5 miles on the southern end, near the farming community of Deerfield, which at that time boasted two general stores.

In December 1911 a dredge working the North New River Canal turned up the body of a Seminole Indian. The man, who had been murdered, was identified as DeSoto Tiger. The Seminole had started down the canal with a load of otter skins belonging to his tribe. Accompanying him was John Ashley. The Ashley family had settled west of Pompano in 1904.

When police later found that Ashley had sold the skins to the Girtman Brothers trading post in Miami, they set out to arrest him. John and Bob Ashley promptly intercepted the police, disarmed them, and sent them back. John left Florida for three years, then returned to stand trial. Before the case was heard, he escaped again, and soon his family began a lengthy series of criminal escapades that earned them fame as the Ashley Gang.

In 1912 the North New River Canal, the centerpiece of the state's drainage program, was finally completed. On April 25 Governor Gilchrist and a press party cruised up the Caloosahatchee River to Lake Okeechobee, spending their first night at the Bolles Hotel, built by Richard Bolles on Ritta Island. When the party reached the northern terminus of the canal, the governor was handed two coconuts, one filled with water from the Atlantic and the other with water from the Gulf of Mexico. These waters were then mixed to symbolize the union of the two coasts via the state's first cross-state waterway.

The group continued to Fort Lauderdale where the arrival of Governor Gilchrist on April 26 was attended, reportedly, by every man, woman, and child in the town. At the foot of Brickell Avenue, on the river, the governor presented Mayor Marshall with a gold shovel.

To the citizens of Fort Lauderdale the visit of the governor and the opening of the canal to Lake Okeechobee must have signaled a glowing future. What lay ahead, however, were glowing embers, the aftermath of

Right and facing page, bottom: Real estate men W. B. Snyder and M. A. Hortt posed on the steps of their new office on Wall Street and Brickell Avenue in downtown Fort Lauderdale on June 1, 1912 (right). That night, Hortt awoke to see the town's business district in flames, and the following morning the two partners posed again by the ruins of their building (facing page). The fire proved to be a blessing in disguise, however, because Fort Lauderdale subsequently gained a fire department, and fireproof buildings replaced many of the old wooden structures that had been destroyed. Courtesy, Fort Lauderdale Historical Society

a fire which burned down virtually the entire business section on the night of June 1, 1912.

Among the buildings that were lost was the Snyder & Hortt Real Estate office. The day before the fire, the two partners had posed for pictures on the steps outside their new building. The next day, only the steps were left. Snyder and Hortt posed again.

The Fort Lauderdale State Bank had been saved by a bucket brigade bringing water from the river. The Osceola Hotel, which also escaped the blaze, ironically burned down a year later. The fire showed the town it needed a fire department. The council promptly authorized the purchase of a gasoline-powered pumper and 1,500 feet of hose. Charles E. Newland was elected the first fire chief.

After the waterway to Lake Okeechobee was completed, a booming trade developed with the lake communities as boats carried produce, catfish, and passengers to Fort Lauderdale. It was not always an easy trip. Dr. Thomas E. Will, a tireless crusader for reclamation, called navigation of the North New River Canal "a combination of heroism and tragedy, including wrecks time without number, the beating and battering of keels and propellors on the rocks that were never blasted out of this canal and the boulders that lay loose in the bottom of the canal."

One of the most beloved of the passenger ships was the *Suwanee*, a 70-foot sternwheeler operated by the Menge Brothers Steamboat Line of Fort Myers. One of its regular customers was Thomas Edison, who wintered in the Gulf Coast city.

Eva Bryan Oliver, who had been married in a rowboat, wrote about the steamboat:

. . . such a grand trip it was. We had our meals on the boat. We left Fort Lauderdale late in the afternoon and arrived at the lake next morning. We began our

Above: Thomas E. Watson, Georgia politician and Populist candidate for the 1904 and 1908 Presidential elections, purchased John McGregor Adams' hunting lodge from Adams' widow in 1905. Maintaining his winter home there until 1914, Watson wrote about Fort Lauderdale from time to time in his Jeffersonian Magazine. *A strong supporter of farming interests, Watson at first praised South Florida drainage efforts. By 1911, however, he had come to regard the Everglades as fit only for "alligators and rattlesnakes and mosquitoes." Courtesy, Georgia Historical Society*

stops at the different farms. At that time sugar cane was three times as high as a person, and the vegetables and flowers were gorgeous. We came back down the canal in daylight and saw thousands of beautiful birds. It was a treat for tourists and many made the trip across to Fort Myers and other points.

The sternwheelers operating on the river carried passengers and supplies to the lake and returned with winter vegetables ready to be loaded onto trains for shipment to northern markets. By 1912 Fort Lauderdale had become one of the largest vegetable shipping centers in the United States.

Docks and packinghouses were built along the river to handle the heavy barge traffic. The town took on a festive air as farmers brought in vegetables and fruit from the Glades for shipment by rail. Local merchants could expect brisk sales as money circulated freely. The flow into town of produce from the Glades, the lake, and the nearby towns of Hallandale, Dania, Pompano, Deerfield, and Zona created new companies, such as the Harbauer catsup plant and the James Carroll Company, which bought locally grown fruit for its guava jelly plant.

Another important source of business from the lake was the fish industry. Fishhouses along New River received catfish from the lake, packed them in ice, and shipped them north. Complaints about the appearance, smell, and sanitary conditions of the fishhouses led to a legal battle between the city and Flagler's old foe, Mary Brickell.

Mrs. Brickell, now a widow, maintained that she owned—and therefore could sell—the riparian rights along the river. To the fishhouse operators she was selling "strips of land of indeterminate width between the city streets and the river with full riparian rights." Her claim was well recognized and generally acknowledged. Many of the town's leading citizens had bought riverfront property, and most of them had paid Mrs. Brickell for the rights in front of their property, even though a street separated their businesses from the river.

In December 1913 Jacob F. Bunn was named town attorney, a post formerly held by J.L. Billingsley, who had been indicted in the Bolles investigation. Bunn's investigation into the question of riparian rights convinced him the city, not Mrs. Brickell, owned these rights. Bunn persuaded the council to let him proceed with a lawsuit in behalf of the town.

Business people who had paid money for the riparian rights were furious. They argued that the fishhouses, no matter how ugly, were vital to the economy of the river port. Those who had not bought riparian rights contended that fishhouses, in addition to their unsightliness, were a menace to sanitation.

Joining Bunn in the legal action for the town was his young law partner, Carl P. Weidling. As her lawyer, Mary Brickell hired Billingsley. Forced to amend his bill of complaint three times before Circuit Court Judge H. Pierre Branning accepted it, Bunn finally brought the case to trial.

The town's key witnesses, Herbert C. Davis and J.H. Gearing, both civil engineers, declared that the plat from which the town had been sold indicated no reservation of riparian rights for individual property owners. Furthermore, they contended, the designation of North and South River streets was marked with a straight line on the land side and by a wavy line at the water's edge, an indication that no land beyond the streets was to be in private hands.

Refuting these claims was a parade of witnesses that read like a "Who's Who" of early Fort Lauderdale—Frank Stranahan, Philemon Bryan, and Tom Bryan among them. All testified that the intention was for the street to be 40 feet wide, leaving the strip along the river untouched. Dade County officials testified they had collected taxes on the strip along the river.

Taking the stand in her own behalf, Mary Brickell testified that she and her husband had had nothing to do with the final platting of the town. That, she said, had been the responsibility of James Ingraham. That revelation proved to be her undoing.

The Flagler executive took the stand and declared it had been his hope that the downtown section of the riverfront would be used for quays and docks. He had not intended for it to fall into private hands. On June 3,

The ease with which vegetables could be barged down the New River to the Florida East Coast Railway tracks made Fort Lauderdale an important shipping point as early as the 1890s. The completion of the North New River Canal enabled farmers in the rich new mucklands on the south side of Lake Okeechobee to transport their produce to the railroad docks at Fort Lauderdale as well. By the time this photograph was taken in the early 1910s, the town was the most important vegetable shipping center on Florida's east coast. Courtesy, Fort Lauderdale Historical Society

Fort Lauderdale's City Attorney Jacob F. Bunn investigated the question of riparian rights that had been raised by opponents of the fishhouses. A circuit court ruled in Fort Lauderdale's favor June 3, 1916. This decision, and resulting municipal control of the riverfront, shaped Fort Lauderdale's future as a boating and sporting center. Before the case was settled, Bunn became the first judge of newly-created Broward County, a post he held until his death in 1917. Courtesy, Ohio Historical Society

Okeechobee catfish, in addition to produce, were barged down the North New River Canal to Fort Lauderdale for packing and shipment. This 1914 view, looking east toward the Andrews Avenue bridge, features the fishhouses lining the banks of the New River. By this time, the odor and unsanitary conditions of these establishments had embroiled the town in a dispute over ownership of the riverfront. Courtesy, Fort Lauderdale Historical Society

1916, Judge Branning handed down a ruling in favor of the town. Appeals added another two years before the decision finally became official. The ruling made it possible for Fort Lauderdale to construct the city docks that would in future years attract thousands of fishermen and yachtsmen.

By 1913 Fort Lauderdale's business community had decided the time had come to break away from Dade County. Four years earlier a new county, Palm Beach, had been carved out of Dade. It included Deerfield and Pompano. Now Fort Lauderdale wanted still another county, to consist of Fort Lauderdale, Dania, Hallandale, Zona, and Pompano. The first effort failed because the southern towns wanted to stay in Dade, and Pompano wanted to remain in Palm Beach.

By 1915 the mood had changed. Dania and Hallandale were now ready to join a new county, and Pompano and Deerfield both wanted to separate from Palm Beach. Furthermore, Miami now had reason to want Fort Lauderdale on the other side of a county line. In 1913 Dade County had held a referendum to decide if the citizens wanted local option Prohibition laws. Miami, a tourist town, favored the wet option, but the county overall voted for Prohibition, primarily because of the heavy dry vote in Dania and Fort Lauderdale.

At a mass meeting in Dania, interested parties from Fort Lauderdale, Hallandale, and Dania voted to provide $300 to defray expenses for Tom Bryan and a distant relative, Frank Bryan, to lobby for the new county before the state legislature. Frank, however, was called home from Tallahassee by the death of his sister.

Tom Bryan found the Dade delegation cooperative, but Palm Beach gave him trouble over the northern boundary of the new county. Both factions agreed to let the Hillsboro Canal separate the two counties in the

Newly-formed Broward County converted the old Central School building into the first courthouse in 1915. This structure stood on the South Andrews Avenue site of Ivy Stranahan's original one-room schoolhouse. It served as the Broward County Courthouse until 1928. Courtesy, Fort Lauderdale Historical Society

This group of original Broward County officials was photographed shortly after the county was established in 1915. From left to right are County Engineer Herbert C. Davis, commissioners C. E. Ingalls of Hallandale, Alexander B. Lowe of Dania, and J. J. Joyce of Fort Lauderdale, and County Attorney W. I. Evans. Courtesy, Fort Lauderdale Historical Society

east, but Bryan's plan to let the border follow the canal as it veered diagonally toward the lake came under heavy fire. His line would have let the county extend all the way to Lake Okeechobee and include the settlement of South Bay. Palm Beach insisted the line continue straight west across the Everglades.

Bryan's people back home authorized him to accept the Palm Beach offer. By unanimous vote the legislature passed a local bill creating the new county. It included the incorporated towns of Dania, Pompano, and Fort Lauderdale as well as the communities of Hallandale, Deerfield, Progresso, Colohatchee, and Davie, as Zona was now called.

The new county was named Broward in honor of the governor whose huge drainage program had begun on the New River and opened up the Everglades to farming. By 1915 all the canals in the county had been completed; the North New River and Hillsboro canals reached the lake and the South New River Canal had been connected to the Miami Canal.

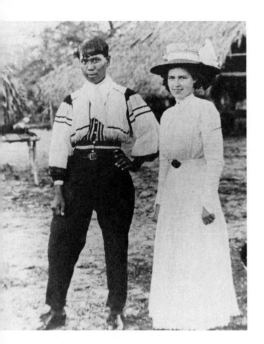

Tony Tommie, an 11-year-old boy when this 1911 photograph was taken, was the first Seminole Indian on Florida's east coast, and the second in the state, to attend a white school. Tommie attended Fort Lauderdale Central School from 1915 to 1917, largely at the urging of Ivy Stranahan, even though most Seminoles at the time frowned on white education. Courtesy, Fort Lauderdale Historical Society

Broward, however, was not alive to savor his triumph. He had died five years earlier. Declared the *Fort Lauderdale Sentinel* of April 30, 1915: "The creation of Broward County gives to Florida's greatest governor a fitting monument."

Prior to its designation as Broward, the area along the New, Middle, and Hillsboro rivers had existed under a huge variety of jurisdictions: Spanish Florida; East Florida (under British rule); St. John's County, 1821; Monroe County, 1823; Dade County, 1836; Mosquito County, 1836; St. Lucia County, 1845; Brevard County, 1860; and Palm Beach County, 1909. In April 1915 the confusion finally ended.

Will Marshall, Fort Lauderdale's first mayor, was elected as Broward County's first state representative. Unlike an earlier representative from New River, one Pig Brown, he served two full terms and then continued to live a long and productive life in his home town.

At Tallahassee, Marshall became chairman of the House Committee on Canals and Drainage. He championed creation of the Everglades Drainage District, a state farmers' market in the county, and the cause of women's suffrage. In backing the women's right-to-vote movement, Marshall may well have been exposed to heavy lobbying from Ivy Stranahan, president of the Women's Suffrage Association of Florida.

David Clifford ("D.C.") Alexander came to Fort Lauderdale in 1909 to visit his parents, among the first of those who saw the area as a retirement haven. While attending Stanford University, D.C. had observed the development of coastal areas in California. Now at Fort Lauderdale he saw an almost totally unused beach he thought even more beautiful than those on the Pacific Coast. To D.C. Alexander, the area had a potential no one had even dreamed of before.

Early settlers had preferred the river, which gave them an avenue for transportation. On the river they could harbor a boat and also farm. The oceanfront, on the other hand, was exposed to storms, and the soil was not suitable for agriculture.

In 1914 Alexander bought Tom Watson's hunting lodge and 32 acres on the beach for $40,000, borrowed from Mrs. M.J. Lawrence at eight percent interest. He platted the tract and called his subdivision Las Olas-by-the-Sea. Watson's hunting lodge was converted into the beach's first hotel—the Las Olas Inn.

Most important of all to the future of the city, he established a street well back from the beach and permitted no structures east of the road. His concept of development preserved for the public what would in later years become the town's greatest attraction—Fort Lauderdale Beach.

Alexander had trouble meeting his monthly payments, since access to the beach was still limited to boats. Progress on a road and a bridge to the beach was moving slowly, a venture that was proving too expensive for private interests. The county then voted its first bond issue, for $400,000, to build roads and bridges to the beaches at Fort Lauderdale, Deerfield, Pompano, Dania, and Hallandale, and to the Davie area.

The contract for building the road across the swamp to Las Olas was awarded to Bryan and Snyder, while the job of building the drawbridge across the East Coast Canal went to Champion Bridge of Wilmington, Ohio, which had built the Hillsboro Lighthouse. In January 1917 the road to the beach was opened to the public. For the town it was a major event. Virtually every operating vehicle in town was recruited for a motorcade. At last, Alexander saw his lots begin to sell, more than 20 of them in the year the bridge was finished.

Overall, the county's transportation was improving. In addition to new roads and bridges and canals in the west, the Dixie Highway had been completed, linking Broward to the northern states. The first car passed through the county on July 22, 1915. That same year telephone service came to the area, as did fresh milk. In Davie, Hamilton Forman established the first dairy, Forman's Sanitary Dairy.

For the Indians the scene was changing, too. Drainage in the Everglades had severely damaged their economy, drying up their canoe trails and their hunting and trapping grounds. Tony Tommie decided the time had come to challenge an old Seminole prohibition. The tribe had always resisted the white man's schools—an Indian had once been placed under a death sentence for attending classes. In 1913 Tommie told the Fort Lauderdale school principal, James Rickard, that he wanted an education. His request presented unusual problems. At that time public schools were segregated; no mixing of races was allowed. There was a further

Above: With hands on hips and eyes gazing into the distance, a youthful D. C. Alexander looks much like the dreamer the residents along New River thought him to be. At a time when Fort Lauderdale's beach was all but deserted and not even incorporated in the city limits, Alexander planned a subdivision there called "Las Olas by the Sea," and awaited completion of a bridge across the Intracoastal Waterway. In the background stands the Las Olas Inn, the old hunting lodge Alexander purchased from Thomas E. Watson in 1914. Courtesy, Fort Lauderdale Historical Society

Left: Described as "rocky, rough, full of potholes (and) narrow," the Dixie Highway was the first major road linking Broward County with the rest of the nation. Built in sections, the entire highway stretched from the Michigan-Canada border to Miami, and was not completed until 1925. The section running through Broward, however, opened in July 1915. Carl Fisher, automobile promoter, developer of Miami Beach, and leading force behind the construction of the highway, led the opening parade, photographed here passing through Dania. Courtesy, Broward County Historical Commission

Numerous Broward County men served in the armed forces during World War I. Some participated in military activities even before the United States entered the world conflict. Company L of the Second Florida Infantry, assembled here at Dolores Mines on the Texas-Mexico border in 1916 or 1917 during the United States-Mexican border dispute, was composed primarily of men from Dade and Broward counties. After the United States entered World War I, the Second Florida was reorganized as the 124th United States Infantry, arriving in France too late to take an active part in the fighting. Courtesy, Fort Lauderdale Historical Society

complication. Since the Seminoles had never signed a peace treaty ending the wars, Tony had no legal status.

Lucien E. Spencer, special commissioner to the tribe, urged that Tommie be enrolled and obtained $150 from the Bureau of Indian Affairs to defray expenses. Tony Tommie, wearing a traditional Seminole shirt and long trousers, entered the second grade as a teenager. He learned quickly, covering two grades in his first year. Intelligent, warm, and friendly, Tony became an influential leader of his people and an important link between the whites and the Indians. He even induced the Seminoles to form a baseball team to play the Fort Lauderdale town team.

For the Indians of the county, a major though unofficial educational resource was Mrs. Stranahan. She developed a deep love and understanding for the Seminoles who came to Stranahan's trading post. Here they could deal with the trader, confident they would be treated fairly, and with the schoolteacher who took it upon herself to instruct them. She taught them in groups of six to twelve at a time, using pictorial Sunday school lessons from the Presbyterian church. Her goals were simple, to teach them to read and write, to instruct them in Christianity, and to help them finally come to terms with the U.S. government.

The growing religious life of the communities indicated that the old pioneer settlements were maturing into organized societies. The first church in the county appears to have been the First Zion Baptist Church, a Negro congregation in Deerfield. Sister Danelia Huntley, one of the founders, recalled those early days:

During the year 1902, I moved to Deerfield, Florida, and at that time there were

four or five white families and not more than forty Negroes . . . Around August of 1902, one Rev. Lawrence and a Mrs. Knight, who were both Methodist leaders, got the people together and began holding services in a bush harbor, built from palmettos by the Sister Knight, and myself, with the help of a few boys.

This "bush harbor," actually just a lean-to, was apparently the first structure of any kind built in the county specifically to serve as a church. The following April the congregation built a palmetto shack for their church.

The Dania Methodist Church was founded in 1903. That same year the Methodist Episcopal Church, South, was established in Fort Lauderdale, and a year later the Piney Grove Missionary Baptist Church, a black church, was organized there. The first building constructed as a church in Fort Lauderdale was the First Methodist Church, South, built in 1905 at Southwest Sixth Street and South Andrews Avenue. The first church in Hallandale, the Bethlehem Lutheran, was organized in 1906. Other early churches in Hallandale included Ebenezer Baptist, St. Ann's Episcopal, and Union Congregational.

In 1911 three new Methodist churches, one to serve newcomers from the North, were organized, and the following year they were joined by a Christian church, an Episcopal church, and the First Presbyterian Church, all in Fort Lauderdale. In 1913 the first Catholic church in Fort Lauderdale opened, followed shortly by the first Christian Science Society.

In 1917 the impact of the world events impinged on the quiet communities of Broward County as America entered World War I. Fort Lauderdale Mayor Will Reed formed a Home Guard, which drilled with wooden rifles at the school athletic field. So many depositers at Broward County Bank in Fort Lauderdale withdrew their savings to buy Liberty Bonds that the bank was forced to merge with the Fort Lauderdale State Bank.

The war had its effect on the county's agriculture, as indicated by an eloquent plea from the onion farmers:

. . . if every family in the city would purchase a hamper, it would be the cause of many a farmer getting a good return for his labor. It would even help to whip the kaiser and make the world safe for democracy, for while you are eating onions, you are saving some other food that could be sent across the ocean to the allies. In fact, it is your patriotic duty to your government to eat an onion every time the opportunity presents itself . . .

On November 11, 1918, the war ended. Broward County celebrated, as did all America, and turned its eyes toward the decade of the 1920s. For the small towns and peaceful communities no crystal ball could have forecast the manic period that lay ahead.

One of five Broward men killed in action during World War I, Coast Guardsman Robert L. Agee lost his life September 26, 1918, when a German U-boat torpedoed the U.S.S. Tampa in the Bristol Channel off the coast of England. The cutter sank with all 118 crewmen aboard. The following year, more than 2,000 people from West Palm Beach to Miami attended the dedication of a monument to Agee in Fort Lauderdale's Evergreen Cemetery. Courtesy, Fort Lauderdale News/Sun-Sentinel

After Fort Lauderdale butcher Egbert L. "Bert" Lasher appeared in the film The Firing Line, *shot near Colohatchee in 1919, he later moved on to his own show business enterprises. Operating a small Seminole attraction on the north fork of the New River in the 1920s, Lasher later took over Miami's famous Musa Isle Indian Village. This 1927 photo of Lasher, taken at Musa Isle, shows him in Seminole costume, accompanied by a small Indian child. Courtesy, Patsy West, Seminole/Miccosukee Photographic Archive, Fort Lauderdale*

Chapter 5

BOOM, BOOM, BOOM

The war was over and a spirit of change was abroad in the land. Ahead for America, and for Broward County, lay an era of prosperity and almost feverish optimism. It would later be called the "Roaring Twenties."

In 1919 Americans who liked to lift a glass lost their right to drink whiskey, beer, or wine legally. Not long afterward, Ivy Stranahan and her fellow suffragettes gained an important right, the right to vote.

Optimistic Fort Lauderdale saw tourism in its future. When a generous man, George Henry of Winchester, Massachusetts, asked M.A. Hortt what he could do for the city, the local real-estate man replied: "Help us build a tourist hotel."

A plan evolved in which Fort Lauderdale citizens agreed to raise $40,000 of the $140,000 needed to construct the city's first three-story tourist hotel. For a city of only 2,000 people, it proved too tough a goal. Fort Lauderdale came up $17,000 short.

The deficit narrowed to $11,000 when a gift of property from Frank Stranahan generated a $6,000 boost to the fund. Stranahan had planned to give the land to the city for a park, then considered selling it with the returns earmarked for the hotel project. When it was learned that Stranahan, as City Council president, could not legally sell anything to the city, he deeded the land instead for one dollar to John Sherwin, publisher of the *Fort Lauderdale Herald*, who sold it to the city for $6,000 for the fund. Hortt then prevailed on Henry to go through with the hotel, pushing to have it ready for the 1919-1920 tourist season.

The Hotel Broward wasn't ready quite fast enough. The greatest of all Hollywood directors, D.W. Griffith, was coming to town to shoot a movie. For *The Idol Dancer* he needed the palm-lined New River to create the look of a South Seas island. He also needed a place for his troupe of 50 to stay.

The kitchen equipment had not yet arrived, hotel manager John Needham explained. No problem, replied Griffith. The film company traveled with its own portable kitchen. The real need was for rooms for such stars of the silent screen as Richard Barthelmess and a rising young starlet, Clarine Seymour.

Even though the hotel was not yet ready for the public, Needham made enough rooms available for Griffith's company. The first signature on the register of Fort Lauderdale's first tourist hotel was one of the most important names in the history of motion pictures—David Wark Griffith.

Film crews had worked in the area before, but Fort Lauderdale had never seen anything like D.W. Griffith. Virtually the whole city turned out to watch, many to act. Marion Reed, daughter of former mayor Captain Will Reed, appeared in the film, as did many Seminoles hired by Griffith through his interpreter, Tony Tommie, to play South Seas natives. Captain James B. Vreeland, Jr., a deep-sea fisherman whose father had been a keeper of the House of Refuge, was engaged by Griffith to transport the troupe to and from the island locations along the river. South Seas villages were built at Will Marshall's farm and among the coconut palms at the Las Olas Inn. Local schoolgirls were hired to appear in the bridal party of a wedding procession.

When Griffith finished shooting, he entertained the city with a

Commodore Auylan Harcourt Brook began his long advertising career as a sign painter. Around the turn of the century, "Mr. Brook of Brooklyn" was responsible for some of the first great electrical display signs in New York. This "fisherman's dream" at the Florida East Coast Railway Station, in addition to mounted fish flanking the approach to the Andrews Avenue bridge, welcomed visitors to Fort Lauderdale in the Roaring Twenties. Courtesy, Fort Lauderdale Historical Society

Thanksgiving Day dance at the Broward Hotel, complete with a five-piece jazz band brought down from Palm Beach. In December local businessmen reciprocated with a dinner for Griffith. He told them he would return for many more pictures:

You people who live here and pursue your daily occupation midst the natural tropical beauty of the country, probably do not realize how wonderful your country is. But to one who has never seen it before it is a revelation. There may be more beautiful rivers in the world than New River, which flows through the heart of your city, but if so I have never seen it.

Griffith was not the first to make films in the area. In the spring of 1919 Western Photo Plays Company shot part of a serial, "The Great Gamble," starring Charles "Daredevil" Hutchison and Anne Luther. Hero and heroine were doomed to be burned at the stake by Tony Tommie and his bloodthirsty band, only be rescued at the last moment. Two desperados escaped from the Broward County jail in a scene featuring wall-climbing by a stuntman, Billy Moran, formerly an English jockey. Still another sequence involved an auto trip over a temporary—very temporary—bridge across Cypress Creek. The bridge, on cue, collapsed and spilled the auto and its inhabitants into the stream.

Within weeks after the serial photography began, Famous Players Lasky brought in the famed dancing star, Irene Castle, and a company of 20 to film scenes for *The Firing Line*, based on a popular novel by Robert W. Chambers. The film employed a number of Seminoles as well as a local man named Bert Lasher, who played the guide to a hunter in scenes shot near Colohatchee. Two of Bert's hunting dogs, Joe and Prince, also had parts. The film company stayed at D.C. Alexander's Las Olas Inn.

Commodore Auylan Harcourt Brook arrived in Fort Lauderdale just in time for the Roaring Twenties. He brought with him the promotional skills honed by his years in the advertising field in New York. One who was to feel the impact of Brook's talents was President-elect Warren G. Harding, who was cruising down the Intracoastal Waterway in early 1921 on his way to Miami. When Thomas Stilwell, who later became the publisher of the *Fort Lauderdale Daily News* and the *Sentinel*, learned about the Presidential journey through the city, he and Commodore Brook came up with a scheme to put Fort Lauderdale on the map.

As the Harding yacht passed through Fort Lauderdale, a large dredge ran aground, effectively blocking the waterway. Suddenly, according to M.A. Hortt, Brook's yacht *Kylo* appeared, ready to take the President-elect and his party away from the mosquitoes and into the city where entertainment awaited. Harding was invited to play a round of golf on the city's new course; he shot a 110.

In the late 1910s and early 1920s, local boosters persuaded D. W. Griffith and several less famous filmmakers that Fort Lauderdale's unspoiled tropical beauty would make a perfect setting for jungle and South Sea island scenes. Griffith (seated) is depicted directing on the banks of the New River in 1919. Filmmaking and the accompanying publicity consequently generated nationwide interest in Fort Lauderdale as a glamorous vacationland, but ironically the ensuing development destroyed the area's original appeal, and moviemaking declined. Courtesy, Fort Lauderdale Historical Society

Above: President-elect Warren G. Harding, sidetracked from a trip to Miami by Commodore A.H. Brook and Thomas Stilwell, visited Fort Lauderdale for the first time on January 28, 1921. At Lake Mabel, the President-elect (third from left) waves from Brook's yacht, Kylo. Courtesy, Fort Lauderdale Historical Society

Griffith's filmmaking and the "visit" by the President-elect brought favorable national publicity to Fort Lauderdale. The ingredients were now in place for the real-estate boom that lay just ahead for Broward County. The census of 1920 reported the population of the new county as only 5,135. Fort Lauderdale showed a population of 2,065, Dania, 762, and Pompano, 630. Precinct 5, Hallandale, contained 516, while Precinct 6, Davie, listed 190. Seminole Indians in the county totaled 22. The stage was set for a sharp population increase. A major highway, a railroad, and the Intracoastal Waterway combined to offer effective transportation to the area. Postwar prosperity gave people money to travel and to buy property.

While transportation overall was improving, one form of transit that had been important to the development of Broward was ending. Silting finally halted the steamboat traffic between Fort Lauderdale and Lake Okeechobee. Skipper Lawrence Will later wrote about the final voyage down the North New River Canal on Christmas Day, 1921: ". . . with this and that, we kept chugging along and finally tied up in Fort Lauderdale at the foot of Brickell Avenue. It was 3:30 Christmas morning. I toted some of the lady passengers' go-way bags to the hotel and I reckon that was about the last time I've walked barefooted up the main street of Fort Lauderdale."

The loss of the picturesque steamboat trade was soon more than offset by a new form of transportation. The age of the auto had arrived, and

with it the first real stirrings of the great Florida land boom. The boom tiptoed in under the guise of a healthy real-estate growth, then swept the area like a raging tropical fever.

As early as mid-1920 people were becoming aware that the world of real estate was beginning to blossom. A three-column headline in the Fort Lauderdale *Sentinel* of July 30, 1920, read:

BUILDING BOOM STARTED
AND WILL CONTINUE

Cited as proof the boom was underway were three separate stories, one on a new home being built for the family of Sam Gillian, one of coquina rock being constructed for John A. Pellett, and a plan of Senator Hilsendegen of Indiana to build seven homes on the south side of the river.

Sellers of real estate felt the need to organize. Eleven men and one woman formed the Fort Lauderdale Real Estate Dealers. C.C. Ausherman, Mary Brickell's agent, was elected president. In August 1920 they assumed the name of Fort Lauderdale Real Estate Board and in November 1921 affiliated with the National Association of Realtors.

Throughout the latter half of 1920 the *Sentinel* ran a steadily increasing amount of real-estate news, including the unveiling of a new development called Norwood on Dixie Highway in Fort Lauderdale. By early 1921 large display ads were beginning to appear, informing potential

Publicity resulting from advertising and visits by famous figures, combined with improved transportation and lodging, sent tourists from throughout the North flocking to Broward County in the prosperous years following World War I. While the wealthy relaxed in newly built private mansions, luxurious hotels, and aboard yachts, visitors of modest means brought their automobiles down the Dixie Highway and parked them at tourist camps such as this one at South Andrews Avenue in Fort Lauderdale. Because they lived on canned food, visitors to the camps were nicknamed "tin can tourists" by local residents. Courtesy, Fort Lauderdale Historical Society

Joseph W. Young's city seems to spring from the wilderness in this November 1921 picture. A closer look shows the hard labor by both man and machine that was responsible for Hollywood's growth. The construction of the city was well documented, as the enterprising photographer on top of the unfinished building demonstrates. Courtesy, Hollywood Historical Society

property owners of such events as the opening of Pleasant Beach, William Harding's oceanfront development in Deerfield, and an oceanfront auction at Pompano Beach-by-the-Sea.

In Fort Lauderdale two significant developments were surfacing, both on land owned for many decades by Mary Brickell. On May 9, 1920, she had filed a plat for a subdivision to be called Rio Vista. The following year Clarence J. Hector, cofounder of the Hector Supply Company, bought the property and proceeded to develop the area on the south side of the river. Rio Vista contained 400 acres, 27 blocks, and approximately 700 lots, many of them waterfront.

Mrs. Brickell also owned property on New River consisting mostly of mangrove swamps and a point of land which hosted one lone coconut palm. M.A. Hortt and his partner, Bob Dye, had bought the land but were short of development money. Tom Stilwell, representing investors from Anderson, Indiana, became interested in the property after he, Hortt, and

Dye visited Miami Beach to observe the technique used to build up marshy areas with river and bay bottom fill. To develop the property, they formed the New River Development Company. They called their new community "Idlewyld," the first in the county to be built on "made" land.

Rio Vista and Idlewyld proved to be highly significant in the residential development of Fort Lauderdale, but they were modest ventures indeed compared to the huge project that burst on the scene in July on lands just to the south of Dania.

Joseph Wesley Young, the man behind the new town, had explored the area between Miami and Fort Lauderdale in the fall of 1920. He was particularly intrigued by the coastal area between Hallandale and Dania, a large stretch of open country used only for farming. Perhaps because of the absence of a large stream, no settlement had grown up in this area. Young and his staff walked and waded through the swampy area as far up as Lake Mabel, and at one point Young swam across the Intracoastal to get a look at the beach. In the marshy wetlands the dynamic Young envisioned a city; at Lake Mabel he envisioned a world seaport.

Young was no stranger to the world of land development. He had already made and lost a fortune in California. In Arizona and Indiana he had developed major subdivisions. Young pioneered marketing techniques that are still in wide use. Instead of simply selling lots and houses, he developed complete communities, with homes, shopping areas, public buildings, streets, and parks. He and his staff conducted salesmanship courses, used giveaways for sales prospects, and provided prospective buyers with transportation to his subdivisions.

Returning to Indianapolis, he developed the grand design for his new city:

There will be a wide boulevard extending from the ocean westward to the edge of the Everglades. Here, one on each side of the boulevard and opening into the Intracoastal canal, we'll create two lakes, each with a turning basin for yachts. The materials dredged from the lakes will be the fill to elevate the lowland occupied by the mangrove swamps. Here, centrally located on this plat, will be the business section . . . This will be a city for everyone—from the opulent at the top of the industrial and social ladders to the most humble of working people.

His staff wanted Young to name the new town after himself. He overruled them and named it Hollywood-by-the-Sea. In contrast to the smaller, more subdued ads other developers used, Young let the world know of his new venture with full-page ads with pictures. He moved ahead, too, with plans to build hotels for his new town, and by December 1922 his Hollywood Hotel was ready for guests. In 1922 nearly

Joseph W. Young, a former California real-estate developer, began work on the new town of Hollywood-by-the-Sea in 1921. Hollywood, as it came to be abbreviated, took its name from Hollywood, California. Young was famous for accomplishments on a grand scale, and his new city was one of the most spectacular developments of the real estate boom. Courtesy, Fort Lauderdale Historical Society

Charles G. Rodes, one of Broward County's more colorful characters, sits on the bank of a canal at his 1921 Venice development. Rodes' Venice pioneered the finger island technique of dredging, and in the process gave Fort Lauderdale the enduring nickname, "The Venice of America." Courtesy, Fort Lauderdale Historical Society

100,000 people visited Hollywood. Young's goal for 1923 was to double that figure.

By 1924 Joe Young was building the Great Southern Hotel in downtown Hollywood, a huge casino on the beach, and a paved Broadwalk where people could stroll along the beach. He also organized the Hollywood Publishing Company to print the endless stream of publications his companies poured forth to promote Hollywood. Young's crews were clearing the land around Lake Mabel for his planned world seaport. Helping clear the area were 10 French-Canadian lumberjacks, the forerunners of an annual French-Canadian visitation to Hollywood a half-century later.

Activity was booming all over the county. Captain Hiram F. Hammon bought 4,500 acres from the Bolles Estate west of Pompano, an area drained by the Cypress Creek Canal. Barkdull Investment Company of Miami announced plans to develop a new town to be called Oakland Park on 810 acres north of Middle River. As agents for Blount Brothers Properties, W.F. Morang & Son announced an "Old Fashion Georgia Barbecue" to sell improved lots on Pompano Beach. Near Rio Vista, Carmichael Development Company presented its "suburb supreme," Placidena, where $40,000 worth of residential lots were sold on opening day.

In late 1922 the *Sentinel* became downright rhapsodic in announcing in its news columns the arrival in Fort Lauderdale of still another venture:

We have many subdivisions here which awaken hope for great things here this winter. But it has been left to Charlie Rodes to plan the greatest of them all. He proposes to make an American Venice. He will have a 100-foot canal in front of each home and 50-foot drive in the rear of the homes. Gondolas with beautiful Italian girls to run them will pass before each door and song and mandolin will stir the soul of man.

A West Virginian, Rodes had come to Fort Lauderdale prior to 1910. He had run a feed store, farmed, and invested in real estate. When the boom arrived, he was ready. From the Beverly Heights Syndicate he bought a mangrove swamp south and east of Las Olas Boulevard and east of the Intracoastal for $400 an acre. Rodes found, however, that neither the river nor the nearby Sospiro Canal could provide him with enough fill to create the amount of dry land he wanted. He turned then to a technique called finger-islanding, in use in Venice, Italy, for more than a century. Finger-islanding required him to dredge a series of parallel canals from Las Olas to the river, thus building up a series of long, thin spoil peninsulas between the canals. By running roads down the middle of each of these peninsulas he developed a subdivision composed entirely of waterfront lots, each with a high degree of privacy since they all dead-ended at the river. For Rodes the technique had the further advantage of keeping his development costs down. Finger-islanding required no floating dredging equipment, just the far less expensive land-based dragline.

Rodes platted the subdivision as "Venice," which he mispronounced as "Venus." He is generally credited with introducing the finger-islanding technique to this country, although some contend he should share the honor with Morang, who was developing Rio Vista Isles along the same lines at roughly the same time. What is not in dispute, however, is that the promotional campaign Rodes launched acquired for Fort Lauderdale the name "the Venice of America."

Meanwhile, the Richlands subdivision west of Fort Lauderdale was offering large lots, 135 by 270 feet, and larger 2.5-acre tracts for truck farming. William Jennings Bryan, Secretary of State in President Woodrow Wilson's Cabinet and unsuccessful candidate for President, bought six lots.

In north Broward the Hillsborough Beach Development Company announced plans for a $6-million hotel and sanitarium in its Hillsborough Beach development, between the Hillsboro Lighthouse and Deerfield. Lake Placid-Cocoanut Grove School for Boys, described as a "millionaires' school," was to be built in the area just north of the lighthouse. By 1925 it had been converted into the Hillsboro Club, the county's most exclusive resort hotel.

Real estate was not the only activity in Broward County. A new inlet was cut just opposite the mouth of New River. Plans were made to blast open the inlet on October 4, 1923, during ceremonies including a luncheon, speeches, and a band concert. But nature failed to cooperate.

Deceptively plain-looking on the outside, the Hillsborough Beach Hillsboro Club quickly earned a reputation as Broward County's most exclusive private resort. The club was situated on the ocean, just north of the Hillsboro Lighthouse, northern Broward County's most famous landmark. Before the establishment of the club in 1925, the property served briefly as the Lake Placid-Cocoanut Grove School for Boys, a school for children of the very wealthy. Courtesy, Fort Lauderdale Historical Society

By the 1920s Fort Lauderdale bore no resemblance to the wilderness river crossing that had greeted Frank Stranahan 30 years earlier. For Stranahan, the rapid growth had brought new business opportunities and accompanying wealth in banking, real estate, and building. During much of the 1910s and 1920s Stranahan served on the City Council, while Ivy Stranahan kept active in a number of civic, cultural, and welfare organizations, including the Florida Equal Suffrage Association, the Audubon Society, and the Friends of the Florida Seminoles. Courtesy, Fort Lauderdale Historical Society

On September 27 the sea washed away the final wall of dirt and opened the inlet.

D.W. Griffith came back to town in 1923 to film *The White Rose*, starring Mae Marsh. Many of the scenes were photographed in and around the Stranahan house. Griffith, however, did not like what the boom was doing to the cinematic tropical island he had first visited just four years earlier. Newly constructed seawalls along the river were robbing the area of its unspoiled, South Seas look.

Another who had misgivings about the changing face of Fort Lauderdale was Frank Stranahan. In the winter of 1923 he wrote to G.C. Varney, "We are getting in too much of a rush here. City life too fast for me."

He had come to the river when no one else lived there. As the settlement had grown, he had stepped in and done what needed to be done to make a riverfront camp into a town and then a small city. He had become the town's postmaster, opened its first store, been elected treasurer of the Board of Trade, and served 10 terms on the City Council, four of them as president. He had invested in the first bank, later becoming its president, in the first company that sought to build a deep-water harbor, and in the first that attempted to build a bridge to the beach. He had donated land for parks, for the Woman's Club Building, and for the first hospital. He had been a vital part of the swiftly moving development that now was becoming "too fast" for him.

Stranahan still remembered the trading post days and the lifelong friendships he had made with the people who poled dugout canoes in from the Everglades. Roy Nash, in a report to the U.S. Senate, wrote: "... many of his neighbors wondered why Frank Stranahan kept a horse long after the automobile had relegated most stables to the past. Few knew of his trips in the dead of night with the old horse to bury some Indian baby or friend who had died in the camps on the edge of town."

If the pace was becoming too fast for Frank, Ivy Stranahan was taking it in stride. Increasingly active in the Florida Audubon Society, she played an important role in catching an illegal dealer in plumes.

Bert Lasher, who with his hunting dogs had appeared in the serial, "The Firing Line," had operated a small tourist attraction on the North Fork of the New River featuring a Seminole camp and a natural slough filled with alligators. His career as an attraction operator was interrupted by a stint in the state prison at Raiford for buying cars he knew were stolen.

After his release from prison, Bert surfaced as operator of the Musa Isle attraction in Miami. One of the Indians who wrestled alligators at Musa Isle was Tony Tommie. Bert was also picking up extra money by illegally buying egret plumes from the Seminoles. From an anonymous informant, probably Willie Willie, who had been deposed by Lasher as Musa

Isle manager, Mrs. Stranahan learned that Lasher had a cache of feathers worth $35,000. Following up on her tip, the federal game warden for South Florida raided Bert's place, seized the plumes, and arrested Lasher. In May of 1926 he was finally convicted and fined $750. That same week any interest his conviction might have stirred was wiped out by a highly publicized event at Musa Isle. Tony Tommie and "Princess" Edna John were "married" at the attraction. The marriage ceremony, repeated many times, became an important part of the Musa Isle show. Two years later the Princess died of tuberculosis, a disease that was also to take Tony in 1931.

Lasher's lawbreaking seemed small, however, when compared with the activities of the area's leading outlaws—the Ashley Gang. For more than a decade the Ashleys had terrorized South Florida with murders, bank robberies, rum-running, hijackings, and jailbreaks. On September 12, 1924, the gang decided to rob the Bank of Pompano. Just before closing time cashier Cecil H. Cates and teller T.L. Myers found themselves gazing at the muzzles of pistols held by Shorty Lynn and Clarence Middleton. From the doorway John Ashley, holding a rifle, called out, "All right, turn around, face the wall, and raise your hands. We won't be long." They escaped with $4,000 in cash plus a $5,000 bond.

But for the Ashley Gang the end was near. Posses were hounding them everywhere they turned. On November 1 an informant told Sheriff Bob Baker of Palm Beach County that the gang would be passing through Fort Pierce that night via the Dixie Highway. At the bridge over Sebastian River the St. Lucie County sheriff, J.R. Merritt, placed a chain blockade.

When they stopped for the chain, the Ashleys were quickly surrounded and handcuffed. What happened next is unclear. One version says that John Ashley made a sudden move and was shot dead immediately. Hearing the gunshots, the other deputies instinctively killed the rest of their captives, who were in handcuffs.

One of the posse scooped out John Ashley's glass eye and sent it to Sheriff Baker, who had boasted that he would someday wear it as a watch fob. He quickly changed his mind and returned the glass eye. He had been threatened by two people he had reason to fear—Ma Ashley and John's moll, Laura Upthegrove.

On one occasion Broward crime was made to serve a useful purpose. In February 1922 a group of well-dressed men rented the Frank Oliver home on New River, a spacious two-story house close to downtown. The men drove high-powered cars, joined the golf club, generally tipped well, and paid their rent promptly. Because they claimed to have access to wires that gave race results, they acquired the name "Wiretappers." Despite the suspicions of the townspeople, Sheriff A.W. Turner of Pompano declined to take any action against them.

WRESTLING PIT
DANGER
DO NOT SIT ON WALL
MUSA ISLE INDIAN VILLAGE
M___FLA.

Indian attractions such as Bert Lasher's village on the New River and his Musa Isle in Miami were extremely popular among tourists in the 1920s. Featuring such events as alligator wrestling and shows demonstrating Seminole wedding ceremonies, the attractions drew severe criticism from those who felt they exploited and degraded the Indians. However, they remained popular for more than 40 years. Courtesy, Fort Lauderdale Historical Society

This photo of John Ashley (left) was taken at the Florida State Prison at Raiford between 1916 and 1918. At the time, Ashley was serving a 17-and-one-half-year sentence for his part in the robbery of the Stuart Bank, a robbery in which he lost his left eye. Escaping after serving less than two years, Ashley returned to a life of crime, robbing a bank at his one-time residence, Pompano, in 1924. Courtesy, Fort Lauderdale Historical Society

Governor Cary Hardee, however, sent a special investigator, Bob Shackelford, down from Jacksonville. Posing as a man looking for a little gambling action, Shackelford penetrated the house. Then on February 19, 1922, he led a raid and captured all but two of the Wiretappers. When the trial was held, the defendants entered guilty pleas through their lawyers and were fined the exact amount of their bond—$18,000.

Although no official records corroborate this, reports persist that the men were let off without prison sentences as part of a deal in which the bond money was earmarked for construction of the county's first hospital on land donated by Frank Stanahan on East Broward Boulevard. In 1923 a special enabling act sponsored by Representative Carl P. Weidling was passed by the state legislature authorizing the county to issue interest-bearing warrants or other evidences of indebtednesses not exceeding $18,000—the exact amount of the forfeited bond.

The hospital became the Edwards-Maxwell Hospital, erected on the Stranahan land in the fall of 1923. It would later become the Edwards Hospital, operated by Dr. Scott Edwards, a son-in-law of Idlewyld developer Tom Stilwell, and still later Memorial Hospital.

Prior to 1920 only one black doctor, Henry H. Green, who moved to Miami, had practiced medicine in Broward County. In April 1922 Dr. James Franklin Sistrunk, a graduate of Meharry Medical College in Nashville, Tennessee, arrived in Fort Lauderdale. When the kindly, white-haired doctor, a native of North Florida, came to Broward, blacks were not permitted to perform surgery. Dr. Sistrunk concentrated on delivering babies—more than 5,000 in his career—and on making house calls to his many patients.

By 1924 the Roaring Twenties were really beginning to roar. It was the time of the flapper and of bootleg hooch. National Prohibition was converting formerly law-abiding citizens into lawbreakers. Drinking in public, frowned on earlier, was becoming fashionable now that it was illegal. Less than 75 miles from Broward lay the Bahamas, British possessions untouched by America's Prohibition. Under cover of darkness, rumrunners' boats cruised through the Hillsboro and New River inlets, carrying whiskey for sale to the eager pleasure-seekers of the Twenties.

But the true mania of the time continued to be the Florida land boom. In Deerfield the Ocean River Corporation and the Ocean Heights Development Company were selling lots on the beach, while farther down the coast the Hillsborough Beach Development Company was moving ahead with its big project, Hillsborough Beach. In Pompano Lettuce Lake became Lake Santa Barbara, a name more conducive to real-estate sales.

In Fort Lauderdale real estate was selling at Rio Vista, Rio Vista Isles, Idlewyld, Venice, and Victoria Park, Alfred G. Kuhn's new development north of the New River area. E.J. "Ned" Willingham, a Georgia peach and pecan grower, was developing Wilton Manors north of Fort Lauderdale and, with M.I. Anglin, the oceanfront subdivison, Lauderdale-by-the-Sea. Morang was hard at work on Harbor Beach and was just getting started on Lauderdale Isles north of Las Olas Boulevard.

The year 1924 brought the start of Fort Lauderdale's biggest development. G. Frank Croissant, who had developed Calumet City, Illinois, for Henry Ford, bought 1,193 acres south of the New River for $1.25 million. Forty years earlier Arthur Williams had platted this land as Palm City.

Croissant, the 1916 winner of the Salesmanship Congress of America's medal as "America's Greatest Salesman," brought 96 of his finest Chicago salespeople to Fort Lauderdale to kick off Croissant Park. They arrived on December 27, 1925. By the dawn of the new year they had already sold $3,184,000 worth of lots.

Croissant Park sold out quickly, and Croissant promptly plowed his profits back into a new subdivision north of Fort Lauderdale. He called it Croissantania and described it as "My Masterpiece." It was to feature a luxurious resort hotel, the Croissantiana, planned to "outdistance every other in elegance, splendor, and design."

Croissant's sales publication, *Post Script*, listed Fort Lauderdale's population as 6,000 in 1924. He predicted it would become Florida's largest city, reaching 50,000 in five years. A small man with a booming voice, Croissant faced the future with faith, confidence, and optimism. Always a hard worker, Croissant nonetheless knew how to enjoy the fruits of his considerable success. He followed the horses and at one time owned a racing stable, a stud farm, and a total of 110 thoroughbreds.

In sheer delight at his own good fortune no one quite matched the joy of Charlie Rodes. The success of Venice and his other real-estate investments in Pompano, Deerfield, Merritt Island, and the Cape Canaveral area had made him a rich man. He once bought a lot for $600 and resold it for $60,000.

Born poor in Gatewood, West Virginia, Rodes decided he was going to share his good fortune with his relatives, many of them still struggling along. His plan was to charter two Pullman cars, round up as many of his relatives as he could, and take them on a grand tour of the country. He located 52 relatives, some from as far away as New Mexico.

The Rodes clan was under orders to "live it up." He laid down only one ground rule—no bickering. Anyone caught arguing would simply be put off the train in the Mohave Desert, no matter what the provocation had been. Consequently, in the whole month-long trip, there was not a single squabble.

The national press followed his progress avidly. More than 300,000 press notices about the trip appeared in papers throughout the country.

James F. Sistrunk was not Broward County's first black physician, but for 16 years he was the only one. In an era when many white doctors refused to treat black patients, Sistrunk's services were especially vital. Practicing medicine in Fort Lauderdale for more than 40 years, he became one of the town's most beloved citizens, retiring shortly before his death in 1966. Courtesy, Fort Lauderdale Historical Society

United Press dispatched the well-known Florida newspaperwoman, Ruby Leach, on the trip. Rodes sent his own cameraman, Eugene M. Kelcy of Fort Lauderdale.

Rodes' only complaint was voiced in California: "I can't spend the money fast enough. Things are too cheap out here. I'm rich and I have more money than I know what to do with. But my relatives are poor spenders. We've got $100,000 to drop—and here the trip is half over with half of it still in my safe."

Back in Broward a luxury yacht from Palm Beach sailed into New River. A woman on board shouted to a young black man on the shore, "Where are we?"

"Fort Lauderdale," he called back.

His answer was a matter of considerable interest to her. The woman was the Countess of Lauderdale. She and her husband, the Earl of Lauderdale, whose title traced back to Scotland, went ashore and explored the area. They were particularly taken with the land south of Cypress Creek—so taken, in fact, that 17 years later in 1926 the Countess formed the British Improvement Association and bought 8,000 acres, including a mile of oceanfront land. Arthur T. Galt, son of Hugh Taylor Birch's law partner in Chicago, sold the company the property for $1 million down, the balance of $6 million to be paid later.

The British Improvement Association involved an interesting group of principals: the Countess and the Earl, Lords Thirlestane and Boulton, Viscount Molesworth, the ex-King of Greece, plus such socially prominent Palm Beachers as Mrs. E.T. Stotesbury, Mrs. Horace Dodge, Samuel E. Vauclain, president of Baldwin Locomotive, and John S. Pillsbury, well known in flour circles.

The Countess' company set about developing a new town to be called

The greatest phenomenon of the Florida land boom in Broward County was the remarkable growth and development of Hollywood. In the four years between 1921 and 1925, Hollywood's population soared from zero to 20,000, making it Broward County's largest city. The established communities of Dania and Hallandale were absorbed into the newborn giant in 1926. This 1925 photo of Hollywood Beach depicts crowds of tourists and new residents congregating in the water, on the Broadwalk, and at the Municipal Casino, a huge public swimming pool. Courtesy, Hollywood Historical Society

Floranada, a combination of the words Florida and Canada. When the town was incorporated on November 25, 1925, it included the successful subdivision, Oakland Park, which had opened in 1923 with one of the biggest barbecues ever seen in the county. With the arrival of Floranada, the days of the down-home barbecue were over. It was the goal of the Countess to create another Palm Beach, a playground for the very rich.

The first mayor of Floranada was Jimmy Cromwell, Mrs. Stotesbury's son and later the husband of Doris Duke, the world's richest heiress. The city commission was stacked with representatives of the development company. The only local resident on the commission was Dewey Hawkins, who owned considerable farmland and other real estate in the Floranada area. Hawkins, who was descended from an old North Florida family, soon joined the company as its purchasing agent. Hortt recalls turning down an offer from Hawkins as an officer of the company to buy a 10-acre tract for $50,000. Two years later Hawkins as a private citizen bought the same land from Hortt for $2,250.

In 1925 Floranada was one of four Broward communities to incorporate. On June 11 some 500 north county residents received a charter for the Town of Deerfield, which extended south from the Hillsboro Canal to the Hillsboro Lighthouse. They chose a mayor-city council form of government and named George Emery Butler the town's first mayor.

Later that year, Davie was incorporated. Davie's residents were concerned about crime; by incorporating they felt they could assure police protection. Mrs. Ed Middlebrooks had written to the Fort Lauderdale Chief of Police:

I want to ask you if you all can't let us have a good man out at Davie for protection. I declare the drunkenness and misbehavior in front of the store I can't

Above: Fort Lauderdale Mayor John W. Tidball presented the key to the city to Gwendolyn Maitland, countess of Lauderdale, in a ceremony at the Rainbow Roof Garden on March 18, 1926. The Scottish countess wintered in Palm Beach, and was a principal backer of the Floranada development at Oakland Park. Although there was no direct connection between the countess' family and the naming of Broward's county seat, the appeal of noble connections and the identical names inspired legends which obscured Fort Lauderdale's actual origins for decades. Courtesy, Fort Lauderdale Historical Society

Fresh ocean breezes rushing through flags, and palm and pine trees, provided atmosphere as Fort Lauderdale residents and visitors gathered by the seaside on July 4, 1923. Broward County beaches, practically deserted 10 years earlier because they were difficult to reach and virtually impossible to cultivate, became popular places to congregate during the land boom. Courtesy, Fort Lauderdale Historical Society

stand and at times they try and do come in the store and cut up, then if a-body tries to get them out, then comes the trouble . . . I cannot put up with the drunkenness, cursing and bad conduct.

On November 16 the vote was held. Twenty-eight favored incorporation; two were opposed. The voters picked as their first mayor the man who had served as chairman of the meeting, Frank Stirling, a horticulturist with the State Plant Board. Aldermen elected were Walter Henry, W.H. Aires, C.E. Viele, Ray Jenne, and William Brumby. C.L. Walsh was designated town clerk and A.C. Brown, town marshall.

On November 25 both Floranada and Hollywood were incorporated. So successful had been the explosive growth of Joe Young's Hollywood venture that Dania, the first Broward town to incorporate, and Hallandale both asked to be annexed into the new city. Not surprisingly, Hollywood's first mayor was Joe Young.

By 1926 Hollywood, which didn't even exist at the start of the decade, may have become the county's largest city, with a population that its boosters estimated at roughly 20,000. Fort Lauderdale, the county seat, probably numbered in the 16,000 range at this time.

In 1925 the boom reached its manic peak. Joe Young was running prospects through Hollywood by the thousands. Early in the boom he ordered the construction of 27 White buses at $8,000 apiece. His buses brought buyers in from the Northeast and the Midwest. Hollywood bus caravans heading south generated excitement all along the way. Selling, unrelenting in the caravans, continued in Florida in sales pavilions, at luncheons, and at the popular marimba band dances. Lecturers assured would-be buyers that Hollywood could never be damaged by a hurricane because the area was protected by the Gulf Stream.

Hollywood and Fort Lauderdale were teeming with visitors, even more than the cities could handle. The boom created so many jobs that employers had trouble finding people to perform the work the boom had brought. Young even had to send buses to Atlanta to bring back enough secretaries to process his mountains of paperwork. The problem was that nearly everybody wanted to sell real estate.

And no wonder. By 1925 the demand had become so great that sellers no longer needed to show property to make sales. More often than not, the buyer wanted the land for a quick resale.

For example, Hortt sold a tract of land near Deerfield for $50 an acre. Two days later he resold the tract for the buyer for $200. In less than a week the acre price had risen to $600, and in less than six months the property sold again for $5,000 an acre. Hortt was kept so busy keeping up with the demand for property that he described himself as "almost a nervous wreck."

At Pompano Beach a 40-acre tract on the ocean that had been sold for $30,000 in 1924 was resold in mid-1925 for more than a million dollars, according to Norbourne B. Cheaney, head of the Broward County Title Company.

Fort Lauderdale no longer bore any real resemblance to the little frontier settlement of 25 years earlier. Hardy pioneers who traversed the river in rowboats had given way to elegant dressers racing up and down the waterways in speedboats. Farmers hauling produce with horses and wagons had been supplanted by big spenders in flashy automobiles. Tar-paper shacks had made way for beautiful Spanish-style mansions designed by such talented architects as Francis Abreu.

In the midst of the frenzied activity, one oasis of uneasy calm held fast. Hugh Taylor Birch refused even to discuss selling his choice two-mile stretch of oceanfront land. A semirecluse, Birch and his faithful servant, "Old Jeff," patrolled the property with shotguns.

To the Seminoles the boom did what the Indian wars failed to accomplish. It forced them finally to leave their old camps on the New River and retire to a reservation. Even the hammocks west of Fort Lauderdale where they camped were swept up in the boom.

Before the turn of the century reservations had been set aside for the Indians. In Broward they retained three small tracts in the Everglades plus 360 acres lying four miles west of Dania. Commissioner Lucien Spencer asked Ivy Stranahan to try to persuade the Indians to move.

The Florida East Coast Railway's freight embargo during the fall of 1925 endangered the already-weakened building boom. Their livelihood crippled by the embargo, several desperate builders managed to bring construction materials in by ship. Here, a three-masted schooner docks on the New River, just east of the Andrews Avenue bridge in downtown Fort Lauderdale. Courtesy, Fort Lauderdale Historical Society

As part of his Hollywood promotional campaign, Joseph W. Young made extensive use of tour buses to sell property. Buses brought prospective buyers to Hollywood from the northern states and other parts of Florida, and salesmen gave guided tours of the town. Double-deck "Tally-ho" buses such as this one, complete with uniformed footmen, transported guests to the links at the Hollywood Golf and Country Club. Courtesy, Fort Lauderdale Historical Society

Believing the reservation offered them the best chance of preserving their culture, she accepted.

One day Ivy drove four tribal leaders to the site. She spoke not a word until they arrived and had a chance to size up the property. Then she said: "This is your land. If you don't take it, someone else will." The Indians' trust in her was so great that they took it. In 1926 the Bureau of Indian Affairs erected 10 one-room cottages and a small administration building on the land.

In the late winter of 1925 vast numbers of "fast-buck" artists began to appear in South Florida, drawn southward by the smell of green money. Their biggest contribution was speeding up the wild speculation that converted boom to bust. To their contemporaries they were known simply as the "binder boys."

A binder is an option on a piece of property. A binder boy would put up a small amount of money to bind a purchase. He might slap a binder of $500 on a property valued at $50,000. He would receive paper stating that he was, in effect, the owner of a $50,000 piece of property on which the next payment of $10,000 or $15,000 was due in 10 days, or possibly 30 days.

The binder would then be resold at a higher price and then resold again and so on. The first genuine installment could not be demanded by the seller until the title had been cleared, a process that took from four to six weeks. Binders were frequently sold as many as eight times before the real purchase took place. The result was chaotic. Prices soared toward absurdity.

The day of the binder boy lasted roughly five months in 1925. The famous author, Kenneth Roberts, in his *Florida*, claims the binder boys met their fate in Broward County. According to this widely circulated version, N.B.T. Roney, a Miami Beach developer, incensed at the chaos created by the binder boys, ambushed them at his new oceanfront development, Seminole Beach, just south of Hallandale. Roney, claimed Roberts, sold strips of land at Seminole Beach, on which the binder boys took options; then he sold parallel strips at sharply lower prices, leaving the binder boys with worthless paper. Chronically low on cash and now unable to sell their binders, they were wiped out and forced to leave town on northbound freight trains.

The truth is that the phenomenal sale of Seminole Beach occurred too quickly to have demolished the binder boys. A number of days would have been required for the alleged Roney plot to have worked its magic. Actually, Seminole Beach sold out in one incredible day.

Roney and James M. Cox, publisher of the *Miami News* and Democratic candidate for President in 1920, bought 115 acres along the ocean from Wade Harley for $3 million. No advertising was published, just a few phone calls to let it be known that Roney was placing an oceanfront property on the market on August 1, 1925.

When the day arrived, Roney's office was overwhelmed by frantic buyers who bought every lot in six and a half hours for $7,645,000. Within a week the buyers had resold the property for $12 million. The first payments were for 10 percent, with a 15-percent payment due in 30 days. Within 30 days, the boom was in retreat. Seminole Beach, one of the most spectacular sales achievements of the boom, reverted to its former owner, Wade Harley.

For people on the scene it was not totally clear that the boom was at last fading. The boom had generated so much energy of its own that people couldn't believe prices could go anywhere but up. By late 1925 they were learning the truth.

Late that summer a number of discouraging events began to close in on South Florida's fantasyland. Agents from the Internal Revenue Service started following up on large real-estate transactions and demanding tax payments in cash from the boom's paper-millionaires. The area was hurt by a wave of adverse publicity, much of it generated by Northern bankers, dismayed at seeing their deposits move to Florida. At the same time the gyrations of the binder boys were stretching speculation to its outer limits.

Then, to throw one more complication into an already deteriorating situation, the Florida East Coast Railway announced a temporary freight embargo to repair its overworked tracks. The embargo stopped the flow of building materials and idled construction projects. Soon railroad cars were backing up all along the rail system. By late fall more than 7,000 southbound freight cars were waiting helplessly outside Jacksonville, unable to continue on down to South Florida.

Despite warning signals Joe Young surged optimistically ahead with his plans to build a world seaport at Lake Mabel. In late 1925 he arranged a three-way deal with the cities of Hollywood and Fort Lauderdale, each of which would contribute $2 million in cash or services. In bond elections in the summer of 1926, voters in both towns overwhelmingly favored the port project. Obviously not convinced the boom was over, they had committed their communities to a large and very bold financial outlay.

That July an event occurred that proved prophetic. In February 1926 Young had opened "Tent City," a motel under canvas just to the south of Hollywood Beach Hotel. Paul Whiteman and his orchestra entertained guests at the grand opening. Then in July the first hurricane to hit southeast Florida since 1910 struck; Tent City was blown away.

Not given to brooding over setbacks or bad omens, Young went to Baltimore to join commissioner A.J. Ryan and Tom Bryan in inspecting a

Davie's first mayor, Frank Stirling, was one of Florida's foremost agricultural experts, dividing his time between his own farming enterprises and working for the State Plant Board. He moved to Davie in the late 1910s from Miami, where he had grown tomatoes near Biscayne Bay. Courtesy, Fort Lauderdale Historical Society

new dredge being built for the port, then continued on to Philadelphia for the heavyweight championship bout between Jack Dempsey and Gene Tunney. He was in Philadelphia when he received word of the catastrophe that told the whole world the Florida land boom was not only dead but also buried under sand and debris.

To Miami weatherman Richard Gray reports he was receiving from ships in the Caribbean were ominous. He telegraphed the barometric pressure readings and wind velocity data to the Weather Bureau in Washington for further analysis.

Just before 6 p.m. on September 17, 1926, he received his orders from Washington—hoist hurricane warnings. Unfortunately, in 1926 there were few avenues for warning people—just one radio station in South Florida and only a handful of sets to pick up its signal. Even worse, most of the people living in the area had never experienced a major hurricane. They simply did not know what to expect or what to do.

On the night of the 17th the wind began picking up, the barometer began falling, and the waters began rising. From the Keys to southern Palm Beach County gale force winds started to buffet the shore. At 2 a.m. the hurricane came ashore. By then southeast Florida was already isolated. Power, telephone, and telegraph lines were down.

Charles Richardson, a carpenter on a pine ridge near Scott Street and 24th Avenue in Hollywood, noticed his house was lifting and falling back on its cement block piers at about 11:30 p.m. He awakened his wife, Mabel. She wrapped their month-old daughter in two blankets and collected a bottle of water and a supply of diapers. Since their bathroom had a sealed cement floor, the Richardsons moved in with a kerosene lamp and a rocking chair.

Below and facing page: Before (below) and after (facing page) scenes, such as these views of Andrews Avenue looking north from 16th Street in Fort Lauderdale's Croissant Park area, dramatically illustrate the destruction caused by the 1926 hurricane. New developments, built quickly during the boom, were especially hard hit. Courtesy, Fort Lauderdale Historical Society

Leo Story and his parents pounded on the Richardsons' door, so Charles brought his neighbors into the bathroom, too. Then the Storys' house smashed into the Richardsons'. The roof broke away, the walls collapsed, and a double bed wedged against the bathroom door, trapping all six people for six hours.

Around midnight the John Anderson family was startled by the sound of flying objects hitting their new home. During the night nearly 30 people joined them in this house, many of them with their clothing torn away by the winds. A cement block crashed through the dining room ceiling, and a stranger who had come in moaned: "Oh, Lord, if you get me through this I'll go back to Alabama and never gamble again."

Arthur Carthon, a night watchman at the Hollywood Country Club, found the water rising around his car. He climbed onto a cement mixer. When a 70-foot steel barge lodged against his truck, he jumped aboard and went below through an open hatch. "I stuck my head out," he recalled, "and saw a big frog. Everytime the frog jumped it would be blown five feet backwards."

T.D. Ellis, Jr., a young attorney who had helped prepare the City of Hollywood charter, was one of three who escaped by floating on a barge up Hollywood Boulevard. That night Ellis' hair reportedly turned white.

The winds pounded Broward, reaching velocities of over 100 miles per hour. Then, at 6:30 a.m., the eye of the hurricane came ashore over Miami. Many were killed because they thought the calm in the eye meant the storm was over. They came out of their homes and shelters to inspect the damage. Then the other side of the hurricane roared ashore with winds even stronger than the first phase, battering Broward this time with winds of 140 miles per hour.

Above: Located on the ocean at the end of Hollywood Boulevard, the Hollywood Beach Hotel was constructed of Belgian cement especially imported by Joseph W. Young during the freight embargo. This 1926 view of the lounge shows the rich ornamentation and intricate detail which characterized the interior of the building. Open for the 1925-1926 winter season, the hotel could accommodate more than 500 guests. Courtesy, Fort Lauderdale Historical Society

DAILY NEWS

Fort Lauderdale, Florida, September 20, 1926

KNOWN DEATH TOLL OF HURRICANE NOW 15 IN LAUDERDALE

With Homeless and Injured Cared For Relief Workers Bend Efforts To Avoid Infections and Establish Sanitation

The 1926 hurricane made headlines across the country, and some northern United States newspapers reported that it had blown South Florida off the map. Fort Lauderdale's Daily News, *although more realistic, was itself a testimonial to the storm's destructive powers. Damage to the presses put the* Daily News *out of commission for two days, and the first post-hurricane edition, printed in Lake Worth on September 20, was a miniature 8½-by-11-inch, four-page issue. Courtesy, Fort Lauderdale Historical Society*

In Oakland Park teenager John U. Lloyd was pinned beneath the roof of an outbuilding when he went out in the storm to tie down the family's windmill. His leg was broken in six places and his skull fractured. He was unconscious for two weeks. He recovered and later became the county attorney.

Tired of driving to temples in Miami and Palm Beach, a group of Jewish citizens decided the time had come to establish a place of worship for themselves in Fort Lauderdale. For the first time in history they met to conduct Jewish services in a place of their own, a second-floor room over a Las Olas Boulevard restaurant. A few hours later the hurricane blew away the second floor of the building where they had met.

Colonel George Mathews, publisher of the *Fort Lauderdale Daily News*, and his family took refuge on the second floor of their home to escape the rising water. So did developer D.C. Alexander and his family. Alexander's daughter, Betty Lou, recalled:

The wind was blowing and the water was coming up and I looked out the wet windows and all I could see was the ocean's waves, merrily rolling through the backyard. In my child's mind I just pictured our house bobbing out in the middle of the ocean. We stayed downstairs until the front door, which was solid oak about an inch and a half thick, broke open and the doorknob flew out and made a dent in the plaster . . . We had 30 windows blown out of the house. One went and the others followed rapidly.

In north Broward the hurricane was less severe. Still, Landrum Blount, a Pompano teenager at the time, recalls pulling the sheet over his face as the window above his bed shattered. He escaped injury, but his brother, Bruce, was less lucky. He was cut by flying glass.

Even the Hillsboro Light went out for the first time. Said keeper Tom Knight: "The big lens shook, stopped turning, and the mercury went out."

By noon Saturday the storm had moved on. The sun was shining, and the breeze from the southeast was gentle and balmy. But all was not well. The hurricane had continued on northwestward to Lake Okeechobee, where its winds and waters broke a dike near Moore Haven. Three hundred people were killed.

In Philadelphia Tom Bryan and Fort Lauderdale City Attorney Lewis Hall were confronted with a frightening newspaper headline: "Southeastern Florida Wiped Out." It was almost that bad. Early reports estimated the death toll in Hollywood at 60, later revised downward to 25. Fifteen were dead at Fort Lauderdale, nine in Dania. In Fort Lauderdale alone the injury toll reached 1,500. For the entire state the death toll was 400.

Property damage ran in the millions of dollars. Early estimates put the figure at $165 million for the area from Miami through Fort Lauderdale. In the county more than 2,700 houses were destroyed, more than 5,650 damaged. It was reported that every house and building in Hollywood and Fort Lauderdale was damaged to some extent. Particularly vulnerable were the less sturdy homes hastily erected during the boom. Davie was badly flooded and Dania severly battered. Hallandale, where most of the homes were of pre-boom construction, fared better. In Pompano and Deerfield, where most of the residents lived on a high sand ridge, damage was less severe, although the Dixie Highway area was under water. At the Indian reservation all 10 of the new cottages were blown away.

Dredges that had been working in Bay Mabel to build the port were blown up on dry land. Pleasure craft were sunk or damaged all over the area. Charles Cory's old houseboat, *Wanderer*, was wrecked as was the *Larooco*, whose final log, written by Franklin D. Roosevelt, indicated that the "good old craft with a personality" wound up four miles inland, at least a mile from the nearest water. Tom Bryan's seaplane wound up in Idlewyld under a 75-foot Coast Guard cutter.

Martial law was declared in Broward as the populace struggled to clean up the debris and then begin the long task of rebuilding the county's communities. What lay ahead, no one could guess, but of one fact the people of Broward were certain. The Florida land boom was over, blown into oblivion by the deadliest hurricane South Florida had ever seen.

After the hurricane ended on September 18, the long, hard task of cleaning up the debris and rebuilding began. Mayor John W. Tidball declared martial law in Fort Lauderdale the day the storm passed, and prisoners were assembled for clean-up duty. Here a group of convicts, dressed in striped uniforms, clean up Wall Street. Courtesy, Fort Lauderdale Historical Society

At 2 p.m., December 5, 1945, training flight 19, composed of five Avenger torpedo bombers such as these, left the Fort Lauderdale Naval Air Station for a two-hour navigation hop over the Bahamas. A series of garbled messages—"All planes close up tight . . . will have to ditch unless landfall . . . when the first plane drops to ten gallons, we all go down together"—were the last transmissions received from the flight. A five-day, 250,000-square-mile search of the Atlantic and Gulf failed to reveal any trace of wreckage. The mystery surrounding the disappearance of the "lost flight" is yet unsolved and has inspired countless legends of the "Devil's Triangle." Courtesy, National Archives

Chapter 6

DEPRESSION, WAR, AND THE DEVIL'S TRIANGLE

For Broward County, the Depression came early. The boom, the bust, and then the hurricane's big blow had left the county battered. Tax collections dropped sharply; mortgage payments were off; and construction work stopped. In downtown Fort Lauderdale, Will Marshall's Will-Mar Hotel paused in mid-air, a skeleton of a building that haunted the city's skyline for years. A bridge Morang had started to build over to his Lauderdale Isles development stood incomplete.

Many, ruined financially, left the county. The population of Fort Lauderdale, which had grown from 3,000 in 1924 to an estimated 13,000 in 1927, leveled off at 8,660 in the 1930 census. Hollywood, estimated to have reached 30,000 in the winter of 1925-1926, had dropped back to 2,869 by 1930.

In the difficult year of 1927 Broward was stunned by two shocking murder cases. On July 7, Bill Hicks, former Broward County chief deputy sheriff and first exalted ruler of Fort Lauderdale Elks Lodge 1517, was arrested on a charge of first-degree murder. The warrant for his arrest had been sworn out by C.W. Barber, brother of the murder victim, Reese Barber, whose nude, mutilated, and gunshot-riddled body had been found floating in the Dania Cut-off Canal by a small boy two years earlier.

Rumors had persisted that the body had been buried after a fake examination. The victim's brother demanded and got an exhumation and proper examination. In short order, the grand jury returned an indictment.

According to testimony, Reese Barber, a carpenter by trade, had been sentenced in July 1925 to seven months in the county jail for petty larceny. While serving time, Barber worked on houses being constructed in

James Horace Alderman, the only man to be legally executed in Broward County, bears little resemblance to a murderer or pirate in this 1929 photograph taken shortly before he was hanged. Alderman, a native Floridian, had a long career of alien-smuggling and rumrunning behind him when he was captured at sea, off Fort Lauderdale, in 1927. In prison the "Gulf Stream Pirate" found religion. Though he died proclaiming his new faith, he never expressed regret for his final murderous acts. Courtesy, Fort Lauderdale Historical Society

Progresso by jailer Hicks. When Hicks failed to pay him, he filed a complaint with the local carpenters' union. In August, after he was released from jail, Barber disappeared from his quarters at the DeSoto Hotel.

Two eyewitnesses testified that they had accompanied Hicks to Barber's room with a fake warrant. They forced the carpenter into a car and drove him to the southwest section of the city, where he was shot, castrated, and dumped into a canal.

Hicks was convicted and sentenced to life imprisonment. On February 13, 1929, his 44th birthday, the verdict was reversed by the state supreme court on a technicality in the grand jury's proceedings. A second trial ended in a mistrial, a third in acquittal for Hicks. He packed up his belongings and returned to his native New York State.

The other murder case resulted from an altercation during the attempted arrest of some rumrunners. For a town that had always voted dry, Fort Lauderdale, like much of America, was finding alcoholic spirits more tempting now that Prohibition had declared them illegal. At this time the city acquired the name Fort Liquordale, partly because its residents lifted many a glass but also because it became an important port of illegal entry for smugglers returning from the Bahamas with boatloads of contraband. U.S. Coast Guard Base Six at Bahia Mar near the old House of Refuge, which had been destroyed by the 1926 hurricane, was a busy scene in the Jazz Age, as its boats and crews struggled to enforce the law.

On August 7, 1927, Coast Guard Cutter 249 set out from Bahia Mar for Bimini. Aboard were the cutter's six-man crew and Robert K. Webster, a secret service agent who was investigating a counterfeiting ring in the Bahamas. At about 1:30 p.m. the crew stopped a rum boat, placed its two operators under arrest, and started to transfer the boat's load of booze to the cutter. One of the men arrested, Horace Alderman, asked to go back for a few personal belongings. What he got was a .45 pistol. Alderman shot the skipper, Sandy Sanderlin, and wounded the motor machinist,

This rare 1926 photograph shows the administration building and parking lot of the short-lived Pompano Race Track. Although this popular attraction was backed by prominent Pompano and Fort Lauderdale businessmen, the state forced the closure of Broward County's first horse racing track. Pari-mutuel betting was illegal in Florida until 1931. Courtesy, Pompano Beach Public Library

Victor Lamby.

When Alderman turned his head to call down to his mate, Robert Weech, in the engine room, the Coast Guardsmen jumped him. Hal Caudle, a 17-year-old from Pompano, described the scene:

The Secret Serviceman was shot down right in front of me. Alderman raised the gun at me and I grabbed the barrel. He shot twice in my face and I don't see how he missed me. I think it was because Johnny Robinson's weight pulled me down, as he climbed over me with the ice pick . . . As soon as I got the gun I hit him in the head . . .

The Skipper and the Secret Serviceman were dead and Lamby wounded [he later died], *the cook wounded, and the bootlegger with ice pick holes in him and a busted head and the other with a busted head.*

In January 1928 in federal court in Miami, Weech was sentenced to a year and a day in prison. Alderman's sentence was death by hanging on May 11 at the Broward County Courthouse. The county commission objected—the county had never performed an execution.

A further search of maritime law revealed that a pirate must be hanged at the port to which he was first brought. Alderman's execution was moved to Coast Guard Base Six on Fort Lauderdale Beach. After appeals and delays, he was transported to Bahia Mar at 5 a.m. on August 17, 1929.

Alderman recognized Dr. Elliott M. Hendricks, a Fort Lauderdale physician and quarantine officer for the base, who had examined him when he was brought to the base two years earlier, bloody from ice pick stabs. Now Dr. Hendricks was here to pronounce him officially dead.

At 6:04, just as the sun rose over the Gulf Stream he had crossed so many times, James Horace Alderman, rumrunner, alien smuggler, pirate, and murderer, dropped through the scaffold opening. Dr. Hendricks declared him dead. Thereafter the doctor was troubled with nightmares. His daughter, Dr. Anne L. Hendricks, said her father remarked, "Alderman was the only calm one at the hanging."

The consumption of illegal liquor brought in by rumrunners in violation of Prohibition was not the only illegal pastime that interested the people of Broward County. As 1926 drew to an end, the county enjoyed a temporary lift from the opening of Broward's first thoroughbred horse-racing track. Backed by such solid citizens as William L. Kester of Pompano and G. Frank Croissant, the Pompano Race Track was built at a cost of $1.25 million. The track was a mile long, 100 feet wide, and surfaced with clay and sand. Its grandstand provided seating for 6,800 spectators, and its stables and service buildings had facilities for 1,000 horses.

Brought in by special buses, the opening-day crowd on Christmas Day,

Fort Lauderdale's Coast Guard Base Six, located at the House of Refuge site on Las Olas Beach, was a busy facility during Prohibition. In 1915 the Life Saving Service, which operated the House of Refuge, merged with the Revenue Cutter Service to form the present United States Coast Guard. Base Six was officially commissioned June 9, 1924. The seaplane hangar where Horace Alderman was hanged is situated in the center of this early 1930s photo. Anchored to the left is the Amphitrite, a late 19th century navy monitor converted to a floating hotel. Courtesy, Fort Lauderdale Historical Society

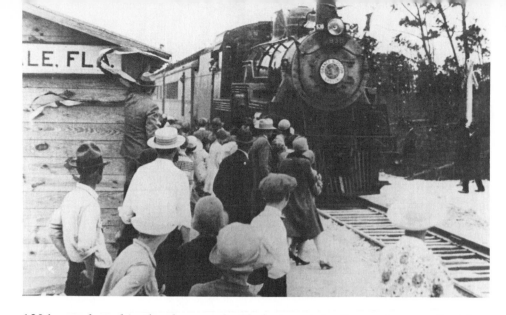

Another gleam of optimism in the dark days immediately following the bust was the completion of the Seaboard Air Line, the second railroad line through Broward County. Crowds gathered at the new station west of Fort Lauderdale to greet the first Seaboard train, the Orange Blossom Special, *on January 8, 1927. The Seaboard served the interior of North and Central Florida, the Atlantic coast from West Palm Beach to Florida City, and the west coast. Courtesy, Fort Lauderdale Historical Society*

1926, numbered in the thousands. Unfortunately, the pari-mutuel betting on which a track's prosperity rests was illegal. This might not have been a problem if the authorities, as they often did in Broward's past, had simply looked the other way. Governor John Martin, however, was not inclined to be lenient. Calling Pompano "a center of lawbreakers," he threatened "to send the militia down there with a tractor and plow up the Pompano track and plant it in cowpeas." Enterprising track operators turned then to other attractions, including boxing matches and South Florida's first dirt track automobile races. Despite its upbeat slogan, "Off They Go at Pompano," the county's first stab at horse racing was doomed.

Other enterprises fared better, however. On January 8 the first Seaboard Air Line Railway train reached Broward. The "Orange Blossom Special" arrived for stops at Pompano and Fort Lauderdale, where welcoming committees greeted the Seaboard president, S. Davies Warfield. In Fort Lauderdale, Thomas E. Hoskins' Trianon Gardens, converted from its original use as "the most elaborate and most beautiful automobile showroom on earth" to "the South's finest ballroom," opened on February 5. The huge room on South Andrews Avenue had a landscaped patio, decorative walkways, and elegant wall and ceiling draperies.

Not all places of entertainment were open to all residents. In 1927 the last remaining integrated public beaches in Broward were segregated by the Fort Lauderdale City Commission, which declared that the exclusive oceanfront area was no place for blacks. Said Blanchard J. Horne, the city manager: "Owners and people along the beach object to the Negroes using the sand in front of their homes for holiday frolics."

Three policemen were assigned to enforce the beach ban. Blacks were only allowed to use a rocky and overgrown section of the beach to the north two days a week. This was land that had reverted to Arthur Galt after the Countess of Lauderdale's Floranada dream died.

Still numb from the bust and the hurricane, the people, the businesses, and the governments of Broward only dimly grasped the magnitude of their problems. The good times were still too recent. Besides, occasional bits of encouraging news obscured the depths of their difficulties.

The year 1927 saw four more incorporated municipalities. In May Hal-

landale, which had become part of Hollywood, seceded and became Broward's ninth incorporated town. The following month, Dania, which Young annexed primarily to extend Hollywood to Lake Mabel, also seceded and reincorporated. In addition, Oakland Park split itself off from Floranada and became a separate incorporated municipality. Then, on November 30, Lauderdale-by-the-Sea became incorporated.

Some Broward Countians, not yet discouraged by the boom's apparent bust, continued on the track of enterprise and development. From his days on J.W. Young's sales force, Floyd Wray had seen first-hand the importance of a concept that could seize the attention of a potential buyer. In 1927 he teamed up with Frank Stirling of Davie and Clarence F. Hammerstein of Hollywood to establish Flamingo Groves on 320 acres of West Davie land purchased from Frank and Mittie Chaplin.

Wray adopted the idea of a citrus-condominium, then in operation at Howie-in-the Hills in Central Florida. Flamingo Groves offered five-acre parcels for $3,750, with a five-year contract to plant, grow, and harvest some 70 varieties of citrus from trees planted 66 to the acre. After five years buyers had the option of reselling their tracts at a previously specified price or receiving pro-rata shares of Flamingo's profits. The sales force of nine included Charles Forbes, who had been a sales manager for J.W. Young.

Stirling, with his strong horticultural background from his days with the State Plant Board, was instrumental in establishing the Flamingo Groves Botanical Garden, an experimental station. By 1930 the botanical garden was receiving foreign plants and seeds from the federal government for test-planting in Florida's subtropical climate.

In his next venture J.W. Young was not as fortunate as his sales force had been at Flamingo Groves. His dream was to reshape the Lake Mabel site into a great world seaport to be called Hollywood Harbor. The lake, large enough to serve as a potential turning basin and dockage area, had the further advantage of proximity to the inlet. A seaport at Lake Mabel, sometimes called Bay Mabel, had been a gleam in the eye of Broward's boosters since the late 1890s. Ed King had first suggested it to Henry Flagler, whose Model Land Company owned the lake and the land around it. Later, in 1913, the Deep Water Harbor Company was incorporated with a planned capitalization of $500,000. Its backers included

Dredges were hard at work converting marshy Lake Mabel into a deep-water seaport by 1927. An ongoing project during much of the late 1920s, the construction of the port, although plagued by financial and technical difficulties, gave Broward County's troubled economy a tremendous boost. Courtesy, Fort Lauderdale Historical Society

some of the biggest names in the community—Will Marshall, president; H.G. Wheeler, vice-president; William M. Heine, secretary; and Frank Stranahan, treasurer—but by the end of 1913 the company had died.

In December 1924 Young bought 1,440 acres in the name of the Hollywood Harbor and Development Company. By 1926 he was under pressure to complete the project since his sales campaigns had made extensive use of the world seaport theme. Unless he could deliver a port, he faced the danger of federal action for fraudulent advertising. The problem facing Young and the cities of Fort Lauderdale and Hollywood was one of funding. The amount of money needed to build the port was enormous for two cities reeling from the collapse of the land boom and the devastation of a killer hurricane.

Trouble began showing up early. On March 11, 1927, Young incorporated the Tropical Dredging and Construction Company to dredge the channel and the turning basin. Since it had no working capital, it was not a bona fide company. Tropical Dredging was dependent on receiving payments in advance, not after satisfactory completion of a given piece of work.

The Citizens Welfare League challenged the role of Tropical Dredging and filed for an injunction even before the company was formed. The bill of complaint sought to enjoin the port from continuing its dealings with Young. The suit, filed purely to get Young out of the picture, failed. Colonel Maxwell Baxter, of the league's law firm of Baxter and Walton, said: "The J.W. Young propaganda in Fort Lauderdale was so thick you could cut it with a knife, and Young didn't have to send any one here to do it for him. It was done by our own local citizens."

Tropical Dredging was unable to raise enough money for a surety bond. The company settled instead for the personal bond of J.W. Young.

On November 3, 1927, a special meeting of the Broward County Port Authority (BCPA) was called to address a pressing financial matter. The First National Bank of Fort Lauderdale reported it could not honor a check drawn by the authority because this would have left the bank unable to honor other withdrawals. To solve the problem, an enormous one not just for the authority but for the whole community, the Fort Lauderdale Bank and Trust Company agreed to buy the deposits of the troubled bank and to merge the two financial institutions.

The Port Authority had another financial problem. Bonds for the port had not actually brought in the funds the BCPA had been told they would. It developed that Young had entered into an agreement with two bond companies to pay a bonus to insure the sale of the not overly attractive bonds. He had done this without the authorization or knowledge of the city commissions of Fort Lauderdale and Hollywood. On October 22, 1927, the BCPA learned that the funds realized from the bond sale were

$400,000 less than it had expected.

Young's problems were increasingly hampering the progress of the port. Of the $2 million that was to have been his share of the costs, only $568,000 was ever paid. The Port Authority finally took over Tropical Dredging, and J.W. Young was out of the picture.

It is a small miracle that the George B. Hills Engineering Company of Jacksonville was able to complete the port. Observers of the progress of the job gave much of the credit to the project engineer, Arthur Solee, who kept the work moving in the midst of unrelenting calamity.

On February 16, 1928, six days before the port was to open officially, the Port Authority and the rest of Fort Lauderdale received a tremendous jolt. The Fort Lauderdale Bank and Trust Company closed its doors. Lost were Port Authority deposits of $151,000.

Despite the bank's failure the port opened on schedule on George Washington's birthday, but even the opening was subjected to still another malfunction. President Calvin Coolidge was to have pressed a button in Washington to set off a dynamite blast at the port. The explosion was to have blown away a small earthen dam, which would have opened a channel to the sea. Whether President Coolidge pressed the wrong button, forgot to punch any button, or whether the long-distance electrical relay failed, no one knows.

Finally, engineers on the scene set off the blast themselves. The crowd, which included practically everyone in Fort Lauderdale, enjoyed one of the few cheers the year 1928 had in store for them.

Warren T. Eller, manager of the Fort Lauderdale Chamber of Commerce, was named port manager. On August 8, 1929, the first cargo vessel arrived at the port, the German S.S. *Vogtland*. The 385-foot ship delivered sheet steel piling for construction work at the port. Later that month the U.S.S. *Antares* arrived, carrying 28 officers and 484 marines. For five months the *Antares'* marines were encamped on the pier south of Slip No. 1, stationed in Southern waters because of troubles in Nicaragua and nearby Central American countries.

The following year the women's clubs in the Port District conducted a contest to pick a new name for the facility. The name selected was Port Everglades.

Broward County needed the lift the port opening gave it. The collapse of Fort Lauderdale's bank left the county with only three operating banks, The Dania Bank, the Bank of Pompano, which the Ashleys had robbed, and the Hollywood State Bank. On May 1, 1912, the Bank of Dania had been established by Georgia's Witham Banking chain. Its first paid employee was I.T. Parker. In 1926 Parker, his brother William S. Parker, A.J. Ryan, and Martin Frost purchased the Witham interests and reorganized the bank as The Dania Bank.

The German ship Vogtland, *seen here approaching the slip at Bay Mabel Harbor (Port Everglades after 1930), was the first cargo vessel and the first foreign registered ship to dock at the new port. At the time the* Vogtland *arrived, in August 1929, the port contained only one slip and few facilities. Note the vacant fields in the background of this photograph. Courtesy, Fort Lauderdale Historical Society*

In February 1924 the Hollywood Bank opened. It was headed by Edward C. Romfh, founder and president of the First National Bank of Miami. Among those involved in organizing the Hollywood Bank was Charles N. McCune, a Fort Lauderdale attorney from the firm of McCune, Casey, Hiassen, and Fleming, which handled J.W. Young's legal affairs. The experience stood McCune in good stead. He knew what was involved in establishing a bank.

When the Fort Lauderdale Bank and Trust Company failed, a crushing blow was delivered to the town. Hundreds of citizens saw their cash reserves and in some cases their life's savings vanish. It was a blow, too, to the confidence of the community. The bank's board of directors included many of the town's leading citizens—Will Kyle, Frank Stranahan, Carl P. Weidling, Tom Bryan, and McCune.

Within 10 minutes of the bank's closing on February 16, a group of prominent citizens began to assemble in the law offices of McCune's firm. The group found they could raise only $50,000 of the $225,000 needed to capitalize the bank. They designated McCune to approach John Lochrie, a Fort Lauderdale winter resident and owner of the Broward Hotel, for possible support. To meet Lochrie, McCune had to drive to Fort Pierce, arriving there at 10 p.m. The two talked into the early morning hours. Finally, Lochrie agreed to head the operation, provided that McCune enlist more investors.

McCune drove all night. At dawn he reached the Hillsboro Club, where he approached William L. Sweet, a New York grain exporter who owned the Sweet Building in downtown Fort Lauderdale, and W.P. Tanner, a New York wholesale grocer. Each agreed to put $10,000 into the new venture.

Later that day Lochrie presided at the first meeting of the new stockholders. They voted to send McCune to Tallahassee that night to apply for a charter. During that frenzied phase, McCune worked more than 48 hours at a stretch. It paid off. A week later the state granted the group a charter.

On March 5, 1928, Broward Bank and Trust Company opened its doors.

Six months later, on September 16, 1928, a West Indian hurricane swept into the South Florida coast. Broward County was spared the fiercest of its winds, which came ashore at Palm Beach, crossed the county, and moved on to Lake Okeechobee. The waters first blown up to the northern end of the lake came roaring back to the south as the winds shifted. They poured over the southern shore of the lake, drowning countless people and animals in Florida's worst natural disaster. The Red Cross set up shelter at the Pompano Race Track to care for more than 1,000 homeless storm victims, and the death toll was estimated at between 1,800 and 2,000.

One of those killed was Ed King, Fort Lauderdale's first builder and president of the first town council. While trying to save two children, he was hit by a timber in the packinghouse of John Aunapu, an Estonian seaman who had operated the first scheduled line of freight boats between Fort Lauderdale and the lake.

The trying times fell hard on yet another of Fort Lauderdale's pioneers. Frank Stranahan had felt most at ease when Fort Lauderdale was a frontier trading post. He was not a man suited to the fast pace of the land boom and the sudden urbanization it had brought. To him the boom had meant wealth but not happiness.

Then the boom collapsed, taking away the wealth, leaving only unhappiness. To make matters worse, the town he had labored so hard to build was deteriorating into an assembly of quarreling factions. Many looked to Stranahan as a possible unifying force. George W. English, a Harvard-educated lawyer who came to Fort Lauderdale in 1925, recalled Stranahan's service on the City Commission:

He was elected on the platform of going in and getting things going again. And when he got in there, Lauderdale people were so mixed up and confused and frustrated after the bubble had burst and the Depression came on that he said to me . . . "George, I don't think Jesus Christ, if He were on earth today, could present anything to this City Commission that would be passed by it."

The burden of Stranahan's own financial problems weighed heavily upon him. Then came the failure of the Fort Lauderdale Bank and Trust Company. Many of his friends had deposited their money in the bank

Revered as Fort Lauderdale's founder and enriched by the town's booming growth, Frank Stranahan suffered severe losses during the bust. By 1929 the collapse of the Stranahan Building Company and the Fort Lauderdale Bank and Trust Company, as well as the impossible task of trying to reconcile quarreling factions in the city government, had broken his health and his spirit. His tragic suicide in the New River brought shock and grief throughout Fort Lauderdale. Headlines flashed the news across the city, and hundreds of mourners gathered for his funeral on the banks of the river where he had lived and died. Courtesy, Fort Lauderdale Historical Society

*With his brusk manners,
Samuel A. Horvitz inspired little love.
When he wrested control of
Hollywood's vast real-estate holdings
away from the genial J. W. Young in
the early 1930s, many residents
regarded him as a villain. In reality,
the situation was a complex one, and
Horvitz's foresight and shrewd
business savvy helped salvage Young's
"dream city." Courtesy, Miami
Herald*

because of confidence in him. Feelings of guilt deepened the depression that was wearing him down.

On March 22, 1929, Will Kyle wrote to the Bank of Bay Biscayne in Miami acknowledging receipt of a letter referring to a Stranahan Building Company note on which $350 was due on March 20. Kyle wrote that Stranahan was negotiating to solve the problem and that a satisfactory arrangement could be expected within 30 days. A week later he wrote again:

...if the note signed by the Stranahan Building Company and endorsed by myself could be extended for thirty days this matter could be worked out. At the present time it is out of the question for the Stranahan Building Company to pay the $100.00 that you ask ... Mr. Stranahan will assume the indebtedness and properly secure or pay all that is due on this note, unless you see fit to force the matter ...

At some future date I will explain in detail why this transaction has been handled as it is being handled.

Then on May 20 Kyle wrote again to the bank: "... Mr. Stranahan has been in the hospital for about ten days due to a nervous breakdown and I have been unable to see him."

On May 22, a Wednesday, Ivy took Stranahan for a drive along the beach about 3 o'clock in the afternoon. He had never learned to drive. When they came back, she drove the car into the garage. Near the porch Frank kept an old wheelbarrow, which held a cast-iron grate. He told Ivy he was going to work around the garage.

Frank found a piece of rope and tied the heavy grate to his foot. Then he leaped into the river.

Ivy's brother, Bloxham Cromartie, saw him and called to him not to jump. Bob Gordon, Winston Stokell, and Mary Taul all plunged into the river and struggled to pull Stranahan out of the 25-foot water. The weight was too heavy. Finally Gordon located a rope, dove in, and tied it around Stranahan's foot. From the shore they pulled his body from the river.

August Burghard, an experienced lifeguard as well as a writer for the *Fort Lauderdale Daily News*, gave him artificial respiration. Some signs of life were detected, but he died soon after being rushed to Memorial Hospital.

Police, firemen, and hundreds of residents jammed the riverbanks and the East Avenue Bridge near the very spot where many years ago Frank Stranahan had operated a ferry across the river, near the spot where the Indians had traded with him for 35 years. The river had been his life, and now it was his death.

On Friday, May 24, 1929, all business in Fort Lauderdale stopped as the city mourned the passing of its founder. Stranahan was 63. He had seen Fort Lauderdale grow from a riverbank camp into a roaring boomtime city. Now what happened would depend on other people. Among those who remained to build a city and a county was his stunned widow, Ivy.

One Broward County builder who, unlike Stranahan, had welcomed the boom met his financial downfall in the hard times after the bust. In 1925 J.W. Young had signed a five-year contract with the Highway Construction Company of Cleveland to build streets and sidewalks in the Hollywood Hills section. The agreement proved his undoing. Heading the Cleveland company was Samuel A. Horvitz, who was not only a paving contractor but also an attorney, a very shrewd one as it turned out. Originally from a background of hardship and poverty, he was also a tough businessman. The Highway Construction Company was already active in South Florida. The company paved a number of major Miami streets, including Biscayne Boulevard, and used Miami as a base for a huge highway construction project in Cuba.

Horvitz's contract with Young called for payment in four installments, but if Young was late on any payment the entire amount became due immediately. Horvitz was concerned about getting paid in a real-estate boom that was showing signs of coming apart. Young, on the other hand, accepted the tough payment clause because he needed paving done quickly to reassure investors and lenders that the great dream was indeed becoming a reality.

Young made his first payment of $2 million on time. He couldn't meet

Parked cars, palm trees, and a variety of businesses line Hollywood Boulevard in this 1930s view looking west. The large, columned building to the right housed the Hollywood Bank and the post office. Courtesy, Miami Herald

the others.

When Young defaulted, Horvitz prepared to sue for "anticipated profits of between $5 to $7 million," but Young's attorney, C.H. "Heinie" Landefeld, Jr., prevented the suit by drawing up a new schedule of payments agreeable to Horvitz. In less than six months, Young had defaulted again.

Construction Company of Cleveland took title to Young's empire at a Sheriff's Sale in 1932. Horvitz acquired 24,000 lots for $35,000. All that was left for Young was his house on Hollywood Boulevard. His other assets had already been foreclosed or conveyed to the City of Hollywood.

"Sam Horvitz had a lot of courage to invest, even at that price," said Landefeld. "Nobody wanted the land after the hurricane, and the thought of paying taxes on it in the future frightened everybody."

One explanation for why Young agreed to the Sheriff's Sale without a lengthy courtroom battle has been given by Young's friend, realtor L.B. "Slats" Slater, who worked for Horvitz. "After the hurricane, a lot of people with faith in Hollywood continued making payments," said Slater. "Mr. Young used their money to keep the development going, but failed to satisfy the basic mortgages before issuing some deeds."

Horvitz pointed out to Young that he had given people deeds but they didn't have good title, which could land Young in prison. Horvitz, according to Slater, then told Young, "If you will not oppose the Sheriff's Sale in any manner, I will give a free deed to every person to whom you have given a deed which does not have a good title."

Horvitz then profited from another deal. From 1929 to 1931 the Hollywood Country Club was operated as a gambling casino by the Chicago mobster, Al Capone. When the Mercantile Investment Company foreclosed a group of mortgages and acquired the country club and the Hollywood Beach Hotel for about $250,000, the Chicago mob moved south to Hallandale. Albert Rosenthal, an Indianapolis furniture dealer who headed Mercantile, had bought tax liens on prime properties for 75 cents on the dollar. Since Horvitz had a $2 million levy pending against Young, and Rosenthal owned tax certificates on some of the prop-

erty in question, the two combined their companies to form Hollywood, Inc.

Out of the bewildering maze of debts and nonpayments Young left behind, Horvitz gained one piece of property that Slater described as a "windfall." In 1926 Young defaulted on mortgages held by a Minnesota corporation on the property from Johnston Street in Hollywood to the fort, which included Central Beach. The company's lawyers did not pursue the $60,000 default. Then in 1946 when Port Everglades wanted to buy 80 acres, it was discovered that a release price would have to be paid to the Minnesota company in order to sell the property. The check was made out, but Horvitz advised against sending it. He had learned that in two months the 20-year statute of limitations would run out on the foreclosure. By waiting it out, he not only avoided paying the $60,000 but also gained clear title to property valued at the time at $2 million.

Young and Horvitz—two men totally different in temperament, style, and appearance. The 300-pound Young was so well liked that many of Hollywood's residents in years to come bore grudges against Horvitz as the man who took away Young's dream. Scowling and gruff, Horvitz was not a man who generated the kind of affection that Young inspired. Yet, people close to Horvitz respected his intellect, his vision, and his toughness. Interestingly enough, the two men got along well. They understood each other.

By the winter of 1933-1934, Young's health was beginning to deteriorate. While working on a development in the Adirondacks, he contracted a severe case of influenza. Weakened by the flu and by a bad heart condition, he returned to Hollywood in the spring to rest and regain his health. Always looking to the future, he was talking with associates on April 28, 1934, about developing an area south of Washington Street that would later be known as Three Islands. Suddenly, he slumped forward in his chair. He was dead of a heart attack at 51. J.W. Young was buried in Long Beach, California, where he had enjoyed his first big real-estate success.

In the boom days a young aviator named Merle L. Fogg had come to Fort Lauderdale to pilot Tom Bryan's seaplane. He built the first airport in the county, a hangar and a simple runway along Las Olas Boulevard near the Intracoastal. A dashing figure, Fogg drove a top-down Reo auto when he wasn't piloting the seaplane or his own "Flying Jenny." He was something of a daredevil, noted for once lassoing an Everglades deer from his Waco biplane, a spectacular feat for a native of Maine.

Above left: A native of Maine and a veteran of World War I, Merle Fogg came to Florida in 1922. After learning to fly at Okeechobee, he moved to Fort Lauderdale in 1925. As the area's first pilot, Fogg flew a seaplane for businessman Tom Bryan and piloted his own JN-4D "Flying Jenny" for a variety of customers, including photographers who wanted aerial publicity shots of new real-estate developments. His flying service was located at Idlewyld, near the Las Olas bridge. Fogg lost his life in an airplane accident in West Palm Beach in 1928. Courtesy, Fort Lauderdale Historical Society

Above: Named in honor of Merle Fogg, Fort Lauderdale's first airport was dedicated on May 1, 1929, and a monument to the fallen flyer was unveiled at the ceremony. Merle Fogg Airport, now the site of the Fort Lauderdale-Hollywood International Airport, was built on the original municipal golf course south of Fort Lauderdale, where President Harding had previously played golf. Courtesy, Fort Lauderdale Historical Society

On May 1, 1928, Fogg was killed at a West Palm Beach orange grove in the crash of a plane flown by a student pilot. The crash also took the life of young Thomas Lochrie, son of the bank president.

One year later to the day the Fort Lauderdale airport, a former well-turfed fairway at the South Side Golf Course, was dedicated as Merle Fogg Field before a crowd of 5,000. In its early days so little activity was generated that the unofficial director of aviation, H. William Langmead, served without pay. Thirty years would elapse before regularly scheduled airlines would begin flying passengers in and out of Broward.

The airport wasn't totally neglected in those days. Bootleggers began using airplanes to bring in whiskey from the Bahamas, landing on little-used airport runways but more often on golf courses, cow pastures, and—in dry weather—the Everglades.

During the summer of 1930 Deerfield residents learned that Al Capone planned to establish a country estate with swimming pools, tennis courts, and a golf course on a 50-acre island located at the confluence of the Hillsboro Canal and the Intracoastal. Nothing ever came of it, but for years the location was called Capone Island.

For a brief time "oil fever" sent a wave of excitement through Fort Lauderdale. When bubbles were seen rising from the New River in front of Commodore Brook's home, the escaping gas was trapped in glass jars. It burned with a blue flame. In 1928 a testing laboratory determined it contained methane (swamp gas) and also ethane, which would indicate the presence of oil. Leases were obtained from the city and state by a group of investors, and drilling began in earnest in Croissant Park. Fort Lauderdale tax bills for 1929 showed a picture of an oil rig. The exhilaration ended when the drilling and the money ran out at 3,000 feet. All that had been found was a vein of sulphur water.

In 1929 Robert H. Gore came to Fort Lauderdale to try to sell publisher Tom Stilwell on an insurance program for the *Fort Lauderdale Daily News*. Stilwell told him, "I don't want to buy any insurance. Why don't you buy my newspaper?" Gore did—for $75,000. To make the purchase he sold 200 shares of stock in a Boston bank at $1,400 per share. Within weeks the stock market crashed, and the price of a share of the stock dropped to $3.

The arrival in town of a man with cash attracted attention. City Attorney George English talked Gore into buying the old Wil-Mar Hotel skeleton for $30,000. Eight more years would pass before he completed the hotel; the early 1930s just was not the time to launch a major construction program.

In 1931 Pompano's only bank, the Bank of Pompano, closed its doors. In desperation Pompano residents turned to the wealthy William L. Kester, who thought he had retired when he came to Pompano in 1923.

Kester, a natty dresser and bon vivant, made it a point never to engage in a business transaction before noon. Born in West Virginia and raised in Pittsburgh, he had run off to Paris to join the French Foreign Legion after an unhappy love affair. He later became managing director of Westinghouse's Cooper-Hewitt Lamp Company and during World War I made a fortune selling heavy equipment. In Pompano he had hoped to spend his time fishing, but he was soon swept up in the excitement of the boom. He remained active till his death in 1954 at the age of 80.

Heeding the community's calls for help, Kester bought the bank's furnishings, building, and land from federal liquidators. He provided half the capital needed, and a little over two years after the Bank of Pompano had failed, the new Farmer's Bank of Pompano opened.

At a time when new construction had virtually stopped, William Kester bucked the trend by building a hundred white frame cottages on the beach and in old Pompano. Built of sturdy Dade County pine, these were known as Kester Cottages. Most of them were rental units, $25 a week on the beach in the winter season.

In the early 1930s Broward County was hurting from the state's Everglades drainage program. The canals that were taking excess water out of the upper Glades near Lake Okeechobee were dumping too much water in too short a time into the farms near Davie. Every fall the area flooded, every spring the Glades dried out and muck fires thickened the air with dense, heavy smoke.

Hamilton M. Forman hated lawyers and engineers, and as a political activist he hated inaction when there was a job that had to be done. In 1932 he was named chairman of the Napoleon B. Broward Drainage District, which included all of Broward County and parts of Dade and Palm Beach counties. He concluded that the devastating fall floods could be brought under control by damming the North New River Canal at Twenty Mile Bend and by cutting spillways in the canal west of the dam to let the waters from Lake Okeechobee spread out in a sheet flow into the open, undeveloped areas of the Glades.

The dam was built in 1932 without the aid of engineers or the rulings of attorneys. "The legality of the dam was a never-never land," recalls Dr. Charles Forman, Hamilton M. Forman's son. "Nobody really wanted to go into that. It was built with dubious legal precedents." The benefits from the dam were dramatic. Water levels in flooded areas dropped quickly once the dam was completed.

Two years later farmers from the Lake Okeechobee region found out about the dam. Afraid it would cause the water to back up and jeopardize drainage of their lands, they descended upon the dam one night and dynamited it.

Forman decided on a new approach. He and Joe Loper designed a dam with spillways, which could be closed by placing heavy horizontal timbers in I-beam slots. Water from the lake could be dammed up while local Broward water was draining off. Then the timber could be removed to permit drainage of the waters from the upper Glades.

Still, he took no chances with dynamiters. First of all, he positioned the dam not at Twenty Mile Bend, which could be reached by car, but at Twenty-Six Mile Bend, which was not served by any roads. And to make sure no visitors from the lake arrived with dynamite, armed guards patrolled the site with shotguns and rifles. Among the people who guarded the dam were Stanley Wimberly, who would later become vice-president of Florida Atlantic University, and Hamilton M. Forman's son, Hamilton C. Forman. The dam patrol worked. Other dynamitings occurred but never when the guard was in place. The design developed by Forman and Loper was later used with modification by the United States Soil Conservation Agency and is still in use in many underdeveloped countries.

The job of keeping law and order county-wide went to Walter Clark in 1933. Sheriff Walter Clark was a good old boy. He understood the county's power structure and in time, some would say, became the power structure and possibly the nearest thing to a political boss the county ever had. He was born in Fort Lauderdale in 1904. In his campaign literature he called on citizens to vote for "the first white male child born in Fort Lauderdale." He was quite aware that this was not true. He went to Beverly McQuarrie, thought to have been the first, and asked his permission to make the claim. He figured it would be good politics. Elected five times, Clark served as sheriff until 1950, and his brother, Bob, served as his chief deputy.

Sheriff Clark presented an affable and friendly image to whites, but to the growing black population of Broward, he presented a different picture. "He was a headbeater," said L.D. Gainey, who later became president of the Broward Urban League. "Clark was a man to be feared if you were black. And, as far as we could see, his tactics had the blessings of the white community."

When Clark entered a room, he expected all blacks to stand up. When John Wooten refused in 1944, he was arrested on a vagrancy charge. He died that night in a jail cell, the result, Clark explained, of falling out of bed on his head. On July 19, 1935, Reuben Stacey, a 37-year-old black field hand, was accused of attempting to rape a white housewife. Three hours later he was hanged by a lynch mob on what became Davie Boulevard, west of 31st Avenue. Blacks claim that Clark came to the ghetto telling them to come with him to see "what happens to a nigger who doesn't stay in his place."

Clark thrived on Florida's loose peonage laws. During harvest, his deputies would routinely round up blacks on vagrancy charges. The blacks would then be given the option of paying a $35 fine, which they could not meet, or working off their debt in the fields. The amount of time needed to earn back the $35 depended on how long it took to finish picking beans, tomatoes, and oranges. The farmers credited the black laborers with only a fraction of what they would have paid whites. After the crops were harvested, the farmers paid Clark $35 for each prisoner.

For Clark, the peonage money was good, but the big returns came from gambling. In the Prohibition era respect for the law took a battering. Bootleggers, with the exception of a few like the vicious Alderman, were regarded as rather colorful rogues supplying a popular commodity. Speakeasies operated openly. It is little wonder that illegal gambling thrived, particularly since gambling casinos meant jobs and the infusion of cash into a depressed economy.

In north Broward the casinos were small, catering to a wealthy winter resident clientele. Two of the most popular were the River View Club, which would later become the Riverview Restaurant, and the Club

Sheriff Walter Clark, standing fourth from the left, poses with members of the Broward County Sheriff's Department in this photo from the 1940s. Walter's chief deputy and brother, Robert L. Clark, stands second from the left. The son of a pioneer Broward family and a former employee of Bert Lasher's butcher shop, Walter Clark served as sheriff from 1933 to 1950. Friendly and informal in manner, he was highly regarded by many, but local blacks thought his administration brutal. Courtesy, Fort Lauderdale Historical Society

111

Broward County's reputation as a lawbreakers' haven grew during bootlegging days, and continued after the repeal of Prohibition. Underworld figure Meyer Lansky, a resident of Hallandale, was closely connected with illegal casino gambling in southern Broward during the 1930s and 1940s. The casinos, although operated by organized criminal elements, were important to the area's developing tourist economy. Courtesy, Miami Herald

Unique, which would become Cap's Place. In the south county the casinos were another matter. These, located in Hallandale and Hollywood, were affiliated with the Mob, which found it could do business with city officials in Hallandale and Hollywood and with the Clark boys.

Even before Prohibition was repealed, a Chicago group was operating the Old Plantation on East Hallandale Beach Boulevard in the midst of tomato and cabbage fields still under cultivation. Appropriately, the head of the operation was named "Potatoes" Kaufman. The Plantation had the biggest play in the area, offering roulette, blackjack, craps, horse parlor betting, and bingo in a no-frills package.

Other casinos were far more elegant, featuring beautifully appointed rooms, elaborate floor shows, and fancy restaurants for a clientele attired in evening clothes. Among these were the Colonial built by the Frank Costello syndicate on Federal Highway in Hallandale, the Greenacres off West Hallandale Beach Boulevard, the Club Boheme at Seminole Beach, the Rainbow Tavern and the Valhalla in downtown Hollywood, and the It Club just outside Fort Lauderdale.

Many well-known names from organized crime were involved: the Lanskys, Costello, Vincent Alo (alias "Jimmy Blue Eyes"), Joe Adonis, and Frank Erickson. The dominant figure overall was Meyer Lansky, operating quietly in the background through local fronts.

Meyer Lansky, the "brain trust" of organized crime, had discovered Florida's Gold Coast in his bootlegging days. Broward, with a sheriff he could deal with, proved a particularly appealing spot. Meyer lived in Hallandale, and his brother, Jake, lived in Hollywood on Harrison Street.

While many were concentrating their efforts on illegal gambling, William Symms, Sr., sought to open the county's first legal wagering operation. On September 8, 1934, the voters of Hallandale approved establishment of a dog track with pari-mutuel betting. On December 12 the Hollywood Kennel Club opened on one of the coldest nights in Hallandale history. With temperatures hovering near freezing, 12,000 fans showed up and bet $12,000.

In the 1930s horse racing also began to pick up. James Bright, a Miami developer who helped found the Hialeah Race Track, bought Camelot Farms on Orange Drive in Davie and trained the first thoroughbred racehorses in the state. Hully Stirling, Frank's son, described Bright's system: "He had a set price for his horses, $1,000. He probably spent $3,000 on each horse, so that was below his costs. But in the sales contract he kept for himself a percentage of every horse's winnings."

But it was not until 1939 that the county had a pari-mutuel horse-racing operation. In the winter of 1939 Jack Horning, owner of a Miami construction firm, introduced thoroughbred horse racing at Gulfstream Park under inauspicious circumstances. So many people showed up on opening day, 15,000 in all, that gates and fences were smashed and proceedings generally disrupted. The real problem was that Horning for some reason had chosen to run the track in direct competition with Hialeah. After three days Gulfstream was declared bankrupt.

One of its many creditors was James Donn, Sr., a Scotsman who headed Exotic Gardens. He became Gulfstream's principal stockholder and president. In December of 1944 the track reopened for a 20-day meet and went on from there to become Florida's most successful racetrack.

In the 1930s racetracks were not the only spots offering diversion from the trials of the Depression years. In 1935 Brownie Robertson came to Fort Lauderdale looking for a nightclub to book big bands for Saturday nights. From attorney C.H. Landefeld he leased the Trianon Ballroom for $50 a month. Club Brownie brought Broward County the best big band entertainment of the day: Duke Ellington, Louis Armstrong, Kay Kyser, Ella Fitzgerald, Sophie Tucker, Cab Calloway, and the Mills Brothers. In time the ballroom reverted to its original purpose, an automobile garage. Brownie's lived on as the town's oldest bar.

The same year Brownie Robertson arrived, Fort Lauderdale held its first Collegiate Aquatic Forum, an event that would have far-reaching consequences. The event held during Christmas holidays provided the original impetus for the annual spring break invasion of college students from the North and Midwest.

The growing importance of Fort Lauderdale to swimming became even more pronounced the following year as Katherine Rawls, who had lived in both Hollywood and Fort Lauderdale, emerged as a major international swimming and diving celebrity. She won 26 national and international championships, held a number of world records, and represented the United States in the 1936 Olympic Games in Hitler's Germany. In 1937 sportswriters voted her "The Greatest Woman Athlete of the Year." Her most satisfying performance, she felt, was in a decathlon celebrating the opening of New York's Jones Beach. She won first place in all 10 events.

Important though recreation was in Depression years, the more serious world of finance was not being neglected. In 1935 Broward County saw the start of two savings and loan associations. A previous building and loan had failed in Fort Lauderdale in the fallout from the real-estate collapse. On January 26, Hollywood Federal Savings and Loan began operations and in the fall First Federal of Broward opened in downtown Fort Lauderdale. Two years later the Barnett banking chain, headquartered in Jacksonville, opened a second Fort Lauderdale bank in the Sweet Building, which had housed the boomtime First National Bank of Fort Lauderdale. The Barnett bank would later also become the First National Bank of Fort Lauderdale.

Legal as well as illegal gambling operations entertained Broward County tourists in the 1930s. The county's first legal betting enterprise, the Hollywood Kennel Club, opened in 1934, three years after pari-mutuel wagering was legalized in Florida. Despite its name, the Hollywood greyhound racing track is located in Hallandale. Courtesy, Hollywood Greyhound Track

Above: Long famous as a center for water sports, Fort Lauderdale became host to the annual Collegiate Aquatic Forum in 1935. The forum, held at the municipal swimming casino on Las Olas Beach, provided college swimmers from the North an opportunity to enjoy open air swimming and sharpen their skills during the winter. It also made Fort Lauderdale a popular gathering place for college students. Here swimmers from a variety of Northern schools line the edge of the casino pool at the second forum in December 1936. Courtesy, Fort Lauderdale Historical Society

Above right: Katherine Rawls, America's greatest female swimmer of the 1930s, lived in Hollywood and Coral Gables before moving to Fort Lauderdale in 1933. She was a member of the U.S. Olympic swimming team at the 1932 games in Los Angeles and at the 1936 meet in Berlin, winning numerous national and world championships. Courtesy, Fort Lauderdale Historical Society

As new businesses were opening, Charlie Rodes, one of the boom's most spectacular millionaires, entered a line of work that would have seemed alien to a man of his promotional talents. In the depth of the Depression he wielded a shovel for the WPA. The irrepressible Rodes would later bounce back and again attain the status of millionaire.

On January 5, 1935, Walter Smith, aged 92, died in Pompano. His death rated front-page coverage because he was the last surviving Confederate veteran in the county. What newspaper accounts did not mention was an event that occurred 30 years earlier and brought nationwide attention to Smith. On July 8, 1905, at Flamingo, Smith had killed the Audubon warden, Guy Bradley, who as a boy had lived at the Fort Lauderdale House of Refuge. Bradley was trying to arrest Smith's sons for killing birds illegally. Though Smith admitted shooting Bradley, he claimed self-defense and managed to escape indictment. Smith came to Pompano in 1906 and subsequently lived a long and law-abiding life.

In the mid-1930s hotel construction finally began to pick up. In 1936 a permit was issued for an 80-room hotel in the 600 block of East Las Olas. It was called the Champ Carr Hotel, taking its name from the manager. Later it became the Riverside.

The following year Robert H. Gore fleshed out the skeleton of the Wil-Mar Hotel, converting the bust's most unsightly legacy into a 110-room hotel called the Governors' Club. Gore says its name came following the 1937 meeting of the Southern Governors' Conference at the new hotel, but most Fort Lauderdale people thought it harked back to his brief stint as governor of Puerto Rico.

When Franklin D. Roosevelt first ran for president, Gore served as his national finance chairman. He was promptly rewarded with an appointment as governor of the island. The job lasted only a year. Governor

ZOO NOW OPEN

CLYDE BEATTY'S ZOO

Famous animal trainer Clyde Beatty purchased the McKillop-Hutton Lion Farm in the present Gateway area of northern Fort Lauderdale in 1939. The farm, established three years earlier, raised lions to sell to zoos and circuses, and offered a small act for the public. Beatty enlarged the attraction and reopened it as Clyde Beatty's Jungle Zoo, Fort Lauderdale's first major tourist attraction. Complaints from new residents in the surrounding area forced Beatty to close the zoo in 1945. In the winter of 1960–1961, he returned to Broward briefly to operate a short-lived attraction called Clyde Beatty's Jungleland on U.S. 1 south of Hollywood. Courtesy, Fort Lauderdale Historical Society

Gore had pushed a law through the Puerto Rican legislature requiring the teaching of English in schools. Eleanor Roosevelt, visiting the islands, sought to have the law repealed.

Gore went straight to the White House. Confronting FDR, he said: "If Mrs. Roosevelt is going to be President, or the Governor of Puerto Rico, she ought to be officially appointed. I'm not going to stay in Puerto Rico as a figurehead." Gore resigned, but the title "Governor" stayed with him.

During the Depression a number of private hospitals had attempted unsuccessfully to provide adequate medical services for the growing Broward community. By 1937 the Broward County Medical Society was convinced that only a publicly supported community hospital could be relied on for continuity of service. A committee of doctors from Fort Lauderdale, Hollywood, and Pompano met to survey the county's needs. From their meetings came the Broward Hospital Association, which included community leaders from the entire county.

Under the leadership of its chairman, James D. Camp, the association concluded that the best approach for providing a community hospital within a reasonable period of time was the renovation of an existing building. They picked the Granada Apartments in Croissant Park. The three-story building contained 16 apartments with wide hallways down the center of each floor and stairways at each end. The location at the time was a central one, lying between Andrews Avenue and Federal Highway in south Fort Lauderdale, easily accessible to Pompano, Deerfield, and Oakland Park on the north, and Hollywood, Hallandale, and Dania on the south.

On September 28, 1937, the City of Fort Lauderdale took title to the building after the association had arranged financing for its purchase for $26,000. Architect Robert Jahelka drew the plans to convert the structure and general contractor George Young, Sr., remodeled the building. Both did their work at cost, contributing their fees to the hospital fund. Equipment for the hospital was donated by the doctors. On January 2, 1938, Dr. R.L. Elliston admitted the first patient to the new community hospital,

By the late 1930s, the staggering effects of the bust and the nationwide Depression had begun to fade, and Fort Lauderdale was once again establishing itself as a seaside vacation and recreation resort. The second half of the 1930s saw several new hotels open, including R. H. Gore's Governor's Club, and the Champ Carr on Las Olas Boulevard, and the Lauderdale Beach Hotel on Highway A-1-A. Courtesy, Florida Photographic Collection, Florida State Archives

which was named Broward General Hospital.

The first floor housed an x-ray room, emergency room, pharmacy, and business office, the second floor rooms for patients, and the third floor a delivery room and an operating room. One patient, a winter resident from Detroit, donated a used air conditioner to the hospital—after having a kidney stone removed in an operating room without air-conditioning.

Prior to 1938 no area hospitals allowed either black doctors or patients. Broward General contained a "colored ward" but did not permit black doctors. As a result members of the black community launched a fund-raising drive for funds to build Provident Hospital in northwest Fort Lauderdale. The hospital, which opened in 1938, was run by Dr. James F. Sistrunk, the county's first black doctor, and Von Delaney Mizell, M.D., the second. Raised in Dania, Dr. Mizell had come back to his home county to practice medicine. His impact on the area would be greater then any black who ever lived here.

On the Seminole reservation, the Indians continued to turn to their medicine men, or in some cases to their medicine women. Two of the most notable of these were Annie Tommie, mother of Tony Tommie, and

Ada Tiger, daughter of the great chief, Tom Tiger, and mother of Betty Mae. In 1967 Betty Mae Tiger Jumper would go on to become the first woman to be elected chairperson, the equivalent of chief.

The Thirties was a difficult time for Jews in Fort Lauderdale. Cleveland Amory, in his book *The Last Resorts*, speaks of "the anti-Semitic reputation" of Fort Lauderdale. Many hotels were "restricted," forcing Jewish travelers and tourists to go south to hotels in Hollywood or the Miami area. The most notable instance involved Henry Morgenthau, Secretary of the Treasury under FDR. Secretary Morgenthau came to Fort Lauderdale on Coast Guard business. When he attempted to register at a hotel on the beach, he was told that the hotel would accept him, but all Jewish members of his staff would have to go elsewhere. The Secretary refused to stay in Fort Lauderdale, preferring to find accommodations for his entire staff a little to the south of the city limits.

When Moe Katz arrived in Fort Lauderdale in 1923 to sell real estate, there were seven Jewish families in town. The first attempt to establish a place of worship had been smashed by the 1926 hurricane. In 1931 the Fort Lauderdale Hebrew Congregation was organized to provide

Broward General Hospital, the county's only public community hospital at the time it was established in 1938, was located in the renovated Granada Apartments in Fort Lauderdale's Croissant Park. Two years after the hospital opened, the county's growth required Broward General to expand. The facility, which has continued to grow, remains Broward's largest hospital. Courtesy, Fort Lauderdale Historical Society

Annie Tommie, known to local residents as "Indian Annie," and her son Tony, who had attended the Fort Lauderdale school in the 1910s, were instrumental in persuading Broward Seminoles to move onto the new Dania Reservation in the late 1920s. The reservation, established in the fall of 1926, was originally intended as a home for sick and indigent Indians, but soon became home to many others displaced by land development along the southeast coast. Courtesy, Fort Lauderdale Historical Society

religious training for children. Through the years Moe, his brother Mack, and his sister-in-law Sadye continued to work toward the formation of a temple in Fort Lauderdale.

I.A. "Pop" Sterling, who had worked South Florida as a traveling salesman since the 1920s, came to Fort Lauderdale in 1935 and opened a men's wear store, Sterling's, selling primarily work clothes. At this time there were still only nine or ten Jewish families in Fort Lauderdale.

In 1936 plans were drawn for Temple Emanu-El, a Reform synagogue. If the luck had been bad for Moe Katz the night the hurricane hit, it now became every bit as good when the founders of Lerner Stores happened by as the foundation was being laid. The 85-year-old Charles Lerner and his son Samuel, in town for the opening of one of their shops, chanced to see it, became interested in the project, and decided to help the 36-year-old Katz, whom Sam Lerner called "Kid." The Lerners, who stayed at the Hollywood Beach Hotel, a gathering place in the 1930s for Jewish tourists from the Midwest and North, helped raise money and arrange a long-range funding plan.

In September 1937 the first services at the new Temple Emanu-El were held. Completed in time for the High Holy Days, the temple housed a congregation of residents of Hollywood, Fort Lauderdale, Pompano, and Boca Raton. Moe Katz became president of the temple and served in that post for 10 years.

In 1939 a building that had served as the private Lauderdale Memorial Hospital and later as the Pine Crest Sanitarium was leased to Mae McMillan. An educator from South Dakota, she had come to South Florida with her husband just before the boom ended. She converted the building into the Pine Crest School, little more than a tutoring service for winter residents at the start but many years later a major Broward County educational institution.

That same year on June 12 the Town of Hillsboro Beach was incorporated, a community of wealthy winter residents who lived along the oceanfront north from the Hillsboro Light to the Deerfield city limits.

By the end of the 1930s most of the worst effects of the Great Depression were behind the people of Broward County. But the future was clouded by the war that had broken out in Europe.

Fort Lauderdale felt that war on December 19, 1939, when the British cruiser *Orion* chased the German freighter *Arauca* into Port Everglades. The German ship was interned at the port. The crew, which came under the watchful eye of Sheriff Clark, remained aboard until April 1941, when they were moved to Dade County Jail and later to Ellis Island in New York.

Not long after the United States entered the war on December 7, 1941, German submarines began attacking Allied shipping off the Florida coast. Broward cities had to be blacked out at night. Armed men patrolled the beach, and the Coast Guard Auxiliary and the Civil Air Patrol kept on the lookout for German submarines off the coast.

Coast Guard Base Six was active, and Port Everglades, with both fueling and repair facilities, was used extensively by the navy. The navy took over the Merle L. Fogg Airfield, and in October of 1942 began work on the Fort Lauderdale Naval Air Station. Satellite airfields for the air station were established at Pompano, West Prospect, and Davie. Naval training schools were set up at the Lauderdale Beach and Tradewinds hotels, and a gunnery range was established on the beach at Lauderdale-by-the-Sea.

The wartime activity brought many jobs to Broward. This offset the loss of tourist trade resulting from gasoline and tire rationing. Broward County, as did the rest of the nation, supplied its share of young men and women to serve in the war. One from Fort Lauderdale, Lieutenant Alexander "Sandy" Nininger, Jr., became the first soldier of World War II to be awarded the Congressional Medal of Honor.

On January 12, 1942, the Japanese threw wave after wave of assaults at the army's 57th Infantry on Bataan. Although wounded three times, Sandy repeatedly attacked Japanese sniper positions, killing more than 20 of the enemy before he was killed.

During the war one of Fort Lauderdale's oldest residents died. Hugh Taylor Birch was 94 when he passed away on January 7, 1943. He had always valued his privacy and proved resentful when a growing population intruded on the solitude of his huge oceanfront estate. Yet he ceded the right-of-way for State Road A1A and leased or gave most of his beach to the city. His estate, however, he gave not to the city against which he had accumulated many grievances over the years, but to the state. It became Hugh Taylor Birch State Park.

On September 2, 1945, the most terrible war the world had ever known ended with the formal surrender of the Japanese. From Broward County, 5,536 persons served in the armed forces. Seventy-six of them died or were killed in action.

A strange, final aftermath to the war occurred at the Fort Lauderdale Naval Air Station on December 5, 1945. Five Navy TBM Avengers with 15 aboard took off on a training mission. From the vicinity of the Florida Keys the tower heard the flight leader, Lieutenant Charles Taylor, declare, "We seem to be off course." They were never seen again; no trace of any of the planes was ever found. A Martin PBM rescue plane with 13 crewmen aboard was sent to search for them from a naval base at Melbourne. It, too, disappeared without a trace.

Those strange, unexplained events became the foundation on which the legend of the Devil's Triangle was built. Some call it the Bermuda Triangle, since its three points are Bermuda, Puerto Rico, and the Miami-

One of Broward County's oldest retail businesses, Sterling's Store for Men and Boys, opened in Fort Lauderdale in 1935, the year Russian immigrant Isadore A. "Pop" Sterling moved south from Palm Beach. Pop's son, Morris Sterling, is shown tending the original store, a converted garage on Andrews Avenue, in this photograph from the late 1930s or early 1940s. Courtesy, Neil Sterling

Fort Lauderdale area.

Many books and articles have been written about the flight of the Lost Patrol, attributing its disappearance to magnetic fields or other natural or unnatural forces, including the Devil. The navy's board of inquiry had a simpler explanation. Its report concluded that the tragedy was a result of inexperienced flyers, who became lost, and ill-equipped planes, which ran out of fuel. When they ditched in the heavy seas somewhere near the Bahamas, the planes "most probably broke up on impact and those crewmen who might have survived the crash would not have lasted long in the cool water."

But the mystery of the Devil's Triangle lives on.

COLOR PLATES

Facing page and top: A brilliant
sunset reflects on Fort Lauderdale's
New River, long acclaimed as one of
Florida's most beautiful waterways.
The river has been an artery for
transportation, a source of
recreation, a means of drainage, and
the center of Broward County's
history from the early years to the
present. Courtesy, Fort Lauderdale
Historical Society

Above: The southeast Florida coast
changed little from the days of the
Spanish explorers to the beginning of
the 20th century. Early settlers
shunned the beaches, considering
them an unhealthy and dangerous
place to live. Recent development has
all but destroyed the natural Florida
beaches. Courtesy, Fort Lauderdale
Historical Society

Above: Taken in the 1930s or 1940s, this postcard shows Fort Lauderdale's New River from the west side of the Federal Highway Bridge. The large building with the belltower in the background is the Broward County Courthouse, completed in 1928. Courtesy, Fort Lauderdale Historical Society

Left: Originally, the South Florida wilderness was a combination of swamps and hardwood hammocks. The many attempts to drain the land for farming and development have altered the natural patterns of vegetation, creating in some cases a mixture of plants not found in historical times. Courtesy, Fort Lauderdale Historical Society

Left: To many, the alligator is the symbol of Florida. For a number of years, the 'gator was under government protection. However, a rapid increase in their population, along with their frequent visits to residential areas via the South Florida canal system, caused the relaxation of the hunting ban. Today, a number of Broward County restaurants serve alligator steaks. Courtesy, Broward County Tourist Development Council

Above: Even the Seminoles' remote Everglades homeland did not escape the great changes of the 20th century. In this 1930s scene, Indians pole their canoes in a South Florida canal, the product of Governor Napoleon Bonaparte Broward's program to drain the Everglades. Courtesy, Fort Lauderdale Historical Society

Right: The Seminole women in this 1938 postcard wear beads and traditional dresses. The beautiful patchwork garments are unique to South Florida's Indians. Courtesy, Fort Lauderdale Historical Society

Right: This tinted 1930s postcard view shows a Seminole family and their dugout canoe against a Florida wilderness background. Florida's Seminoles were scattered through parts of South and Central Florida during this period, but Broward County was home to many. The Dania Reservation (now the Hollywood Reservation) was established in Broward in 1926. Courtesy, Fort Lauderdale Historical Society

Above: Seminole Indians had a village in Fort Lauderdale when this photograph was taken in the 1920s. With their colorful clothing and chickee huts, the Seminoles were popular with tourists and could often be seen strolling and trading in downtown Fort Lauderdale. Courtesy, Fort Lauderdale Historical Society

Left: In this 1977 photograph, the Miccosukee tribal leader Josie Billie confers with Joe Dan Osceola, then president of the Seminole tribe. Born in the 1880s, Josie Billie shunned the urban reservation in favor of the Everglades. He embodied the old traditional ways of the South Florida Indians. Courtesy, Jordan Denner, Fort Lauderdale Historical Society

Left: Seminole families gather for a special occasion at the Seminole Indian Reservation. Although many Seminoles have accepted a place in Broward County's urban culture, many remain true to the traditional ways and seek the isolation of the reservations in the Everglades. Courtesy, Jordan Denner, Fort Lauderdale Historical Society

125

Above: The Hollywood Beach Hotel, built by founder Joseph W. Young in 1925, accommodated more than 500 guests. This postcard from the 1920s or 1930s shows the hotel as it appeared at the height of its popularity. Courtesy, Fort Lauderdale Historical Society

Right: Elegant visitors, golf bag on the runningboard of their car, watch speedboats racing down New River in this idealized scene from a 1920s tourist brochure. Actually, the river was much narrower than this and was used by pleasure boaters and fishermen, rather than racers. Attractive advertising such as this brought tourists to Fort Lauderdale by the thousands. Courtesy, Fort Lauderdale Historical Society

Above: Connecting the Everglades and the Atlantic Ocean, the New River winds its way through Fort Lauderdale in this aerial view from the late 1930s or early 1940s. By this relatively late date, Fort Lauderdale's beach was still largely undeveloped. The river empties into the ocean at New River Inlet, at top center, and the city's downtown bustles in the lower left corner. Courtesy, Fort Lauderdale Historical Society

Top left: In the years immediately following World War I, the Idlewyld residential subdivision became Fort Lauderdale's first "island" development. Many of the houses built there remain among the most desirable in the area. The house seen here, constructed in 1921, was the first residence in Idlewyld. Courtesy, Fort Lauderdale Historical Society

Center: One of Broward County's most recently acquired historic landmarks is the Bonnet House. Originally owned by Hugh Taylor Birch, the estate was donated to the people of Florida in 1983. The extensive grounds constitute one of the last stretches of undeveloped property on the Southeast Florida coast. Courtesy, Vivianna Ramirez, Fort Lauderdale Historical Society

Bottom: One of Fort Lauderdale's last landmarks is Casa Sonriendo, the "house of smiles." Built in 1925 by pioneer resident Albert Erkins, the house was typical of the luxurious style of the 1920s Florida land boom. The house was demolished in 1964 to make way for a parking lot. Courtesy, Fort Lauderdale Historical Society

Above: Mounted fish greeted motorists driving south across the New River on the Andrews Avenue Bridge in the early 1920s. Excursion boats, such as the one seen here, carried passengers up the New River Canal to Lake Okeechobee and then on to Florida's west coast. Courtesy, Fort Lauderdale Historical Society

Top Right: As the New River flows from the Everglades to the ocean, it passes through some of the most attractive residential areas in the county. Here can be seen the boats, palms, and the brilliantly colored Royal Poinciana, all typical of tropical Fort Lauderdale. Courtesy, Dan Hobby, Fort Lauderdale Historical Society

Center: Bathers at Fort Lauderdale's Las Olas Beach view a passing ship as it prepares to enter Port Everglades. The shipping lanes off the southeast Florida coast are among the busiest in the world, as they have been since the days of the Spanish treasure fleets. Courtesy, Fort Lauderdale Historical Society

Right: High-rise buildings along Broward County beaches have inspired mixed feelings. Although they tend to destroy much of the natural beauty that drew people to this area, they allow a greater number of individuals to reside near the ocean than would be possible in lower density developments. Large concentrations of high-rise buildings, such as these along Hallandale Beach and at Galt Ocean Mile have brought about counter-efforts to preserve remaining undeveloped beachfront property in its pristine state. Courtesy, Florida Division of Tourism

Above: Broward County's oldest surviving structure, the 1901 Stranahan house, is shown against a colorful sunrise in this New River scene. At the time this photograph was taken in the 1940s, the building served as the Pioneer House Restaurant. Courtesy, Fort Lauderdale Historical Society

Top Left: One of the first historic preservation projects in Fort Lauderdale was the restoration of the King-Cromartie House, made possible by moving the structure out of the path of development. The house was barged up the New River to the Fort Lauderdale Historical District. Here, the house movers take a break from their sometimes arduous task. Courtesy, Fort Lauderdale Historical Society

Center: For decades, horseracing, the "Sport of Kings," has been a Broward County fixture. During the racing seasons, both residents and visitors lined the seats at Gulfstream and Pompano Park to watch some of the best horses and riders in the nation compete for money and glory. Courtesy, Broward County Tourist Development Council

Bottom: Broward County has long been recognized as a sporting center. Currently two major league baseball teams are headquartered in the county for spring training—the New York Yankees in Fort Lauderdale and the Texas Rangers in Pompano Beach. Courtesy, Paragon

Above: This Pompano Beach postcard from the 1960s or 1970s shows the view north along the Intracoastal Waterway. Boating along the Intracoastal and other waterways is a popular pastime throughout Broward County. Courtesy, Fort Lauderdale Historical Society

Above right: The urban sprawl of metropolitan Fort Lauderdale can be seen clearly in this view from space. Much of the recent development has taken place in the western part of the county. Courtesy, EROS Data Center

Right: Port Everglades is recognized internationally as a world cruise port. It serves as port-of-call for liners sailing to the Bahamas, Caribbean, West Indies, Central and South America, Europe, the Far East, and around the world. Here, one of the liners takes on passengers at night. Courtesy, Port Everglades Authority

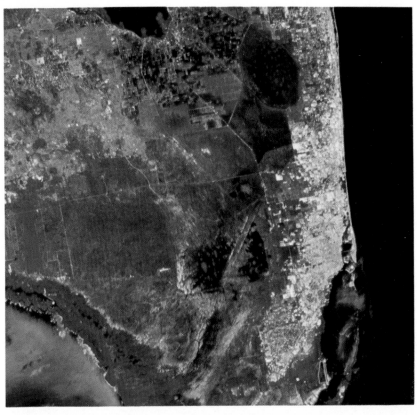

Above: A full moon, strings of colored lights along the banks, and numerous boats sparkle in this New River scene from the 1930s. Recovering from the depression which followed the collapse of Florida's real estate boom, Fort Lauderdale and the surrounding area combined a friendly small-town atmosphere with a reputation as a yacht and pleasure-craft center. Courtesy, Fort Lauderdale Historical Society

Above left: The brightly colored patch of land on the east coast of Florida marks the South Florida megalopolis. Currently, approximately four million people live in this narrow coastal strip. To the west, the darkness of the Everglades proves that not all of Florida has been lost to urbanization. Courtesy, EROS Data Center

Left: Looking west across the Intracoastal Waterway at the 17th Street Causeway, the hotels and homes shine like jewels in the night. To the left is the northern edge of the Port Everglades Complex. Courtesy, Florida Division of Tourism

Above: Broward County's Courthouse, with its imposing belltower, was a landmark to Fort Lauderdale boaters on the New River. This view, looking west toward the courthouse, captures the quiet beauty of the river during the 1940s and 1950s. Courtesy, Fort Lauderdale Historical Society

Left: Among the most colorful and popular events in Broward County are the annual Christmas Boat parades held in both Fort Lauderdale and Pompano Beach. Each year, hundreds of boats vie for the honor of being judged "best in the show," as thousands of spectators view the brightly decorated vessels. Courtesy, Fort Lauderdale/Broward County Chamber of Commerce

Left: The setting sun silhouettes the skyline of Fort Lauderdale. In recent years, both residential and commercial buildings have been going up at a rapid rate throughout the county. The construction of modern glass and steel high-rises, especially along the beachfront, has caused concern as to their ability to withstand the effects of a tropical hurricane. Courtesy, Broward County Tourist Development Council

Facing page: The Landmark Bank building, Fort Lauderdale's first "skyscraper," is seen here behind the banners of the Fort Lauderdale City Park, a new parking garage and shopping complex. The development of downtown Fort Lauderdale has challenged urban planners and architects to provide for more people and vehicles in a way that does not create a sterile complex of office buildings. Courtesy, Terri Horrow, Fort Lauderdale Historical Society

The downtown buildings of Fort Lauderdale are seen from across the Intracoastal Waterway. Increased traffic on the Intracoastal has recently led to the imposition of speed limits and marine patrols in order to insure the safety of boaters. Courtesy, Paragon

Chapter 7

ONE MILLION PEOPLE

The rains started early. On March 1, 1947, a line squall dumped half a foot of water on the upper Glades. By July the Everglades Drainage District was holding flood emergency sessions. On September 17 a hurricane entered the lower southwest Gulf Coast and poured more water onto the Everglades. Less than a month later, on October 11, another wet hurricane struck, passing across Broward County and dumping more rain on an already saturated area. The October hurricane deposited 11 inches of rain on Fort Lauderdale in less than three hours, submerging the downtown area under two feet of water. New River poured over its banks.

Davie and the farming sections were hit even harder. Water was polluted as septic tanks overflowed. High canal banks became refuges for cattle and horses but also for rattlesnakes, wildcats, and deer.

And still the rain kept falling. Unnaturally high fall tides slowed the runoff. There was simply nowhere for the water to go. Three million acres in Central and Southern Florida were flooded for months. Coastal rainfall is normally about 60 inches; in 1947 several coastal stations reported over 100 inches.

At Twenty-Six Mile Bend the angry dynamiters were on the move again. The Everglades Drainage District, which now had jurisdiction over Broward, didn't want any dynamiting, but it did want the control structure kept open. The faction that wanted it closed plugged it up with stoplogs and dumped timbers, sandbags, and concrete blocks around it. The group that wanted it open came with explosives. Both sides were heavily armed.

The controversy raged so intensely that the Broward County grand jury issued a report calling on all factions to support a flood-control plan now pending before the federal government to solve the problem that

had hurt all sides for so many years. In 1949 Congress authorized the creation of the Central and Southern Florida Flood Control District, giving the new organization jurisdiction over 1,340 square miles of land. It would not solve all of Broward's water problems, but once in place the flood-control project would open vast acreages in west Broward for development. Many years later Dr. Charles Forman, whose father had worked mightily to bring about the Flood Control District, would remark: "Eighty percent of the people who live in Broward today couldn't live here without flood control."

As the flood receded, a new era was dawning for Broward. The war was over, the Depression a thing of the past. The county began by facing up to two of its biggest problems—flooding and corruption.

In the postwar era the Mob stepped up its illegal gambling operations in Broward. This apparently was fine with Sheriff Clark. He left them alone, and at the fancy Colonial Inn, just south of Gulfstream Park, he supplied armed deputies to guard the illegal casino and to protect its armored cars. In return, he was permitted to operate a numbers racket from his office and control slot machines under the name of the Broward Amusement Company, later called the Broward Novelty Company.

Hollywood was wide open. A slot machine was once placed in the men's room at the city hall. More and more people became alarmed about the Mob and the corruption that was infecting county and local governments. Both the *Fort Lauderdale News* and *The Miami Herald* began exposing illegal gambling activities.

Then, on February 12, 1948, the assistant state attorney, Dwight L. Rogers, Jr., went to circuit court and called for a civil injunction against the operation of the Colonial Inn, the Lopez Restaurant, and Club Greenacres. Meanwhile Fort Lauderdale turned to frequent arrests and heavy fines for bookmakers. Lee Wentworth, former tax assessor whose family came to Florida in 1840, led a group of Hollywood citizens who sought injunctions in their city.

In 1949 Jake Lansky called on Wentworth and offered him a $25,000 bribe. Wentworth turned and went back in his house. Two or three nights later, strangers called. One showed him a shoebox and said: "We have $25,000 here. You know how these things end—either with a silver bullet or a silver dollar."

Wentworth went back into his house and got the shotgun he kept near his front door. "I'm going to count to five," he told the three men in the car, "and then I'm going to start shooting." The men drove away and never returned.

The reform movement, however, sputtered. It did not regain momentum until a lanky senator from Tennessee brought his Senate Crime Investigating Committee to Miami in 1950. Senator Estes Kefauver, thriving on the national publicity the probe was bringing to his Presidential candidacy, aimed the pitiless glare of nationwide television coverage on Broward and Dade counties. Walter Clark looked particularly evasive on TV.

Said Clark: "I let them have what they want for the tourists down there."

When Senator Kefauver asked him about the casinos, Clark replied: "Four or five clubs, yes; but not gambling places to my knowledge. They are clubs."

The chairman then asked: "You have never known that there was gambling in those places?"

"Rumors," said Clark, "but no actual evidence of it."

Sheriff Clark skillfully avoided embarassing questions by pleading a poor memory, but Kefauver finally nailed him hard with income tax records that showed an annual income of $35,000. The sheriff's job paid only $7,500.

Governor Fuller Warren suspended Clark and appointed Amos Hall of Hollywood to succeed him. Then on August 18, 1950, the Broward County grand jury indicted Clark on 14 counts of possessing slot machines. The sheriff struggled into the courtroom on crutches, favoring an arthritic leg and hip. He was acquitted on all 14 counts. The sheriff did not enjoy his victory for long—within a year he was dead of leukemia.

Facing page: Although Broward County felt the effects of eight hurricanes between 1945 and 1950, the 1947 storms had the most destructive impact. The swollen New River overflowed its banks and transformed downtown Fort Lauderdale streets into waterways. In the Davie area, flood waters inundated vegetable fields and citrus groves, causing major crop damage and intensifying growers' pleas for an effective flood control program. Courtesy, Fort Lauderdale Historical Society

Commodore Auyland Harcourt Brook, a leading figure in promoting the 1920s boom, was preparing for new postwar growth when an overly energetic 80th birthday celebration cost him his life in 1946. In this 1941 photograph, the Commodore cuts the cake at a more restrained birthday party. Although he did not live to see Fort Lauderdale's greatest period of growth, the Commodore, with his promotional expertise and relentless optimism in the city's future, established the groundwork for a new generation of boosters. Courtesy, Fort Lauderdale Historical Society

An ironic footnote to the winding down of Broward's era of wide-open gambling occurred on October 29, 1949. The Collier Construction Company of Cleveland incorporated the Town of Hacienda Village on State Road 84, west of Fort Lauderdale. Its mission was to be a casino town. Its casino, the Hacienda Inn, operated only briefly, then ran afoul of changing times. The casino later became a country music hangout.

After World War II, the census of 1950 revealed that Broward's population had reached 83,933. Fort Lauderdale, with 36,328 residents, was now far ahead of Hollywood, the second largest city with 14,351, and Pompano with 5,682. The county was beginning to mature, and none too soon. Just ahead lay a massive land rush.

Early in the postwar era Victor Nurmi, a native of Finland, made his contribution toward starting a new boom. In 1944 he had purchased the four spoil islands that Morang had abandoned just north of Las Olas Boulevard. Left over from the bust, these islands had deteriorated into overgrown dumps, made all the more unsightly by four humpbacked concrete bridges that failed to connect with the boulevard. Nurmi put a crew of 55 to work building new bridges, seawalls, and streets. By February 1, 1946, he had lots for sale on Nurmi Isles. In six weeks 75 percent of them were sold.

Commodore Brook, the ebullient symbol of boomtime Fort Lauderdale, looked ahead with typical enthusiasm but made a serious miscalculation. "I made it," he cried out in joy when he reached his 80th birthday. To dramatize his perpetual youthfulness, the Commodore proceeded to show he could still stand on his head. The feat ruptured some blood vessels, and a few days later he died—on April 1, 1946.

That same year James Hunt of Detroit, believed to be the nation's largest Chevrolet dealer, Joseph Taravella, who had served under him in the navy, and Stephen Calder, a Fort Lauderdale real-estate man since 1920, teamed up to form Coral Ridge Properties (CRP). In the next three decades the company developed most of northeastern Fort Lauderdale, north from Sunrise Boulevard to Pompano Beach, an area containing some 8,000 homes and 7,000 luxury oceanfront apartments and comprising a third of the assessed valuation of the entire city of Fort Lauderdale.

In 1953 the company put together the largest private land transaction ever completed up to that time. For $19,389,000 CRP bought 2,466 acres from Arthur Galt, who had taken the property back from the Countess of Lauderdale during the bust. Included in this property was a particularly prime piece of land which would become the Galt Ocean Mile, a row of oceanfront luxury condominiums where an isolated beach for blacks had once been located.

The postwar years brought an upsurge in real-estate activity throughout the county. Municipalities began to spring up. Some, like

Wilton Manors, arose from the wishes of older communities to incorporate, usually to block annexation by larger cities. Most began as new developer towns. In 1947, eighty-six freeholders signed a petition to incorporate Wilton Manors, which had started as an E.J. "Fred" Willingham subdivision in 1924. Its first mayor was Dave Turner, a sixth-generation Floridian whose father had been the county's first sheriff. In the 1940s Dave Turner was the largest private landowner in the state, with more than 10,000 acres.

In the 1950s, ten new municipalities were incorporated, seven of them in the west where improved flood control opened the door for developers. The year 1953 saw the start of the new wave of towns, with Plantation, which would become the largest city in the west, and Lazy Lake, which would steadfastly maintain its position as the county's smallest municipality.

As far back as 1911 the area just to the north of Davie was called the Old Plantation Water Control District. In 1941 Fred C. Peters, whose family had large agricultural interests in south Dade County, bought 10,000 acres from Dewey Hawkins, Oakland Park's mayor for 26 years. When the tract proved less suitable for cattle ranching than Peters had expected, he asked Chauncey R. Clark, Sr., a Miami developer, to plan a city called Plantation. Clark's concept called for a city of one-acre lots with homes in front and orchards in the rear. The first houses were built on East Acre Drive.

Unfortunately, the floods of 1947 and 1948 slowed the project down. When the new development flooded in 1948 for the second time in two years, Clark's company, Plantation Homes, Inc., was unable to sell prop-

Above: During the war years, four abandoned, garbage-strewn, man-made islands north of Las Olas Boulevard remained as unsightly reminders of the "bust" and Depression. But a booming postwar economy guaranteed that such valuable waterfront property would not remain idle for long. By 1946 Finnish-born Victor Nurmi had cleared and subdivided the islands, selling lots to eager buyers. With the development of Nurmi Isles, the last of Fort Lauderdale's famed Las Olas Islands was completed. Courtesy, Gene Hyde Collection, Fort Lauderdale Historical Society

Above left: Stephen A. Calder, James S. Hunt, Arthur T. Galt, and M.A. Hortt (left to right) stopped their Fort Lauderdale and Broward County land development activities long enough to pose for a group photograph in the early 1950s. Galt, a Chicagoan who had purchased 8,000 acres along the Intracoastal Waterway during the 1920s land boom, had battled both Fort Lauderdale and Oakland Park to prevent his vast property holdings from being incorporated into either city. Courtesy, Coral Ridge Properties, Inc.

erty. The company's assets reverted to Fred Peters.

By 1951 the population was only 98, but two years later Plantation's roughly 475 residents concluded it was time to incorporate. The city was chartered on April 30, 1953. Eleven days later the first formal council meeting was held in an old feed warehouse near the intersection of East Acre Drive and Broward Boulevard. Named as mayor was Ellsworth Gage, president of the Plantation Homeowner's Association.

The Plantation Golf Course and Country Clubhouse, constructed in 1950 on lands where Seminoles once roamed, has a distinctly Indian flavor. The 14th hole, it was discovered, contained an Indian burial mound. All 18 holes were given "Indian" names; for example, the 14th is Funnee-Okko-Pokko (Bone Head Burial Mound) and the 3rd is Kotok Taikee (Hidden Lake, after a water hazard).

Lazy Lake began life in December 1946 as a small subdivision, 13 acres on a spring-fed lake. It incorporated on June 3, 1953, primarily to avoid annexation by Wilton Manors, which completely surrounds it. In the 1960 census Lazy Lake's population was 49. By 1980 it had dropped to 31. Basically the village wants to be left alone. In the early 1970s residents decided not to accept federal revenue-sharing funds—too much paper-work, too much government interference. The village's share of funds would have been $1,200.

In its first 30 years, Lazy Lake proved to be almost crime-free. The first arrest came when a villager illegally placed four swans in the lake. The second, 10 years later in 1969, involved the apprehension of two people who rented an apartment in the home of an unsuspecting Lazy Lake police chief and used it as the base for a bookmaking operation.

In 1954 a southwest Broward dairy farmer named Henry Perry sold a square mile of land to Abraham L. Mailman, who had retired to Florida after making a fortune from the manufacture of Persona Razor Blades and a line of shoes and boots. Involved in the project were Bob Gordon, Mailman's Harvard-educated son-in-law, and his partner, Hy Siegal.

The deal carried with it a strange twist. Perry agreed to sell only if he could serve as foreman on the housing project. Perry was a versatile man—dairy farmer, carpenter, banker, and influential politico.

Gordon sought to develop "an inexpensive, bedroom blue-collar" community. The first weekend the development was open Gordon and Siegal sold 150 homes in a new community to be called Miramar. The town was incorporated on May 26, 1955. Gordon served as the first mayor, presiding over commission meetings held in an old barn. In land area Miramar became the largest city in Broward and the third largest in the state. Starting from a population of 200 at incorporation, Miramar had grown to 32,813 by the 1980 census, even though only 30 percent of the city's land had been developed.

Just four days after Miramar became an official city, the town of Margate was incorporated, encompassing 1,900 acres just west of Pompano. Originally planned as a city of 10,000, Margate expanded its land area over the years and by 1980 had grown into a city of 36,044.

Margate had started in the 1890s as Hiram F. Hammon's farming community, Hammondville, but the father of the modern city is generally felt to be Jack Marqusee. In 1957 the IBEC Corporation, headed by Winthrop Rockefeller, bought 640 acres north of the Margate city limits to develop into home sites in an area adjacent to what later became Royal Palm Boulevard. Marqusee, a New Yorker who had come south for health reasons, joined with IBEC in developing the area, later annexed into Margate.

Just north of Pompano on the west side of the Intracoastal lay a stretch of sparsely settled land that looked straight across at the Hillsboro Lighthouse. The area's 107 residents voted to incorporate under the name of Lighthouse Point. The date of incorporation was June 13, 1956. The first mayor was Russell Clarke. An affluent bedroom community, the town had grown to 11,488 residents by 1980.

In the 1920s Lighthouse Point had been the scene of a popular fishing camp and of the Club Unique, a gambling casino catering to the wealthy clientele of the Hillsboro Club. Known even then simply as Cap's Place, the casino, accessible only by boat, later became one of the area's best-known restaurants. Over the years Cap's has attracted Presidents Roosevelt and Kennedy, Winston Churchill, Jack Dempsey, General George Marshall, and Lord Beaverbrook, among many others. Cap—Captain Eugene Theodore Knight, brother of the lighthouse keeper—used to feed the rich and famous in his overalls.

In the early part of the 20th century a group of farmhouses in a farming area west of Hallandale acquired the name Pembroke, a designation that some observers think may trace back to the days of Sir Edward Reed, since Pembroke is a county in Wales. At any rate, the farming settlement influenced the naming of two Broward municipalities, which were incorporated within two years of each other.

Pembroke Park, primarily a mobile home community at the time, was incorporated on December 10, 1957, "to stop the spread of noxious industries," according to its city manager, Hewitt Wagner. Rendering, acid, and chlorine plants along the railroad track alarmed the tiny community. Today the town of roughly 5,000 consists of 13 mobile home parks, a number of townhouses, and an industrial section limited to light industry. Pembroke Park annexed a small incorporated town, Hollywood Ridge Farms, on July 1, 1970.

For the people of Pembroke Pines the task of incorporation proved much more complicated. Many in West Hollywood and the area that is now Pembroke Pines wanted to create a new city called Hollywood

Heights. They were fearful of being annexed by the City of Hollywood. The *Hollywood Sun-Tattler* favored one large city for all of south Broward, which would be preferable, the paper felt, to a group of proliferating municipalities that would make the county ungovernable. A "don't go to the polls" campaign blocked the incorporation attempt, since Florida law calls for the approval of two-thirds of the eligible, registered freeholders.

Among those standing for election, unsuccessfully, was Dr. Walter S. Kipnis. He was active in a second incorporation effort, this one directed toward encompassing a smaller area to be called the Village of Pembroke Pines. In a close, mud-slinging election, the pro-incorporators won—but not quite. The vote was close, the number of eligible freeholders was not determined precisely, the legal description of the town was not accurate, and Dr. Kipnis was improperly named chairman of the balloting committee. Judge Richard Sauls de-incorporated the village.

By now Kipnis, who had been named mayor only to have his village shot out from under him, and his supporters were learning how to do it. Once more they tried, carefully addressing each point brought out in the court case. On January 1 the incorporation won easily, and Kipnis continued as mayor. A village of only 200 people at the start, Pembroke Pines had grown into a city of over 40,000 by the early 1980s.

Nestled in a secluded spot between Lake Placid and the Intracoastal Waterway in Lighthouse Point, Cap's Place was an exclusive gambling house in the 1930s and 1940s. With its beautiful, isolated setting and proximity to large Gold Coast resort cities, Cap's Place, now a restaurant, has been a favorite stopping place for the wealthy and famous. Longtime cook and bartender Al Hasis stands at the bar in this 1965 photograph. Courtesy, Gene Hyde Collection, Fort Lauderdale Historical Society

Two west Broward municipalities were incorporated on June 20, 1959—Cooper City and Lauderhill. Lauderhill, with only eight homes in the newly developed area, became a town at a time when residents could still ride horseback on the undeveloped land within its boundaries. The population was only 132 in 1960. Twenty years later it was approaching 40,000.

The largest development in Lauderhill is Inverrary, the home of Jackie Gleason and for many years of the Inverrary golf classic, which attracted not only the best golf pros but also celebrities from other sports, the entertainment field, and even politics. For instance, ex-President Gerald Ford competed in the Inverrary Celebrity Golf Event.

In 1958 Morris Cooper, a Miami Beach developer, cleared a four-square-mile area west of Davie and named it Cooper Colony Estates. Of the two main access roads at that time, Stirling Road was a trail through the swamps, and Griffin Road was still unpaved. By 1959 the city had 85 residents. On June 20 the town was incorporated as Cooper City.

The city's beautification plan includes planting trees along South New River Canal, Cooper City's northern boundary, and requiring builders to plant at least three six-foot trees on each lot. Cooper City in the 1980 census had a population of 10,140.

One of Broward's smallest municipalities, Sea Ranch Lakes, was incorporated on October 6. Governor Gore, who developed the affluent community, had bought a half-mile of ocean frontage just north of Lauderdale-by-the-Sea for $25,000 in the early 1940s. The property extended from the ocean to the Intracoastal. On the Intracoastal side, Gore developed Sea Ranch Lakes, an exclusive, walled community that numbered only 170 people in the 1960 census and less that 600 twenty years later. On the ocean side of the property Governor Gore built the Sea Ranch Hotel, a beautifully landscaped hotel, which in its day hosted both Franklin Delano Roosevelt and Winston Churchill.

One other small community incorporated in the 1950s and then disincorporated on July 1, 1970. Ferncrest Village, which was essentially the Forman dairy property, was incorporated in 1953. Hamilton Forman served as a commissioner from its founding until September 16, 1961. On that day, while driving home from work along State Road 84, his car blew a tire and plunged into the North New River Canal. His death in the canal was particularly ironic—he had given a lifetime to the control and management of water.

Activity in the 1950s encompassed far more than simply the opening up of new towns. Within such established towns as Fort Lauderdale and Hollywood, real-estate development was moving ahead vigorously. In Fort Lauderdale, Coral Ridge Properties was the principal developer in that decade, while Hollywood, Inc., awakened from a long quiescent

Mayor Walter Seth "Doc" Kipnis and Finance Director William Francis White stand in front of Pembroke Pine's new city hall in this March 1962 photograph. Kipnis led the struggle to incorporate Pembroke Pines and served as the city's first mayor. Pembroke Pines' incorporation battle was typical of the fight waged by several developments in western Broward County to preserve their identity, as older, larger communities attempted to absorb them. Courtesy, Gene Hyde Collection, Fort Lauderdale Historical Society

Golf has been an important part of Broward County sports and recreation since the early 1920s, when President-elect Harding played on Fort Lauderdale's original municipal course. By far the most famous Broward golfing event has been the Inverrary Classic in Lauderhill, originally sponsored by entertainer Jackie Gleason. Here Gleason watches Jack Nicklaus' shot during the March 7, 1979, pro-am competition which preceded the tournament. Courtesy, Miami Herald

Christmas decorations stretch across Hollywood Boulevard in this January 6, 1959, view looking east from 21st Avenue. Hollywood, relatively stable since the Depression, saw renewed growth in the 1950s as Sam Horvitz's company, Hollywood, Inc., opened several new developments. Courtesy, Hollywood Historical Society

period and began the development of Hollywood in earnest with the appointment in 1953 of young William Horvitz, Sam's 27-year-old son, as president.

During the troubled Depression years Sam Horvitz held back on new developments. In 1939 he built only about a dozen houses, and then he had a hard time selling them. Such was not the case in the 1950s. Starting with Orange Brook Golf Estates in 1954, the company went on to develop Emerald Hills and Hollywood Hills, and later moved into Cooper City to build Rock Creek.

In Dania Broward County's first jai-alai fronton was opened on December 28, 1953. Jai-alai is an old Basque game, played with a very hard ball and a woven basket, the cesta, which is used for catching and throwing the ball against the walls of the court. By the 1980s more than a million people a year were watching jai-alai at Dania, making the sport Broward County's leader in total attendance. The Dania Fronton became the county's third legal pari-mutuel gambling enterprise, joining Hollywood Kennel Club and Gulfstream Park.

At the end of 1955 the City of Fort Lauderdale finally gained full possession of Bahia Mar, a yachting marina of such excellence that the National Association of Engine and Boat Manufacturers voted it "the Outstanding Achievement in Water-front Development Programs in the United States." Following World War II Coast Guard Base Six was declared surplus. After months of negotiation City Attorney George English, with the aid of U.S. Senator Claude Pepper, induced the government to lower its price from an unattainable one million dollars to a possibly attainable $600,000. Even then the city couldn't raise the money. Private citizens pitched in to subscribe the money, starting with a $250,000 lead-off contribution from Governor Gore. The final funds needed to meet the price were raised just minutes before the option expired.

For the next eight years the city struggled through a series of suits, countersuits, bitter arguments, and hassles as the ownership, management, and funding of the facility became a roiling sea of controversy. Through it all, yachtsmen were discovering Bahia Mar with such enthusiasm that Fort Lauderdale became known as "the Yachting Capital

of the World." Bahia Mar, once the home of the House of Refuge and later the Coast Guard base, acquired one unexpected bit of fame when the noted Florida writer, John D. MacDonald, made Bahia Mar the home base for his popular fictional hero, Travis McGee.

As the decade drew to a close, Fort Lauderdale launched a major project, born once again out of controversy. Heavy traffic on U.S. 1 created the need for a larger bridge over the New River. Or would a tunnel be better? From 1940 till 1955 the bridge-vs-tunnel battle raged. The city commissioners called for a referendum. When the votes were counted, the tunnel had won—7,000 votes to 6,443. Work started on the project on October 13, 1958, and the tunnel was opened to traffic on December 9, 1960. It was then, and still is, the only public highway tunnel in the state of Florida.

The census of 1960 showed the effects of the new towns that had been formed in the 1950s. A four-fold increase in population sent the county's total to 333,946 people.

In the decade ahead seven more municipalities were incorporated, two of them—Sunrise and Lauderdale Lakes—on June 22, 1961. When founded, Lauderdale Lakes had approximately 600 residents. Its principal early developers were Harold Diamond, Herman Corn, and Oriole Homes. Among the largest communities in Lauderdale Lakes are Hawaiian Gardens, Somerset, and Cypress Chase. By the 1980 census Lauderdale Lakes had moved past 25,000 in population.

The City of Sunrise began life as Sunrise Golf Village. In 1960 developer Norman Johnson bought 2,650 acres for $9 million, just north of Plantation, where he lived. Since the property was contiguous to an existing golf course, he called his new town Sunrise Golf Village and introduced it to the buying public with a gimmick so outrageous that it still had people talking two decades later.

In 1960 Johnson, a sports car enthusiast, was driving along Miami's 36th Street, an area of multiple automobile dealerships. When a traffic jam slowed him down, he assumed an accident had occurred. The cause

actually turned out to be an upside-down car on a dealer's lot—an inspiration for Johnson.

At a cost of about 20 percent more than a conventional house, Johnson proceeded to build an upside-down house at Sunrise. Furniture was bolted to the floor, a Pontiac convertible was attached to the floor of the carport, and small trees and bushes were even planted in an upside-down position. Only the plants resisted. In time they began to change direction and reach upward.

The upside-down house rated a two-page spread in *Life* magazine. Aircraft pilots began using the house as a visual checkpoint when approaching the airport. Best of all, from Johnson's point of view, the upside-down house sold homes.

Appointed the first mayor of the village by Governor Farris Bryant, Johnson served until 1967 when John Lomelo was elected mayor. The strong-willed Lomelo would emerge as one of the county's political powers, annexing more and more territory as Sunrise grew in less than two decades into the second-largest city in west Broward, with a population of just under 40,000 in the 1980 census.

For more than three decades Bud Lyons acquired land in west Broward, through tax sales or in trades for mules or old Model-T Fords. At his death in 1952 Lyons, nicknamed "the Titan of the Beanpatch," owned the largest bean farm in the United States, 20 sections of land stretching west of State Road 7 from Fort Lauderdale almost to Deerfield Beach.

In 1962 Lena Lyons, Bud's widow, sold 5,000 acres in north Broward to Coral Ridge Properties. An additional 400 acres were purchased by the company from Rodman Rockefeller in the Margate area to extend Royal Palm Boulevard from Margate into the new city, which would be named Coral Springs. On July 10, 1963, Coral Springs was incorporated. Since five legal residents were required to constitute a city, the residency requirement was met by locating company employees in the new municipality. The five who first moved into the undeveloped open country of Coral Springs were George Porter, Mrs. Val Baker, Mr. and Mrs. James Novotny, and Gordon Ickes, a company vice-president. Since those five first settled there, Coral Springs has grown to a population of 37,349 according to the 1980 census.

To stimulate sales in the early years, Coral Ridge Properties made use of celebrities, in particular Johnny Carson, to attract crowds to company auctions. For the first 15 minutes of a sale, lots were sold at a discount. When the gong sounded, prospective homeowners, real-estate buyers, and investors made a mad rush to the auctioneer's platform to buy lots in Coral Springs.

Incorporated on the same day as Coral Springs, North Lauderdale had

to wait a little longer for its day of growth. Cattle owners still had lease rights on much of the land until 1968. The following year the pace quickened with the announcement that Morris Lapidus, who had designed the Fountainbleu, Eden Roc, and Americana hotels on Miami Beach, had been engaged to create a $100,000 gateway into North Lauderdale. In describing the 12 separate towers of poured concrete in his gateway, Lapidus said, "Each tower consists of four gracefully tapering shafts, looking like the landing legs on a space capsule."

By the 1970 census North Lauderdale had already attained a population of more than 1,000 and in 1980 had reached 18,479. The principal developer in North Lauderdale has been the Tam O'Shanter Development Corporation, which attracted national attention in 1976 by becoming the first large developer to make solar hot-water heaters standard equipment in new homes. Sunshine has been an important thread in the history of North Lauderdale. The first purchase of land in the town's eventual area, a 3,190-acre parcel owned by Lena Lyons, was made by Solar Estates, Inc. Then in 1971 two city officials became the first people in Florida cited under the state's new "Government-in-the-Sunshine" law, which stipulates that government bodies must transact public business in the open.

In northwest Broward, just north of Coral Springs, lies the town of Parkland, the third-smallest municipality in the county with a population of little over 700. Incorporated on July 10, 1963, Parkland began to develop as a community when Bruce Blount of Pompano Beach started selling off parcels of land in the 1950s. His original deed restrictions called for a minimum lot size of two-and-a-half acres. The first residents wanted to maintain small ranches and enjoy owning a few horses.

A project of Fort Lauderdale's Coral Ridge Properties, Coral Springs, like several other western Broward developments, was constructed on part of a vast agricultural tract that had been owned by the Lyons family of Pompano. Lots sold rapidly as a result of Coral Ridge Properties' skillful promotions. Land sales, such as this March 1965 event, featured celebrities, barbeques, persuasive sales talks, and 15-minute discounts, attracting hordes of prospective homeowners. Courtesy, Coral Ridge Properties, Inc.

The original Parkland contained 330 acres. In 1973 the town annexed 660 acres to the east, zoned for 1.5 units per acre. In the area near Parkland, Leadership Housing purchased 4,000 acres but later had to default on its purchase. Since Leadership's default, the future development of Parkland has been complicated by lawsuits regarding the density to be allowed in the 4,000-acre tract.

On August 15, 1963, Tamarac became Broward County's 28th municipality, incorporated by five registered voters, all employees of the developer, Behring Properties. Ken Behring, in addition to developing the city, established a large factory to produce "manufactured housing." He was successful in introducing a number of innovative mass production techniques, but manufactured housing did not prove a viable industry. Behring later sold the bulk of his land holdings to Leadership Housing and his manufacturing facility to Visual Graphics, Inc., a manufacturer of photo typesetting equipment and industrial cameras.

Tamarac's population had grown to almost 30,000 by the 1980 census. It is basically a low-density residential community with nine golf courses and 70 acres of land for parks and recreation centers.

In 1956 Robert E. Bateman bought land east of Margate and south of Hammondville Road, which would form the original development of Coconut Creek. It was first called Edgefield, then switched to its present name in 1959. After John W. "Jack" Brown joined Bateman, the community was promoted heavily by water-skiing exhibitions on the man-made lakes and canals.

In 1963 both Pompano Beach and Margate made preliminary efforts to annex the community. As a result, the Coconut Creek Home Owners Association formed a committee to explore the development's options. In the incorporation election of February 19, 1967, more than 98 percent of the eligible voters turned out. Incorporation won, gaining just three votes more than the necessary two-thirds. In short order Coconut Creek again

faced the threat of being absorbed into a larger unit. In 1970 the county's Governmental Efficiency Study Commission recommended the reordering of the county into eight municipalities. For example, Coconut Creek, Margate, and North Lauderdale were to be merged into a single unit called "North City." Adverse reactions throughout the county forced the abandonment of the plan.

With the incorporation of Coconut Creek on February 20, 1967, a 20-year period of new city formation in Broward County came to an end. Since it became the 29th municipality, no other city has been created. Nor is it likely that others will be established in the foreseeable future. Present state law is designed to halt the proliferation of small cities, while consolidation of existing municipalities has run afoul of strong territorial feelings.

Social as well as physical changes affected Broward County in the second half of the 20th century. In the 1960s the civil-rights movement, which had begun to build in the 1950s, started to produce results for Broward blacks. On September 5, 1961, the school color line was broken without incident when 15 black pupils entered Rock Island Elementary School, six others began classes at Everglades Junior High, and Rosamond Pappy enrolled as a freshman at St. Thomas Aquinas High School.

In 1966 Boisy Waiters, a teacher from Dania, became the first black elected official in the county when he joined the Dania City Commission. Andrew DeGraffenreidt, also a teacher, followed as the first black elected to the Fort Lauderdale City Commission. In 1974 Kathleen Wright became the first to win county-wide office when she was elected to the Broward County School Board. The following year Sylvia Poitier became the county's first black mayor when voters in Deerfield Beach picked her to head their city government. Alcee Hastings became the first black

Fort Lauderdale's northwest area, a mainly black community since the early 20th century, was the scene of rioting in September 1969. Although this violence and a similar disturbance in Pompano Beach came as a surprise to many residents, Broward County's rioting was not an isolated local event, but part of a continuing struggle against racial discrimination in the South and elsewhere in the United States. Courtesy, Miami Herald

Above: Dr. Von D. Mizell was Broward County's most prominent figure in the struggle for civil rights in the 1950s and 1960s. Mizell, who grew up in Dania, helped found Provident Hospital in 1938, and the Broward Chapter of the National Association for the Advancement of Colored People in 1945. Courtesy, Fort Lauderdale Historical Society

Above right: Dr. Von D. Mizell led Fort Lauderdale's last major protest march July 4, 1961, which culminated in a wade-in at Fort Lauderdale's "white" beach. The protest was organized in response to the city's failure to provide an accessible beach for blacks after their former swimming area had been developed as Galt Ocean Mile. As blacks continued to use the white beach, integration was gradually accomplished without incident. Courtesy, Miami Herald

federal judge in South Florida—and then the first to be indicted. He was later acquitted of the charge of accepting a bribe. In December 1962 George Allen became the first black to earn a law degree from the University of Florida. Eight years later, as attorney for the Broward Chapter of the NAACP (National Association for the Advancement of Colored People), he brought the case, *Allen* vs. *The Broward County School Board*, which resulted in the integration of all public schools in the county.

During the first week of September 1969, years of discrimination and escalating protests erupted into race riots. In Fort Lauderdale alone 34 people were injured, and many businesses—owned by both blacks and whites—were looted and burned in the city's predominantly black northwest section.

Through all the civil-rights battles of the postwar period the name that always loomed largest was Dr. Von D. Mizell. He helped found the local NAACP chapter in 1945 and served it as president until his death three decades later. A militant and a battler, Mizell infuriated the white power structure and particularly members of the Broward County Medical Association, who at various times charged that he was incompetent or that he was performing unnecessary operations.

Dr. Mizell prevailed, however, and on July 4, 1961, he led Fort Lauderdale's last great protest. After blacks lost their beach at Galt Ocean Mile, the city promised them an accessible new beach south of the Port Everglades inlet. When the city dragged its feet in providing anything more than access by boat, Dr. Mizell led a Fourth of July wade-in at the Fort Lauderdale Beach, despite threats of violence.

"I was scared that day," he recalled later. "I had to walk through a little corridor there with a human wall on both sides. It was tense and one little spark could have started a riot. I had to look straight ahead, and I was not at ease at all."

Within two weeks the city had pledged to build a road to make the

black beach more accessible, but this action still did not address the issue of segregation. Black people eventually integrated all the beaches over a period of time, simply by using them.

The Fort Lauderdale Beach had been in the news before, when what started quietly as the Collegiate Aquatic Forum led in the 1950s to an annual springtime invasion of college students. A 1959 *Time* article on the phenomenon quoted a young woman's explanation of why she came to the beaches of Fort Lauderdale: "This is where the boys are."

Where the Boys Are became the title for a mildly risqué novel by Glendon Swarthout and then a 99-minute motion picture produced for MGM by Joe Pasternak. Starring Paula Prentiss, Jim Hutton, Delores Hart, and Connie Francis, the film was unveiled to the world at a premiere at the Gateway Theater on December 21, 1960. Three months later the beach was mobbed when 50,000 kids showed up on spring break.

The Aquatic Forum that spawned *Where the Boys Are* also gave Fort Lauderdale Beach an important swimming and diving attraction. In 1962 the Amateur Athletic Union picked Fort Lauderdale as the site for the national Swimming Hall of Fame. On December 27, 1966, ground was broken for the new Hall of Fame complex, consisting of a museum, an auditorium, and an Olympic-size swimming pool. Named to direct the Hall of Fame was William "Buck" Dawson, who over the years has been actively associated with the University of Michigan swimming program.

Before his death in 1961 Hamilton M. Forman set in motion forces that in time would sharply upgrade Broward's higher educational facilities. In World War II he had sold land to the navy for one dollar for an airfield with the proviso that the land after the war could never be used for anything but education. The General Services Administration set about overriding this to obtain a higher return on the land. Forman, backed up strongly by Senator George Smathers, battled the GSA all the way. The problem for Broward was the requirement that land acquired from the GSA must have a completed building on it within a year.

Senator Smathers asked the Broward delegation what it could build in a year. Myron Ashmore, superintendent of schools, suggested one portable elementary school building. Proceeding from that point, the Broward delegation moved ahead with what would become the South Florida Education Center. The center when completed included Nova University, the second-largest independent university in Florida; Broward Community College, which enrolled 3,200 students at its opening in August 1964; four experimental public schools, Nova High, Nova Middle, Nova Blanche Forman Elementary, and Nova Dwight D. Eisenhower Elementary; and the University of Florida Agriculture Station, which was transferred from Peters Road in Plantation.

The 1970 census reported a Broward population of 620,100. Both Fort Lauderdale and Hollywood had moved past the 100,000 mark. As Broward grew, it became concerned about transportation. In addition to such serviceable north-south roads as U.S. 1 and State Road 7, by 1970 Broward also had two limited access roads, Florida's Turnpike and I-95. East-west was another matter. The county had been unable to cope with the huge migration that brought nearly a quarter of a million people into the west.

Port Everglades, after its shaky start, had become the state's deepest harbor, with a depth of 37 feet. The port has become an important South Florida facility for petroleum shipments. Luxury cruise liners are increasingly utilizing Port Everglades, already one of only five principal cruise ports in the United States.

Fort Lauderdale/Hollywood International Airport now hosts virtually every major U.S. airline, in addition to Air Canada and Bahamasair. General aviation airports include Fort Lauderdale Executive Airport, North Perry Airport in south Broward, and Pompano Air Park, which also is home base for the Goodyear Blimp.

Although the area had not lacked famous winter residents and retirees, growing Broward County finally got around to producing a few celebrities of its own, most notably one Christine Marie Evert, better known as tennis star Chris Evert. Trained from childhood by her father, Jimmy Evert, teaching professional at Fort Lauderdale's Holiday Park Tennis Center, Chris went on to win every major women's tennis title and to attain the Number 1 ranking in the world by 1974 while still a teenager.

A tragic sports hero was Brian Piccolo, a football star at St. Thomas Aquinas High School, which Chris Evert also attended. Brian was an All-

American at Wake Forest University, where he led the nation's colleges in rushing and in scoring. With the Chicago Bears of the National Football League, he played in the same backfield and roomed with the Bears' star running back, Gale Sayers. Piccolo's career was cut short by cancer; on June 16, 1970, he died at age 26. The story of his tragic death and his friendship with Sayers became the subject for a film and for a hauntingly beautiful musical theme, "Brian's Song."

From Pompano Beach's northwest section came Esther Rolle, the ninth of eighteen children of Bahamian immigrants. In "Good Times," one of the earliest television series featuring black actors, Rolle became the show's Emmy Award-winning star as the mother whose first name was, appropriately, "Florida."

In the face of the west's enormous growth, the cities in the east assumed different roles. Fort Lauderdale, the county seat, began to

develop as the area's business and financial center. Downtown Fort Lauderdale, after two decades of doldrums, began to display a skyline as skyscraper office buildings were added to the local scene. In previous years the county's skyscrapers had been highrise beachfront condominiums. In addition, the city began to attract high-technology industries, many of them in the electronics and computer fields.

Dania, the first Broward community to incorporate, underwent the most complete transformation. In its early days agriculture had proved so important that each year the city observed "Tomato Days," a three-day festival that featured, among other things, tomato-throwing battles. Then came saltwater intrusion, which destroyed the agricultural foundation of Dania. In 1945 Jeanette Ely and her husband, Willard, started an antique store on Federal Highway in downtown Dania. Thirty years later nearly 50 antique stores were operating in Dania, which called itself "the Antique Capital of the South."

There was no suspense. Advance estimates made it clear that the census of 1980 would show that Broward County had become a metropolitan area of a million people. The official returns showed the figure as 1,018,200. No one knows who the one-millionth person was, someone who was born in Broward or someone who moved here. The chances are that the one-millionth person was a new citizen who moved here from a Northeastern state and settled in west Broward.

The county had started as a strip along the coast. Now roughly half the population lived west of State Road 7. It is not a world the early settlers would have recognized, any more than the newcomers would have recognized the settlements of Frank Stranahan, Andrew Frost, the Blounts and Hardys, or the camps of Sam Jones.

Still, there are touches that reach back into the past. A major restoration project is the Stranahan House, which the Fort Lauderdale Historical Society and the Fort Lauderdale Board of Realtors through the Stranahan Foundation are restoring to its 1913 configuration. Farther west, the P.N. Bryan family houses on the river are being renovated as restaurants, near the already restored New River Inn and the King-Cromartie House. In Deerfield Beach the old schoolhouse opens a window to the past, as do

With the coming of the jet age, Fort Lauderdale-Hollywood International Airport, formerly the Fort Lauderdale Naval Air Station, became an important port of entry for Broward County. Mackey Airlines, founded in 1952 by aviation pioneer Colonel Joseph C. Mackey, was headquartered at Fort Lauderdale-Hollywood International, and ran the first scheduled flights from South Florida to the Bahamas before merging with Eastern Airlines in 1967. Courtesy, Fort Lauderdale Historical Society

the Kester Cottages preserved in Deerfield and Pompano. In Dania, Pompano Beach, Hollywood, and Hallandale active preservation programs are planned or are already in motion.

In far west Broward, Interstate-75, a road designed to cross the Everglades and travel south through the western part of the county and down into Dade, uncovered reminders of Broward's past. In 1967 Hully Stirling, son of Frank Stirling, asked the Broward County Archaeological Society to excavate a site on his property in western Davie. Radiocarbon dating indicated an Indian camp was in existence as early as 1100 B.C. In 1977 Stirling advised the archaeologists that the site, generally called Peace Camp, would be destroyed by the interstate. After a hard battle, the society succeeded in its effort to save the site. The highway was routed around the camp, which Stirling said was called "Camp Where Indians Talk and No Make War" by Indians he knew—and by some white men as Council Island.

By the start of the 1980s the Seminoles were learning what they called "the white man's game." As an outgrowth of their increasing political awareness, the Indians organized a main governing body, officially chartered as a legal entity in 1975. Today Seminole Tribe, Inc., is a successful business enterprise, producing income for the Indians from cigarette sales, bingo, and land leases. Tribal revenues had increased from $600,000 in 1968 to more than $4 million by 1977. Increased wealth for the tribe has been gained at the loss of many old Seminole values and traditions.

Anthropologist Margot Ammidown writes: "So once again, the Semi-

One of Broward's most colorful and remarkable personalities is the beloved Easter Lily Gates, whose role in the county's history spans more than 60 years. After her husband died in 1926, she became the county's first female school bus driver, and in 1928 was elected supervisor of registration, a post she held until 1969. During much of her tenure, Broward was almost exclusively Democratic. Courtesy, Broward County Historical Commission

nole Indians find themselves in a state of transition with important and difficult choices to make. One path threatens to lead to the complete assimilation of the Seminole Indians as a distinct cultural entity, but provide greater financial security, the other towards a less profitable economic outlook, but a stronger tribal identity. Admirers of the Seminole cultural heritage hope for the latter.''

Discovery of shipwrecks also led today's Broward County back into an earlier time. In 1977 on Hillsboro Beach Veronika Stalcup found a coin dated 1824. Investigation by the Marine Archaeology Advisory Council of the Broward County Historical Commission raised the likelihood that the ship was the *Gil Blas*, the vessel that Cooley was salvaging in 1836 when the Indians massacred his family. In 1981 that same beach was the scene of a terrible tragedy. On August 26, thirty-three Haitians drowned and were washed up on the beach. In fleeing from oppression and poverty in Haiti they had tried to make it across the Gulf Stream and had died in the attempt. One hundred and forty-five years earlier Seminole

Negroes had fled across those same waters to escape oppression. The difference was that they were fleeing from the United States.

In the life of Broward County, the role of water remains central to all that has happened or is likely to happen. Since the earliest times Indians lived along the New River and on the islands in the Everglades. The early settlers had been drawn here first by the clear, sheltered waters of the New River. Later groupings of pioneers settled on the Hillsboro River and later still on Cypress Creek and Lettuce Lake.

In time the waters of the ocean became the moving force that drew people to eastern Broward County, while too much water kept them from moving into the Everglades. When the waters in the west were brought under more effective control, new migrations poured into the western reaches of the county.

From time to time the waters have reminded their too complacent guests of their awesome powers. New River Inlet moves when it wants to; in the past 150 years it has been located in three different places. Severe floods, too, have come to Broward, some rolling in from the ocean on hurricane winds and tides, and others falling in torrents from the skies. Over the years the river has claimed the lives of three of the county's most notable citizens, men who symbolized the spirit of their times: Cap Valentine, who toppled into the river while drunk; Frank Stranahan, who flung himself into the river; and Hamilton Forman, whose car plunged into the waters of North New River Canal. The waters give. They also take away.

If the waters have sometimes brought tragic events to Broward, they have more than offset these by the bounty they have provided: beaches, clear, beautiful waterways, and to the west a unique watery wilderness known as the Everglades. These, coupled with the immensely agreeable weather of the area, have helped shape a one-time frontier settlement into a thriving business, financial, and manufacturing center—and a world-famous resort.

Chapter 8

PARTNERS IN PROGRESS

In the beginning, of course, they came for the sun. The shimmering brilliance, the seductive gleam of eternal summer. It is difficult, in retrospect, to underestimate the intensity of the sun's allure or how pleasant it must feel to be permanently paroled from winter's prison.

And, too, in the beginning, in the days of Wilson and Harding and Coolidge, and flappers and bootleg whiskey, in the days when real estate sired and then slew fortunes overnight, they came for money. Some, the philosophic gunslingers, those dedicated to the short term, came for easy money.

Others came with a notion to settle a community, to open businesses, to raise families, to build churches and schools and hospitals and banks and, eventually, a tradition. That they succeeded, and in less than 60 years, is a tale brow-deep in improbabilities.

Fort Lauderdale and Broward County pioneers found more than sunshine when they arrived on these gleaming sands. They found mosquitoes large enough to cast shadows. They found swamp and mangrove and a silent, sodden, torpid, asphyxiating heat that arrived each summer with all the oppressive predictability of a despised relative.

They found hurricanes and hard times. And they found a place that was not just unfinished, but practically unfurnished. Fort Lauderdale had a port, but it was not developed. It had a railway, but it was only passing through. It had no natural resources to speak of (except sun, sea, and sand), no lumber, no oil, no coal, no quarries, no mines, and, while agriculture would become a major industry, more than half of Broward's 400 square miles was swamp.

Indeed, stuck as it was between the burgeoning city of Miami to the south and the fatuous opulence of Palm Beach to the north, Fort Lauderdale even lacked a sense of its own identity. It was, simply, a place between places. But that wouldn't last for long.

Between 1930 and 1980, a mere blink in the histories of most cities, Fort Lauderdale and Broward County grew from nothing to a suburban megalopolis of more than one million people. It was one of the most astonishing stories of growth not only in Florida but anywhere in America.

And at the vortex of this protean growth was Broward industry: the developers and bankers, brokers, realtors, lawyers, manufacturers, restaurateurs, hoteliers, designers, architects, engineers, construction companies, laborers, and service groups. For the excesses which must, inevitably, occur during times of unfathomable growth, industry has taken its share of blame. But industry must also be given a disproportionate share of credit for making Broward County and Fort Lauderdale what it is today, a major southeastern city of vast, virtually limitless potential.

If there is a common thread to the corporate histories that follow, it is that Broward's businesses, like the pioneers who settled here, came to create a future. That they are doing, every day, in the brilliant heat of our endless summer.

FORT LAUDERDALE HISTORICAL SOCIETY, INC.

Not to know what happened before one was born is to remain a child. —*Cicero*

In February 1962 three Fort Lauderdale pioneers, George W. English, Jr., August Burghard, and Carl P. Weidling, Jr., eased themselves down into the overstuffed leather luxury of English's law office and began to contemplate the solution to an inevitable problem.

Time had become an enemy. Fort Lauderdale's generation of pioneers, those who came to the region before the great hurricane of 1926, those who had struggled to build a community among the swamps and insects and heat, those who had slogged through booms and busts, those people were dying.

When they did each took with them priceless first-hand recollections. Fort Lauderdale's history, the three men could see, was dying with them.

They agreed that a historical society would be the most effective way to preserve the area's heritage. English prepared the papers for incorporation, and, on February 23, 1962, the Fort Lauderdale Historical Society was delivered, an organizational infant with a man-size job.

Not surprisingly, those who became a part of the Historical Society in those early days were many of the people who had created the community's history: Mrs. Ivy Stranahan, Tom Bryan, Mrs. Annie Beck, Mrs. Florence Hardy, N.B. Cheaney, R.H. Gore, James S. Hunt, and Congressman Paul G. Rogers, to name a few. Burghard became the first president and they established an office at 315 Southeast Sixth Street in a county-owned apartment.

The trustees moved swiftly. By June 1962 the Society had signed a contract with Burghard and Weidling to assemble, edit, and write a history of Fort Lauderdale. The result was *Checkered Sunshine* and it went on sale in August 1966. Through the years the Society would publish several books, including a biography of Ivy Stranahan, a historic guide to the city, the memoirs of Seminole Indian agent James L. Glenn, and this volume, its most ambitious project, a complete history of the city and county.

The Society received financing from the city but was not a public agency. It made money from membership dues, an endowment fund, sales in its store, fund-raising events, its publications, and grants.

In 1965 the Society moved to new headquarters in an old recreation building in Holiday Park and in 1978 moved into its own building in the historic section of old Fort Lauderdale. Early in 1979 the Society opened its historical museum, offering residents and visitors a unique look at the heritage of the region. The Historical Society has been active in the field of historic preservation also. In 1975 it purchased the oldest structure in the county—the Stranahan House—and took the necessary steps to ensure its restoration.

The Historical Society continues to carry out the mandate of the original charter: "To . . . maintain, preserve, and disseminate the history of the city . . . to record current and future information and events. And to encourage and arouse the interest of the inhabitants of the city [in its] history."

Carl P. Weidling, Jr. (foreground), George W. English, Jr. (standing), and August Burghard, founders of the Fort Lauderdale Historical Society.

Every year thousands of children learn about their heritage at the Fort Lauderdale Historical Museum.

HOLLYWOOD FEDERAL SAVINGS AND LOAN ASSOCIATION

The Hollywood Federal Savings and Loan headquarters is located at 1909 Tyler Street in downtown Hollywood.

If the early 1930s were difficult years for business in America, they were virtually impossible years in Broward County. Broward was hardly more than a smudge on the road between Miami and Palm Beach in 1933, and the tiny town of Hollywood had fewer than 4,000 year-round residents.

Nevertheless, it was in 1933 that paint and electrical appliance dealer William A. Michel turned to his friend, attorney T.D. Ellis, Jr., and asked what would be required to start a savings and loan association. Michel felt that the city needed a new source of first mortgage loans that could help Hollywood recover and add stability to a local economy still reeling from the effects of the Depression.

Ellis, it turns out, knew the answers to Michel's questions and the two were joined by R.W. Dilg, a banker, and Dr. B.F. Butler. Together they drafted, signed, and sent off for approval the first federal savings and loan charter application in Hollywood's brief

history. It was approved in January 1934.

On February 27, the first official board of directors met to plan the association's future.

The first few years of Hollywood Federal's existence were difficult indeed. Savings were hard to come by, and by the end of 1934 the association had less than $12,000 in assets and $5,000 in total loans and investments. But those figures were hardly a portent of things to come.

Year by year, inch by inch, it seemed, Hollywood Federal began to grow. By 1946 it had moved from the Dixon Building on Hollywood Boulevard to 1901 Tyler Street.

In April 1956 E.F. Weigle, a former examiner on the Federal Home Loan Bank Board, became president of Hollywood Federal. By then Hollywood Federal was one of Florida's largest associations, with a solid reserve-to-savings ratio and one of the most respectable loan portfolios in the state.

A West Hollywood office was opened in 1958, soon to be followed by the Dania branch in 1960. By 1969 Hollywood Federal had opened its Davie branch, employed 110 people, and had more than $200 million in assets.

Under the leadership and direction

of James M. Blanz, who succeeded Weigle as president in 1972, the association committed itself in the mid-1970s to one of the most progressive consumer concepts in the industry: Electronic Funds Transfer System. In late 1974 it introduced statement savings and, in conjunction, it also introduced a telephone bill-paying service, the first of its kind in the nation.

Called the Plus Account, the new service allowed anyone to pay their bills automatically by telephone, eliminating checks, stamps, envelopes, and coupon stubs. In less than eight years the service would be paying more than 170,000 bills a month.

After introducing statement savings and telephone bill paying, Hollywood Federal pioneered self-service terminals, placed within supermarket chains.

By the early 1980s Hollywood Federal had 560 employees and more than $1.2 billion in assets, making it one of the biggest and most progressive associations in the state, an institution with its roots buried deep in Broward's past but with its sights set constantly on its future.

All Hollywood Federal offices are designed to provide customers with a relaxed and comfortable setting.

NOVA UNIVERSITY

The Mailman Hollywood Building, at the main entrance to the campus in Davie, houses the University's administrative offices, the Behavioral Sciences Center, the Learning Technology production studio, and the University's main computer center.

Nova University is Broward's university. It is the second largest independent institution of higher learning in Florida today. Nova continues to grow, to add programs of study, and to expand its services to the citizens of Broward County.

The University is accredited by the Southern Association of Colleges and Schools. The Center for the Study of Law is accredited by the American Bar Association, and the doctor of philosophy program in clinical psychology in the Behavioral Sciences Center is provisionally accredited by the American Psychological Association.

In 1961 the executive committee of the Broward County Board of Public Instruction was authorized to establish Nova University. In 1964 Nova University was chartered by the state of Florida, becoming the only member of the South Florida Education Center

that was a private, nonprofit, coeducational institution of higher learning.

Nova University, though located on land adjoining the central campus of Broward Community College, has quite a different history and purpose. Chartered in 1964 as Nova University of Advanced Technology, it was planned for graduate students. In 1966 a Physical Oceanography Center was launched with a two-year contract for

$350,000 from the Office of Naval Research and the National Science Foundation. The Broward County Commission deeded the University 10 acres of land at the Port Everglades inlet for the construction of permanent oceanographic facilities. Initial funding for these facilities was made by Charles and Hamilton Forman, who have carried on their parents' interest in civic and, especially, educational affairs.

Field offices were opened on Las Olas Boulevard in Fort Lauderdale in 1965. The Rosenthal Building was completed two years later and the first class of doctoral students entered Nova. The Parker Physical Sciences Center was opened in 1968 and the entire administrative operation moved to the 200-acre Davie campus west of Fort Lauderdale.

Though originally established as an institution for on-campus graduate study, in 1970 Nova joined in an educational federation with the New York Institute of Technology which offered undergraduate programs. The more recent outgrowth of this continuing affiliation is Nova College,

Students have the opportunity to participate in various roles in simulated cases under actual courtroom conditions in this classroom-courtroom in the Goodwin Law Center.

the undergraduate division of the University.

As the University approached the end of its second decade, it had 7,500 students in its on- and off-campus programs supported by a faculty and staff of 650.

In its first 20 years Nova pioneered many educational models and especially innovative ways to deliver programs. It has expanded from its 200-acre main campus to include three other locations in Broward: the Oceanographic Center, Nova University at Coral Springs in north Broward, and the Center for the Study of Law in downtown Fort Lauderdale. Consistent with its mission to provide education to students wherever they may be, the University also offers degree programs and continuing educational experiences throughout the state of Florida and in 20 other states.

Among its major successes as an innovator in higher education was its development of cluster programs for

Hamilton Forman (left) and Dr. Charles Forman (right), Fort Lauderdale philanthropists, with Nova University president Dr. Abraham Fischler at the dedication of the Forman Building at the Oceanographic Center.

professionals who prefer to study without interrupting their careers. This delivery system was first used by a single doctoral program in education. The practicality of the system brought about its adoption by many on- and off-campus programs.

Traditional programs include the J.D., for law students; the Ph.D. in clinical psychology; bachelor's programs for postsecondary students; and The University School, which

offers innovative alternatives in primary and secondary education to more than 1,300 children from preschool through grade 12. Nova's range and variety of programs make it a university for all ages.

A major event occurred in 1979 that greatly aided in the success of the Law Center and of the University. Nova received a $16-million gift from the estate of Leo Goodwin, Sr., the founder of GEICO insurance and an educational philanthropist. Part of that bequest permitted the University to acquire the downtown property that houses the Law Center.

In addition to its many academic, degree-granting programs, Nova University sponsors cultural events and programs for students, faculty, administration, and the public; an annual art show; a film series; breakfast and lunch forums featuring informative and entertaining, nationally known speakers; an author series; and a program of winter concerts by the Nova University Community Singers.

Nova University's Leo Goodwin, Sr., Law Center is in downtown Fort Lauderdale.

ACR ELECTRONICS, INC.

Letters. In a sense, the history of ACR is told in letters. Letters on the walls of its corporate waiting room, from the Smithsonian Institution thanking ACR for donating to its space exhibit, from astronauts Lovell, Haise, and Swigert of *Apollo 13* thanking ACR for its contribution, from scores of Broward County charitable organizations thanking ACR for its support.

And then there are the letters you can't see, letters from men and women whose lives have been saved by the rescue lights and beacons ACR has manufactured for more than 25 years. All letters that say, "thank you."

In the beginning, of course, there were no letters, only the mind and resolution of one man: David H. Rush. He began in his camera shop in Manhattan in 1953, a technologically gifted young man, given to tinkering with cameras. His tinkering extended to photographic lighting and resulted in the first use of dry-cell batteries for electronic flash units.

Before long he had designed for use by the National Aeronautic and Space Administration the first camera to take pictures from outer space. This camera is now in the Smithsonian Institution's National Air and Space Museum.

Rush began to solicit government agencies in the rescue and survival field. His approach was to "discover a need and then fill it." He initially found a life-saving need for downed pilots—a compact, high-intensity strobe rescue light.

Other new products followed. Rush created survival radio beacons that could broadcast distress signals for hours over distances exceeding 100 miles; he designed floating survival lights for frogmen trapped under water; he went to jungle school and visited the front in Vietnam to experience first hand the rescue and survival needs of the military; and he designed products to satisfy those needs.

In 1973 Rush moved ACR from its headquarters in Carle Place, Long Island, to Hollywood, Florida, bringing to Broward County one of the most significant rescue light, beacon, and marine electronic rescue and survival companies in the world. It presently is one of the larger employers in Broward County.

In less than a decade Rush became one of the community's most dedicated civic activists. He is a member of an impressively large number of major business, charitable, and cultural enterprises in Broward County. That is Rush's way of saying thanks to what Broward County has given him and ACR.

David H. Rush, president of ACR Electronics, Inc.

HOLY CROSS HOSPITAL

To many people it seemed a ridiculous idea at the time. A major hospital between Fort Lauderdale and Pompano Beach? Absurd. That was nowhere. A place between places. Nothing but pine forest.

But others felt differently back in 1950, the year the idea of Holy Cross Hospital was conceived. Those who did included some of the county's most important community leaders: R.H. Gore, former governor of Puerto Rico and owner of Broward's largest newspaper; James Camp, president of the Broward National Bank; and James Hunt, head of Coral Ridge Properties.

After two years of exploring possibilities, the group contacted Archbishop Joseph Hurley of the Diocese of St. Augustine, then Florida's southernmost diocese. Archbishop Hurley agreed, in 1952, to build and operate a 150-bed, $2.5-million hospital provided that the community could assume half the cost.

By December of that year $300,000 had been raised and 22.5 acres of land acquired between Fort Lauderdale and Pompano Beach. The site was desolate and, at the time, remote. Still, fund raising went on until, by April 1953, the community's economic goals were met. By November, ground was broken for a 100-bed adult medical and surgical hospital with additional floors "shelled in" for expansion.

On December 8, 1955, the first five patients were admitted. At the time the medical staff had 145 physicans and surgeons and a lay staff of 133 people, including the Sisters of St. Joseph assigned by the diocese to administer the hospital.

Since it opened more than 400,000 patients have been admitted, 31,000 babies born, more than one million patients treated in emergency, and two million seen as outpatients. The medical staff now has nearly 400 physicians and specialists and the lay staff has increased tenfold.

To be sure, such spectacular growth did not come without problems. By the late '50s Holy Cross wallowed in debt and had few patients and an unhappy medical staff. It was unclear if the new hospital had a future at all. The problems drew the attention of the new diocese of Miami's Archbishop Coleman F. Carroll. The Right Reverend Carroll turned to the Religious Sisters of Mercy in Pittsburgh, one of the world's most respected nursing orders, for help. In July 1959, 10 Sisters from Pittsburgh, headed by Sister M. Innocent Hughes, came to Fort Lauderdale.

Lack of patients, Sister Innocent soon discovered, was only one of the hospital's problems. The staff resented the change in leadership and, later, Sister Innocent's no-nonsense, tight-fisted, pay-as-you-go financial approach. It was only a matter of time, however, before the hospital's new fiscal policy began to show results and the staff responded to make the '60s a time of growth and prosperity for Holy Cross.

Holy Cross, now a 597-bed facility, is noted for its programs in surgical replacement of damaged joints, eye

Holy Cross Hospital, then a 100-bed facility, was nearing completion when this 1955 photo was taken. The stretch of undeveloped beach at the top is Galt Ocean Mile.

surgery, laboratory medicine, nuclear medicine, diagnostic radiology, cancer therapy, and open-heart surgery, and has become a referral center for Florida and Latin America. It also is noted for accomplishing the objective it set for itself when it opened in 1955: to provide the highest-quality care and to serve all who come there with kindness and mercy.

Holy Cross Hospital today is a 597-bed facility. Galt Ocean Mile, with its luxury residential high-rise buildings, is at the top.

HARDRIVES COMPANY

The smoke, the dirt, and the grayness of Pittsburgh finally got to Robert "Bob" Elmore, and in November 1946 he headed south to look over Florida for a new location for his modest driveway paving company. After graduating from Penn State University in 1941, Bob spent five years as a metallurgist with U.S. Steel and had resigned in June to start Hardrives Company with one small roller and one used dump truck.

The first month operating his own business was very difficult because it had rained incessantly, no jobs had been completed, and his bank account had shrunk to $16 on the fourth Friday—which was payday for his two employees. That Friday the rain stopped, the sun came out, and the asphalt surface was laid on Hardrives' first driveway. When the job was completed, the homeowner looked over the work, announced that it was the best-looking driveway he had ever seen, and paid in full on the spot.

"I could have kissed him," Elmore recalls, "but I didn't. . . . I went back twenty-five years later, and the driveway was still there and in good condition."

The November trip resulted in Elmore selecting Fort Lauderdale by a wide margin over other towns because "there were beautiful homes with beautiful lots and beautiful yachts, and they all had terrible driveways." On his third day in Fort Lauderdale, Elmore sold 17 paving jobs to potential customers on South Federal Highway from Road 84 to Las Olas Boulevard. He went back to Pittsburgh, picked up his equipment, brought it south, and his wife Gerry and their 10-month old daughter Chris flew down the next week. Thus began a career that would make Hardrives one of South Florida's most successful and best known road builders and engineering contractors, and Elmore one of the most respected businessmen and civic workers in the community.

Hardrives started with driveways and has expanded to highways, and the company's own quarry and rock-mining operation was followed later by fill pits and an asphalt plant.

In its 37 years of operation in Broward County, Hardrives has constructed many thousands of jobs with over 98 percent customer satisfaction. These contracts range from small sealcoat and patchwork to four sections of I-95 and many miles of quality paving on Road 84; U.S. 1; Pembroke and Davie roads; and Hillsboro, Atlantic, Commercial, Oakland Park, Sunrise, Broward, and Davie boulevards. There are also thousands of parking areas for large and small shopping centers, office and professional buildings, condominiums, parks, and recreational areas on the completed job list.

The firm's growth from two employees and two pieces of equipment to 235 employees and over 200 pieces of major equipment in Broward County has become one of

Robert Elmore, founder and chairman of the board of Hardrives Company.

the success stories of this thriving and vibrant area. In January 1982 Elmore became chairman of the board and Robert C. Platt, a civil engineering graduate of West Point in 1960, became president and chief executive officer. Platt promises to lead the respected Hardrives Company to even higher achievements.

A Hardrives Company crew working on a paving job is a familiar sight around the Fort Lauderdale area.

GULFSTREAM LAND & DEVELOPMENT CORP.

*Henry D. Epstein, founder of Gulfstream Land &
Development Corp.*

*Abraham "Abe" L. Mailman, founder of
Hollywood Bank and Trust (now Barnett Banks),
was part of the team that formed and
incorporated Gulfstream Land &
Development Corp.*

The founder of Gulfstream Land &
Development Corp. was Henry David
Epstein, a Philadelphia-born New
Yorker who was to have powerful
influence on the growth of Broward
County while remaining quietly in the
background.

When he died suddenly at age 59 in
July 1980 at Bennett Community
Hospital in Plantation, his extensive
obituary in *The New York Times*
revealed a man who, having started
with $2,000 in borrowed capital, was
known for purchasing whole
communities and towns.

According to the *Times*, "In 1948
(when he was 27 years old) he
acquired the town of Norris,
Tennessee, from the Tennessee Valley
Authority. Four years later he
purchased 5,400 single-family homes
in Levittown, Long Island, New York,
for $42 million. He converted them
from rentals to individually owned
homes and sold out the entire project."

Twenty years later he founded Gulfstream Land & Development Corp.
with land that is part of a 10,000-acre
tract originally owned by Fred C.
Peters, Sr., the Florida pioneer, farmer,
and landholder. Peters asked longtime
Miami resident Alex Youngerman, a

real estate broker, to sell the land for
him at $1,000 an acre. But Peters died
before that could be accomplished,
leaving 5,700 acres of unsold land in
Plantation.

There followed a period when the
land was in the hands of a Baltimore
syndicate. But Youngerman entered
the picture again as broker for the
property and was able to persuade
Epstein, a longtime client, that this was
the opportunity of a lifetime.

With the aid of John Cleary, an
attorney who had been with Mobil
Oil, and A.L. Mailman, a legendary
figure who founded Hollywood Bank
and Trust (now Barnett Banks),
Epstein formed a public company
called Gulfstream Land &
Development Corp. and began to sell
stock.

Together they raised $3 million
through private stock sales to friends
and acquaintances and bought back
the remaining Peters land.

Although the property was
considered remote and nearly
worthless at the time, Henry Epstein
had the vision and sophistication to
know he could create value by
building a fine golf course and clubhouse and surrounding it with first-
class homes. The formula was such a
success that the first 156 homes at
Jacaranda Country Club sold in six

months.

The company was underwritten in
1971. Its 310,000 shares of stock sold
out overnight and the stock soon split
two-for-one. In 1974 Gulfstream's
landholdings, including the site of the
Broward Mall, were annexed to the
City of Plantation.

Today Gulfstream continues to sell
improved land to builders as well as
develop residential communities such
as Parc Village, a successful multi-
family community on University
Drive just north of Broward
Boulevard. One of the last projects
Epstein worked on was the master
plan for a major commercial office
park which will soon become a reality.
His dedication and business expertise
were proven correct.

The company also has active
community developments in
Jacksonville, Orlando, and Sarasota, as
well as two major construction
companies—Robert L. Turchin, Inc., in
Dade County and Current Builders in
Broward County. In central Florida,
Gulfstream has a major single-family
home building subsidiary called Bel-
Aire Homes.

167

LAGO MAR

It was quite a way to spend a vacation. Here it was 2 a.m., August 28, 1964, in a premier oceanfront hotel in Fort Lauderdale and all the guests were gathered in the lounge, shoring up doors, sealing windows, and settling in for a long, harrowing night.

Outside the 140-mile-an-hour winds of Hurricane Cleo fulminated against the Lago Mar Hotel, tearing out vegetation and filling the hotel's two swimming pools with tons of sand and debris. Inside, the Sidney Banks family, owners and operators of Lago Mar for five years, had to be wondering if they had done the right thing.

Their decision to move from Virginia Beach, Virginia, to Fort Lauderdale had been a traumatic one. Banks, a Virginia hotelier and entrepreneur, owned and operated two of that state's finest properties, The Cavalier in Virginia Beach and The Jefferson in Richmond. A move to Fort Lauderdale and the relatively untested Lago Mar Hotel was a huge business risk.

On the other hand, Banks, his wife Florence, and teenage son Walter had been vacationing in Fort Lauderdale each year for nearly 15 years. They loved the city and Banks thought that the Lago Mar Hotel, a sprawling, 11-acre, 110-room complex on 600 feet of oceanfront in a posh residential neighborhood, had excellent possibilities. So, in 1959, he bought Lago Mar and the family left Virginia forever.

Constructed in 1952, Lago Mar was two buildings separated by a common recreation area. When the Banks moved in they built a 32-room addition with meeting rooms and banquet accommodations that joined the original facilities. From the beginning, Banks was determined to market Lago Mar as a quality resort hotel for affluent families and corporations, to keep a well-trained staff, and to hope for return business and referrals. It turned out to be a remarkably successful formula.

In 1959 they began the Lago Mar Beach Club with 29 members. Today that club's membership is at its maximum and most of those who become members have done so because they once were hotel guests. Indeed, 10 years after opening the club, the family built Lago Mar Place, a cooperative apartment complex adjacent to the hotel property. Most of those buyers had been hotel guests. Today Walter Banks, now president of the hotel, says that his family's legacy to the community is the families and current property owners who first saw Fort Lauderdale by way of Lago Mar.

In 1967 Banks began construction of 12 suites at Lago Mar because he sensed an untapped demand in consumers for more than just quality hotel accommodations. The idea was so successful that today the hotel has 77 apartment-size suites for guests.

Over the years Lago Mar grew to be more than a hotel—it became something of a local institution. In 1968 the Banks began building Lago Mar Country Club, a golf course and residential property in west Broward County. In 1980 they sold it to the membership.

In 1983 the Banks still reigned over one of the county's unique resort hotels, convinced that, Hurricane Cleo or no, leaving Virginia for the beaches of Fort Lauderdale was a wise decision after all.

Lago Mar is one of Fort Lauderdale's oldest and finest resort hotels.

JUNGLE QUEEN

For Earl Faber the *Jungle Queen* was a new wrinkle for his act and, it turned out, would make him a star long after he stopped performing.

Before the Depression, Faber and his wife Margie had been a top-draw vaudeville act. He was a singer, dancer, and comic whose best friends included Jack Benny and Milton Berle and whose act was known throughout the industry. But the Depression, and the responsibilities of three children, ended his stage career and the family moved to Long Island where Faber began a successful insurance business.

Years later, while vacationing in Fort Lauderdale, Faber happened to see the *Jungle Queen*, a small tourist boat owned by a man named Al Starts who had founded the business in 1945. The boat plied Fort Lauderdale's New River several times a day with fewer than 100 passengers and limited entertainment.

To Faber the idea of owning the *Jungle Queen* seemed perfect. First, it was a magnificent way for visitors and tourists to see the city. They did not, after all, call Fort Lauderdale the "Venice of America" for nothing.

Since 1945 the Jungle Queen *has made countless trips down Fort Lauderdale's New River, and has become a local institution.*

Meandering along the winding New River, past the magnificent waterfront homes, beneath quaint drawbridges, near huge marinas with yachts of incredible opulence, the *Jungle Queen* showed off Fort Lauderdale as no other vehicle could.

Second, it provided him, once again, with a stage. So, in 1958 Faber bought the *Jungle Queen*. At the time it was a tiny business. He put on a vaudeville show of his own, greeting passengers personally as they came on board, telling jokes, doing song and dance routines. The enterprise grew nicely during the first years and the *Jungle Queen* rapidly became not just an attraction for tourists but a local institution.

In 1962, however, Earl Faber died and it was not until two years later that his son Jerry left the advertising field in New York and came to Fort Lauderdale. Jerry Faber began a promotion and marketing program that drew visitors to the *Jungle Queen* not only from around America, but from around the world. The company's growth accelerated.

He commissioned the building of another boat, a double-decked steel vessel that would hold 550 passengers. People suggested he was moving too far, too fast, with the *Jungle Queen* but

he persevered. Together the boats made three trips a day, including the evening dinner cruise, and the business grew from a relatively small family operation into a multimillion-dollar, international tourist attraction entertaining hundreds of thousands of people each year.

For its millions of passengers, its 200 employees, the city of Fort Lauderdale, and the Faber family, the *Jungle Queen* has been just what Earl Faber had always wanted it to be: a very hard act to follow.

From a small family-owned venture, the Jungle Queen *has become an international attraction.*

Earl and Margie Faber were a top vaudeville act before the Depression. Owning the Jungle Queen *put Earl back on stage.*

NOVATRONICS, INC.

Part of the original Novatronics team (left to right): Becky Hall, A.J.W. Novak, and his father A.J. Novak.

There were few moments of self-doubt among the risk takers who founded Pompano Beach's Novatronics, Inc. But among those few, surely, was the corporate necessity to help chase rattlesnakes out of the ladies' washrooms during the company's early days.

That was an unlikely activity indeed for the firm's founder, Albert John Wittmayer Novak, a tall, courtly, Harvard-educated physicist who possessed a gift for technological wizardry and the nerve of a riverboat gambler.

Novak came to Broward County in 1962 from Timonium, Maryland, as general manager of the electronics division of the Hoover Company. Along with 10 other employees, he set up shop in a warehouse in the swamp west of Pompano Beach. There they began to make telemetry equipment for the burgeoning space industry and, during the rainy season when water surrounded the plant, it was there they spent mornings shooing rattlers from the ladies' room.

During the summer of 1964, after a dispute with Hoover over management priorities at the Pompano plant, Novak broke with the parent company. With borrowed money, the help of his father (who became the first corporate treasurer), and the pledges of fealty from fellow Hooverites Don Dodd, Becky Hall, and Joseph A. Cianciarulo, he bought the division and began operations as an independent electronics manufacturing firm, one of Broward's first. It was a small group, but ambitious and, as Novak would agree years later, one with "more guts than sense in those early years."

They prowled the country searching for clients, sometimes finding jobs larger than they could handle. They took them anyway. A midwestern customer gave them a contract so big that Novak had to borrow money to complete it. The amount he borrowed exceeded Novatronics' net worth. The lender was the customer. "The strange thing about that incident was that we paid them back and finally made a profit on the contract," Novak recalls.

In 1965 Novak merged his organization with Spectran Electronics Corporation of Maynard, Massachusetts, and began to increase production of military electronic systems. It was one of many calculated risks Novak would take over the company's history.

Novatronics acquired a Canadian firm in 1969 to increase its component-manufacturing capability. Novatronics of Canada Ltd., since has become a leading supplier of digital indicators for commercial and military markets and has developed a line of circuitry for microcomputers. In 1976 it created Novatronics East, Inc., of Dover, New Hampshire, to market the Canadian plant's products. In 1980 Novak bought William L. Rose & Associates and its subsidiary, Precision Electronics and Instrument, in Delray Beach, Florida, and formed Novatronics Group, the parent organization for the growing firm.

The company's growth was spectacular, increasing nearly 30 percent a year until what had begun as a $500,000-a-year entrepreneurial experiment had matured into a $15-million operation that is one of the oldest electronic manufacturing firms in Broward County.

Before and after at Novatronics. The plant site in the mid-1960s was surrounded by nothing but swamp directly west of Pompano Beach. (Inset) The Novatronics facility today.

FPA CORPORATION

The World of Palm-Aire, a half-billion-dollar residential/resort development in Pompano Beach, is the flagship community of FPA Corporation.

FPA Corporation has helped shape the framework of Broward County. Its primary business involves the acquisition of land and the subsequent design, development, and construction of planned residential communities.

The World of Palm-Aire, a half-billion-dollar residential/resort development in Pompano Beach, is the flagship community of FPA. It is vast in dimension with five golf courses, 37 tennis courts, two clubhouses, restaurants, a beach club, and a world-famous spa coupled with an elaborate hotel and conference center.

In 1965 Philadelphia developers Marvin Orleans and Alfred P. Orleans, his father, bought controlling interest in the Florida Palm-Aire Corporation. The initial acquisition consisted of a resort facility with a 50-room motel, an 18-hole golf course and clubhouse situated on 137 acres, plus the 300 acres adjacent to the club. Florida Palm-Aire changed its name to FPA Corporation in 1969, at which time public issues of stock were offered over the American Stock Exchange.

With the goal of creating the ultimate in leisure living, a master plan was developed and additional land acquisitions were made, totaling 2,500 acres. The World of Palm-Aire was developed on 1,500 of those acres. The largest parcel, 1,700 acres, was purchased from McArthur Dairies in 1969. Two other important additions were also purchased that year. Some 113 acres were bought from Claude Lanier and another parcel of 165 acres was acquired from land holdings of Mississippi State University. Some of the remaining 1,000 acres were sold to other developers; 600 acres were developed into FPA's Palm-Aire Village and 260 acres were sold to Broward County for a park.

The first products introduced at The World of Palm-Aire were condominium homes in apartment buildings. Townhomes and villas were added a short time thereafter and eventually some single-family homes rounded out the product mix. Construction was performed by FPA's own subsidiary, Orleans Construction Company of Florida.

The world-famous spa was added to the community in 1971. It combined the best in fitness training, diet, and luxurious personal treatments, and established a reputation as one of the finest health resorts in the world. To accommodate its guests, a multi-million-dollar hotel complex was built adjacent to the spa.

By 1973 The World of Palm-Aire attained the highest sales volume ever recorded by a single condominium developer in the county. Residents of Palm-Aire were attracted by the diversity of the amenities offered and the beauty of the condominium homes which were picturesquely set along golf course fairways.

FPA acquired other undeveloped land on which to build its life-style communities. In addition to The World of Palm-Aire, other developments bear FPA's distinctive mark of quality housing in a leisure setting.

By 1983 FPA Corporation had delivered nearly 10,000 housing units in Florida, Pennsylvania, and New Jersey, with two-thirds of those residences lying within Broward County's borders.

The initial acquisition of FPA Corporation consisted of a 50-room motel, an 18-hole golf course and clubhouse on 137 acres, plus 300 acres adjacent to the club.

CORAL RIDGE PROPERTIES, INC.

The history of Fort Lauderdale since 1946 could not be written without frequent references to the contributions of Coral Ridge Properties, Inc., and its principals in its growth and development. The company's internationally known developments of Galt Ocean Mile and Coral Ridge consistently contribute one-third of the assessed valuation of the entire city. Coral Ridge Properties' luxurious new development of Port Royale comprises 42 acres on the Intracoastal Waterway, which the firm currently is developing as an exclusive, high-rise apartment community.

Coral Ridge Properties became a wholly owned subsidiary of Westinghouse Electric Corporation in 1966 and continues as the cornerstone of Westinghouse Communities, Inc., with H.J. Frazier as president of that corporation and as chairman of the board of Coral Ridge Properties, and with Werner Buntemeyer as president of Coral Ridge Properties. Coral Ridge

Properties has been profitable every consecutive year since its founding.

Moving aggressively into the '80s, the company is concentrating on the continued planned development of the city of Coral Springs which was incorporated in 1963. The formative years of the '70s saw the successfully phased residential, commercial, and business development and concomitant social, civic, and recreational amenities established and enhanced.

In 1983 Coral Springs welcomed its 50,000th resident, representing approximately one-third of its planned size. An elected city mayor and commission are leading Coral Springs from its adolescence into its maturing status with business expertise and dignity, aided by a highly competent administrative staff. The city's 10 new Broward County public schools and 5 private schools are acknowledged among the finest in the state.

Special attention currently is being given to the development of the almost-mile-square area of Eagle Trace. This sophisticated and exclusive private community is being developed in conjunction with the Eagle Trace

tournament golf course, recently purchased by the PGA TOUR. Eagle Trace will be the scene of the Honda Classic in 1984.

The completion of Coral Square, the largest regional mall in Broward County, with its surrounding commercial and business potential; the new 200-bed hospital in the center of Coral Springs; the further development of the city's Park of Industry; the regional parks; and other exciting developments will mark the '80s as a keystone decade for what is destined to become one of Broward's foremost cities.

Westinghouse Communities, Inc., is progressing profitably: Pelican Bay at Naples, Florida, with three miles on the Gulf of Mexico; the new Westinghouse Gateway community near Fort Myers, Florida; Spring Lake; Miles Grant at Stuart, Florida; and Half Moon Bay Properties, 8,200 acres, south of San Francisco. H.J. Frazier has also revealed other substantial proposed acquisitions of acreage in Broward and Palm Beach counties.

The headquarters of Westinghouse Communities, Inc., of which Coral Ridge Properties is a wholly owned subsidiary, is located in the Coral Springs Financial Plaza Building.

H.J. Frazier, president of Westinghouse Communities, Inc.

MODCOMP: MODULAR COMPUTER SYSTEMS, INC.

There is something magical about the beginnings of companies and always something wistful in how those who helped nurture it through its first years reflect on the "early days."

That is certainly the case with Modular Computer Systems, Inc., a firm specializing in real-time computer systems. It grew, in less than 15 years, into one of the world's major computer manufacturers with offices throughout the world.

But in the early days, it was simply eight founders and 12 employees who came to the small Broward city of Wilton Manors with some ideas, some ideals, and a lot of energy. Their first plant was a converted drugstore near the town's main intersection, and the immediate concerns of management and labor were not public stock offerings, major marketing decisions, international banking deals, and controlling a space shuttle. That came later.

Their immediate concerns were if they could do low-temperature equipment testing in a borrowed, grocery store meat locker (Answer: yes), and if they could knock a hole in the wall to expand production space without dust ruining all the test equipment? (Answer: yes; just give a cofounder a scuba suit, air tank, mask, and cement saw, seal him between the walls with heavy plastic tape, and have him cut his way to freedom).

It was an innovative and exciting place to work with a management willing to take risks. Perhaps its most crucial computer was the first, the MODCOMP III, built around an experimental computer chip. Its success ensured the success of the company, but even more, it reinforced a corporate determination to listen closely to its customers and be ready to respond to their needs.

That philosophy helped the firm double its revenues each year for the first five years, until it had grown from 20 employees to 500 and, in 1972,

moved into a new plant west of Pompano Beach.

By 1980 MODCOMP was listed on the New York Stock Exchange and had become one of the best-known names in the computer industry with systems on five continents, 1,200 employees, and more than $92 million in revenue.

It maintained that status by excelling in the markets in which it competed: industrial, scientific, space exploration (in 1983 MODCOMP computers monitored every phase of the *Columbia* space shuttle launch), telecommunications, laboratory automation, defense, and more.

MODCOMP also remained in touch with its tradition, showing its willingness to diversify, to take risks, to serve the market's needs. In 1983 it acquired, for example, Telcon Industries, manufacturer of Zorba, a personal computer system. For MODCOMP it was a totally new

From NASA's space shuttle launch control to the Pioneer, Viking, and Helios Jet Propulsion laboratory space missions, MODCOMP's computer systems make the difference in performance, reliability, and value. Photo courtesy of NASA.

From its inception in the 1970s, MODCOMP has been dedicated to the design, development, and support of real-time computer systems. These MODCOMP pioneers were among the employees who built and marketed the company's first computer, MODCOMP III.

market. It also completed its range with Classic II/15 and 32/85, machines that are models for the industry.

As it had since its inception in a tiny drugstore in Wilton Manors, MODCOMP continued to lead the way into the last half of the 20th century. The days of meat locker tests and scuba suits were only lovely recollections, but the company's vitality, innovation, and responsiveness would never be a memory.

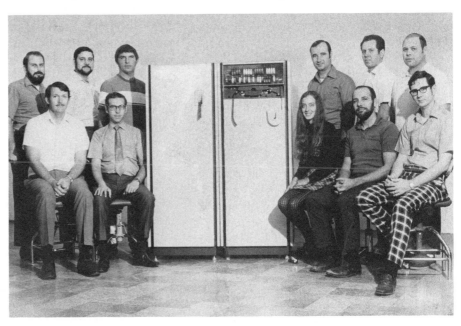

LABONTE DIVERSIFIED HOLDINGS, INC.

LaBonte Diversified Holdings, Inc. (LDH), is a growing, dynamic, private holding company, specializing in land development, manufacturing industries, and selected supporting services. This vigorous, growth-oriented organization, headquartered in Fort Lauderdale, is deeply responsive to its customers, markets, suppliers, and the general public.

With more than 30 years of outstanding performance in real estate, manufacturing, and service industries, LDH has created a tradition of excellence and corporate achievement in a variety of markets.

Jack LaBonte, chairman of LDH, was the guiding influence in the development of homes for 20,000 residents. In Florida, LaBonte has established his status as a quality real estate developer and LDH, directed by president Jim LaBonte, was founded to coordinate the firm's vast real estate and land development projects.

Early Florida projects, among them communities such as Hollybrook, condominiums like the Sea Monarch and Ocean Monarch, and the Pinecrest apartments, confirmed the reputation that the LaBonte name meant quality in every detail.

Reflecting the company's commitment to excellence is the prestigious Sanctuary and luxurious Boca Grove Plantation. The Sanctuary is an exclusive single-family waterfront development in Boca Raton where homes range in price from $600,000 to $5 million, and Boca Grove Plantation is Boca Raton's most elegant country club community with homes priced up to $2 million.

The Sanctuary Realty Division, which handles marketing for all LaBonte projects as well as the projects of other developers, had a sales volume of nearly $100 million in 1983.

In conjunction with the tremendous growth of commercial land development in Florida, LDH has

Boca Grove Plantation, Boca Raton's most prestigious country club community.

expanded in the commercial real estate area and developed over 250,000 square feet of prime commercial office space during 1983. LaBonte Diversified Holdings is dedicated to the future for the continued development of superior, high-grade office facilities in Florida.

In addition to its development division, there is also LDM, and its primary division, LaBonte Precision, Inc., a high-technology manufacturing firm serving the aerospace and medical industries. Major machining and fabrication contracts for the firm have included high-technology gas turbine engine parts for the General Electric Company and United Technologies (Pratt Whitney), precision parts for the C.A.T. Scanner for the Medical

The luxurious Sea Monarch is one of LDH's early Florida projects.

Systems Division of General Electric, machine parts for Teledyne Ryan, and parts for Avco Lycoming.

As the holding company and its subsidiaries grew, Jack LaBonte's four sons and son-in-law assumed increasing responsibilities in the business. Family members also played active roles in the community and cultural affairs of Broward County. The LaBonte family is a major contributor to the arts, and to civic and social services. They have offered their talents and support to the Florida Chamber Orchestra Association, Fort Lauderdale Symphony, American Symphony Orchestra League, the Oral School for the Deaf, and the Broward Civic Center.

CAUSEWAY LUMBER COMPANY

If there is a single entity in Broward County that can be called representative of the area's billion-dollar construction company, it is the collection of yards, sheds, and structures on South Andrews Avenue in Fort Lauderdale that make up the Causeway Lumber Company.

The vast complex is the focus of a $50-million annual trade in building materials carried on by more than 300 employees.

Gene A. Whiddon, son of the company's founder and now president, sees both Causeway and Florida standing on the brink of a new threshold of economic development.

The Causeway Lumber Company in Fort Lauderdale is the heartbeat of the construction economy in its region. It is, to a considerable extent, the heartbeat of the civic and cultural

community as well. Because of the involvement of Gene Whiddon and his wife, Angelyn, in such activities as the First Baptist Church, Broward Community College, the Fort Lauderdale Historical Society, the Opera Guild, the United Way, the Museum of Art, the Chamber of Commerce, the Freedoms Foundation of Valley Forge, and countless charities, many decisions affecting the quality of life in the community are quietly made in his office.

Few movements of any consequence are launched without at least some input from the Whiddon circle; his influence reaches statewide proportions through his association with governors and Florida's highest ranking executives, his membership on the Florida Council of 100, and the Southeast Florida Coordinating Council. As a board member of the Freedoms Foundation Whiddon meets with generals, admirals, congressmen, and captains of industry at the Fortune 500 level, not infrequently at the White House. Civic awards and service plaques literally cover the walls of his offices, sharing space with a variety of reproductions of the American flag as a symbol of his continually demonstrated dedication to free enterprise and fundamental

American traditions.

It is, however, his real loves—the company and lumber—that bring Whiddon to the office every morning before daylight and keeps him there many an evening past dinner. He runs the operation with a small executive staff that includes his sons, Scott and Gene Jr., and his nephew, Joel Ashe.

The stature of the enterprise is such that Citicorp, the New York-based financial giant, produced a booklet about it in 1980, saying Causeway at that point was "experiencing the highest profit level in its history," with a high market share that was attributed to "quality and quick service, not price."

Inherently, Causeway Lumber Company has been built upon the population growth and economic expansion of South Florida and the rest of the state, and its future is keyed to confidence in decades of future development. But service to causes is woven deeply into the corporate charter along with faith in free enterprise and the traditions of the nation's founding fathers.

Gene A. Whiddon (left), president of Causeway Lumber Company, and his son, Scott.

O.R. Whiddon, founder of Causeway Lumber Company, with the firm's first lumber truck, circa 1939.

BROWARD FEDERAL SAVINGS AND LOAN ASSOCIATION

It was March 31, 1978, and Ira Carlton Hatch, Jr., attorney-at-law from Broward County, Florida, was on a death watch at the Federal Home Loan Bank Board in Washington, D.C.

The application for Broward Federal Savings and Loan, a venture Hatch had helped to form and finance, was up for review. Its chances did not look good.

Already the board's regional office in Atlanta had recommended denial of Broward Federal's application for charter. Hatch had no clue why Atlanta had denied it. Surely, he thought as he sat in the gallery waiting for the national board to vote on his future, West Broward *needed* a savings and loan. None existed in the west part of the county and the last savings and loan to receive a charter in Broward County did so in 1966. Since then the population in Broward had exploded, making it the fastest growing area in America. Most of that growth had occurred in Broward's western reaches.

These circumstances had made Broward Federal's application seem like a good bet to Hatch. And so, in 1976, he took the idea to three of his

Broward Federal Savings and Loan Association, 3000 North University Drive, Sunrise.

friends: realtor and former County Commissioner Hugh Anderson, Mrs. Angelique Stahl, who would later serve at the United Nations under President Jimmy Carter, and attorney/ businessman Ross Beckerman. The original four were joined later by furniture magnate Allan Baer, attorney W. George Allen, contractor Ronald Bergeron, and architect Emanuel Abraben.

Hatch and friends plunged ahead, hired an economic consultant to prepare the charter application, and, by August 1977, were involved in oral hearings before the Federal Home Loan Bank Board office in Atlanta.

Predictably, competing local institutions challenged the application. Atlantic Federal Savings and Loan argued against Broward Federal at the Atlanta hearings. Nevertheless, Hatch felt confident that Broward Federal would be granted its wish.

The blow fell in October 1977, when the Atlanta review board denied the request and sent it to Washington with a recommendation it be denied there as well. Hatch flew to Washington on March 31, 1978. He was prepared for the worst.

The Broward Federal petition, entitled *Ira Hatch, Jr.,* et al, was fourth on the agenda. When the two-man national board unexpectedly approved it, Hatch "felt my heart jump into my throat. I went into shock."

Broward Federal opened for business November 6, 1978, with $2 million in deposits and a trailer for an office. Mrs. Stahl served as chairman of the board and then, in 1982, became chief operating officer. Her marketing concept of drawing customers to the bank through "community rooms," paid for by Broward Federal and made available for activities of community groups without charge, had proven immensely successful.

Within five years Broward Federal had more than $300 million in assets, annual after-tax profits of $6 million, and new branches in Deerfield Beach, Lauderhill, Tamarac, and Pembroke Pines. The institution also had a new central headquarters building at 3000 North University Drive.

After less than seven years, the plot that Ira Hatch concocted that day in 1976 seemed complete, secure, and successful beyond even his expectations. And its place as the first savings and loan in west Broward County seemed assured.

Broward Federal Savings and Loan Association, with its community rooms available for civic activities without charge and such conveniences as drive-in facilities, is a customer-oriented facility.

DANIA JAI ALAI

In 1953 a flamboyant, former circus owner named Roy McAndrews built the original Dania Jai Alai Palace just east of Federal Highway between Fort Lauderdale and Hollywood.

The sport was as unique as the location. Dania was Broward County's oldest city—one of its most colorful. Jai alai was one of the world's oldest sports, invented by Spanish Basques, but in 1953 it was, in America, something of a cultural oddity.

Over the next decades, however, Dania Jai Alai (jai alai is Basque for "Merry Festival") would attract athletes and celebrities by the score to the Gold Coast and make the game one of the great entertainment media in Broward County.

It was called the fastest ball game in the world (*Ripley's Believe It Or Not* clocked the "pelota" at over 180 m.p.h.) and its excitement and business potential attracted new ownership in 1970. The group was led by Steve Snyder, a former world-class sprinter at Yale University and sports enthusiast, and not long after they

purchased the company they began its major expansion phase.

Dania Jai Alai became the first jai alai company to introduce matinee performances. Believing that a great sport deserved a great arena, Snyder's group renovated and expanded the fronton several times in the '70s, until it was more than double its original size, had a luxurious new clubhouse and restaurant, and boasted a two-level bar overlooking the court.

They formed a new company named Carrousel Concessions to manage all of the food and beverage operations previously done by an independent food service company. Additionally, they established a minor league jai alai training facility in Spain where the game is the Basques' national sport.

In Florida, however, statutes limited the season to four and one-half months. So, in an effort to extend its operating time, the company formed Dania Jai Alai of Connecticut and, in 1977, opened Milford Jai Alai in Milford, Connecticut. The new fronton

won several architectural awards, but it also allowed the firm to operate from December to April in Florida and from May to November in Connecticut. By so doing it created year-round revenues, jobs, and a singular, gypsy-like caravan between the two states as players and equipment traveled back and forth.

Three years later the company won a state license for a summer jai alai season at Dania and, by 1983, it had sold the Connecticut operation so that it could concentrate its efforts where they began.

By the end of its first 30 years, Dania Jai Alai had become an international landmark. It had tradition, tough competition, superb athletes, and provided not only thrilling entertainment for the tourists and residents of Broward County but more than 500 jobs and millions of dollars in annual tax revenues.

One of the great entertainments in Broward County is Dania Jai Alai, located in Dania.

GOULD INC., S.E.L. COMPUTER SYSTEMS DIVISION

The year was 1961 and for nine young engineers with bright new ideas, the notion of staying at Radiation, Inc., an electronics firm in Melbourne, Florida, just didn't compute.

So they joined together and left Radiation, Inc., with hope and some ideas of how to design and create "specialized electronic digital data-acquisition and -processing systems." They took that idea to a small manufacturing plant at 4066 Northeast Fifth Avenue in Fort Lauderdale.

They began their specialized trade in 1961 with William W. Dodgson as president and chairman of the board, a position that would change hands many times. With Dodgson were J.P. Knight, A.G. Randolph, Thomas J. Sullivan, and John T. Jackson on the board of directors. They called the venture Systems Engineering Laboratories, Inc., or S.E.L. Their goal was to produce custom-designed data-acquisition systems for defense, space exploration, and industrial uses and after less than a year in Fort Lauderdale it appeared S.E.L. would succeed beyond anyone's imagination.

By the mid-1960s S.E.L. had begun to manufacture the first high-speed minicomputers in Florida. Called the 800 Series, they were designed for engineering, scientific, and industrial uses, or what is now known as the "real-time" market. S.E.L. sold its first computer to Alcoa Aluminum in 1965, the same year it moved into a new, 50,000-square-foot plant at what was then the end of Sunrise Boulevard in Plantation.

Also in the mid-1960s, S.E.L. was undergoing management philosophy changes. A.G. Randolph had taken over as president and chairman of the board and, with the success of the 800 Series, S.E.L. began an assault on the digital computer market and began to de-emphasize its custom operations. By the time it was seven years old S.E.L. had become Broward County's fourth-largest industrial firm, had

A.G. Randolph (right) proudly watches the ticker tape on June 20, 1968, the first day of trading S.E.L.'s stock on the American Stock Exchange.

sales and service in 22 cities in America, Canada, Europe, and Japan, and was making dramatic inroads into minicomputer markets.

After three years in office, Randolph, one of the founders, had taken the company from 362 employees and $5.2 million a year in business to more than 800 employees and $17 million. Yet, as the organization matured into a minicomputer company rather than specialized computer services, Randolph expressed a need to step

down as president. "I think a person more experienced in the computer business could move the company faster than I," he said. And so, in 1969 at the age of 38, Randolph retired.

He was succeeded by Sheldon Eglash, who embarked almost immediately on an aggressive expansion campaign. S.E.L. already had acquired 47 acres of land near the Fort Lauderdale Executive Airport, anticipating future growth. Eglash began to acquire subsidiaries around the country.

Then the economy turned and Eglash and S.E.L., whose acquisitions would have made good management sense in a strong economy, suddenly found themselves in a desperate cash-flow bind. Eglash resigned and C. Edwin Griffin took over. He immediately instituted an austerity program that meant trimming the work force, cutting development

This aerial view, taken in early 1983, shows the sprawling 36-acre Plantation campus. The headquarters building (lower left) dates back to 1965 when it was at the end of Sunrise Boulevard, a two-lane road.

programs, cancelling some planned programs, and trying to divest the firm of its unprofitable businesses.

It was a dark and uncertain time. By the end of 1971 S.E.L. had gone from 1,200 employees to 525 and from a profit to losses exceeding $12 million. But Griffin's program began to take hold. S.E.L. sold the land near the airport to relieve some pressure on the company's cash flow. In 1972 S.E.L. had stabilized, realized a small profit, and the worst was over; but the competition was moving ahead.

At his own request, Griffin resigned the presidency in October 1973 but stayed on as executive vice-president. The board of directors then summoned A.G. Randolph back to restore S.E.L. to health. With no new products in development, and a big debt, Randolph had his work cut out for him. First, he arranged for new financing by showing the banks progress each and every quarter. It was also a time when all employees would meet each quarter on the manufacturing floor to measure the progress, and to set new goals for the

Governor Robert Graham, posing with employees, visited Gould's Plantation facilities in May 1982 to sign a piece of legislation into law that would exempt development projects from Florida's sales tax.

next quarter. With financial backing, Randolph then turned his attention to new-product development.

In almost complete secrecy, a new family of state-of-the-art 32-bit computers were developed with the help of a California consultant. The result of this gamble was the S.E.L. 32/55, the industry's first true 32-bit super minicomputer. Announced in January 1975, the 32/55 was an immediate success. Being there with the right product at the right time was important; but good fortune also played a part. Xerox, one of S.E.L.'s biggest competitors, got out of the business and opened up opportunities for the new 32/55. The company had

truly turned around.

Between 1976 and 1980 S.E.L. grew steadily from $20 million per year to over $79 million. The company was profitable, and its stock on the American Stock Exchange reflected what was happening. This captured the attention of one of America's most respected firms, Gould Inc., of Rolling Meadows, Illinois.

The decision to merge S.E.L. with Gould, a $2-billion business with operations around the world, would "open up new markets for our products and new career opportunities for our people," Randolph told the press. And so, in December 1980, Gould acquired S.E.L. and in March 1981, once again , A.G. Randolph retired.

C.S. James who had been S.E.L.'s chief financial officer, replaced Randolph as president, and with the additional resources provided by Gould proceeded on an aggressive expansion program.

The product lines from Gould's Computer Systems Division grew to include the CONCEPT 32/8780—the world's fastest super minicomputer. Markets expanded by the introduction of engineering work stations. Manufacturing operations expanded to include facilities in Melbourne, Florida; Puerto Rico; and Ireland.

By the end of 1982 James could brag that the Fort Lauderdale division, the child of the original S.E.L., had sold over $170 million in minicomputers to customers around the world. These systems helped to put the Space Shuttle in orbit, to control the world's first large Tokamak Fusion Test Reactor at Princeton's Plasma Physics Laboratory, and to find new oil and gas deposits.

These achievements were noteworthy; but James was most proud of the fact that in his first two years he led one of the fastest-growing companies in the minicomputer industry.

In October 1980 W.T. Ylvisaker (center), chairman, and David Simpson (right), president, both of Gould Inc., met with C.S. James (left), then secretary/treasurer of S.E.L., to discuss the pending merger of the two corporations.

MAYHUE'S

In 1938, 19-year-old C
opened a grocery store on the corner of
Northwest Fourth Street and
11th Avenue in Fort Lauderdale, thus
beginning what would become one of
the city's most colorful and, it
sometimes seemed, most improbable
success stories.

Mayhue knew nothing of the
grocery business, yet when the old
Chancey grocery store went up for
sale, he borrowed $1,500 from a bank,
and bought the property. He arranged
with suppliers to stock his store,
promising to pay his lenders back at
one dollar a week each, until the debt
was retired.

*The original Mayhue's, located at Northeast
Fourth Street and U.S. 1, was the first "Super
Liquor Store" in Florida.*

For two years, business grew until
its value was more than $10,000 and
Mayhue's future seemed assured.
Then fate, in the garb of the federal
government, arrived on his doorstep.
Mayhue's property was condemned to
make room for a low-income housing
project. They paid him $3,000 and
dispossessed him.

Angry, somewhat bitter, but still
determined, Mayhue spent $2,500 of
the money the government had paid
him for another piece of property at
Northeast Fourth Street and U.S. 1 in
Fort Lauderdale. He built a new store
with his own hands and opened his
second grocery store. Two years later,
he was drafted to serve in World
War II.

While he was in the service, his wife
Fern ran the store. When he returned
he decided to add a small liquor store
adjacent to the grocery operation, by
converting one of the bedrooms of his
apartment. There was only one other
liquor store in town, and that belonged
to the father of his brother-in-law.

The liquor store flourished and sales
grew so rapidly that Mayhue decided
to abandon the grocery part of his
operation completely in 1949. He filled

the former grocery shelves with every
conceivable distilled product and
created the first "Super Liquor Store"
in the nation.

Liquor prices were fair-traded. Still
he offered liquor at cut-rate prices. His
was the first retail liquor store to
advertise cut-rate liquor in newspapers
in the state of Florida. Advertising
liquor was not acceptable to the
distillers. They sued Mayhue under
the Fair Trade law. Mayhue won.

What was popular with customers
was not popular with a growing list of
competitors. In the early '60s a group
of retailers pressured wholesalers to
boycott Mayhue's operation. For 30
days, at one point, only one wholesaler
would sell to Mayhue's.

Then Mayhue appealed to the U.S.
Justice Department. The federal
government came to his aid. Mayhue
won his right to advertise and sell
discounted liquor.

During the next 20 years his "Super
Liquor Store" grew from the one store
on U.S. 1 to the largest locally owned
company of its kind, with nine stores
located in most major cities in Broward
and Palm Beach counties.

*Carl L. Mayhue, owner and founder of the liquor
stores that bear his name.*

MAI KAI

It is not careers most high school and college students are hunting when they stalk the beaches of Fort Lauderdale during spring vacation time. And, in truth, finding a place to settle down for the rest of his life was not precisely what was on young Bob Thornton's mind when, in 1948, he first browned himself on the city's sands.

Thornton was from Chicago and just a high school senior. But the two weeks he spent vacationing in Fort Lauderdale left an indelible impression. Though young, he was perceptive enough to realize that there was more to the city's potential than glistening beaches.

During his college years at Stanford and Lake Forest, Thornton and his brother Jack continued to take their spring breaks in Fort Lauderdale. And through those years and visits a vision of Thornton's future began to grow.

They had always been impressed by the bucolic—almost South Sea island—charm of Fort Lauderdale. Although its population was just 25,000 in 1948, they also saw it had strong potential for growth. Its languid, warm atmosphere would be a perfect place, the brothers thought, for a Polynesian-theme restaurant like Trader Vic's in San Francisco or Don the Beachcomber's in Chicago.

"We thought it would work," Bob Thorton recalls. At the time, he didn't know the half of it.

Thornton was discharged from the Army in 1955 at age 24. With three friends, and $2,000 each, he became part-owner in a 42-foot sportfisherman docked at Bahia Mar on the Intracoastal. There he lived. During the day the friends chartered the boat to tourists. During the night he tended bar along Fort Lauderdale's beachfront. And through it all he planned the Mai Kai.

In 1956 his brother Jack moved to Fort Lauderdale, they borrowed money on their idea, and bought

Mai Kai's owner Bob Thornton came to Fort Lauderdale as a high school senior from Chicago. His love affair with the city has lasted for more than three decades.

property along North Federal Highway in Fort Lauderdale. At the time the location was nothing but pastureland. But the price was right.

They opened in 1956 with 60 employees, a 325-seat restaurant, a 17-stool bar, and no entertainment. By the early 1980s the Mai Kai was an enduring success story. What began as a four-room complex was a sprawling mega-restaurant with nine dining rooms, a 150-seat bar/lounge, a full gift shop, a landscaped tropical garden with waterfalls, excellent Cantonese and American cuisine, and a 200-person staff. One member of that staff is Mireille Thornton, Bob's wife, a Tahitian dancer who has choreographed the Mai Kai's Polynesian revue and made it the longest-running show in Florida history.

In its first 26 years the Mai Kai served more than seven million dinners and won enough awards to fulfill the most grandiose dreams of any Chicago high schooler. Even Bob Thornton.

Tommy Eng (left), chef for 20 years, and some of his staff in the Mai Kai's recently remodeled kitchen.

LANDMARK FIRST NATIONAL BANK

The old Sweet Building at Las Olas Boulevard and Andrews Avenue, where First National Bank was started on March 17, 1937. Courtesy of the Gene Hyde Collection, Fort Lauderdale Historical Society, Inc.

Towering 28 stories above downtown Fort Lauderdale, Landmark First National Bank is the symbol of financial and corporate power in Broward County. But it had its humble beginning on St. Patrick's Day, 1937, when six employees opened for business on the ground floor of the old Sweet Building on Las Olas Boulevard.

There was little money in the community then. Many property owners couldn't pay their taxes. Fort Lauderdale and South Florida were still in the grip of a major economic depression, caused by a killer hurricane and the historic land bust of 1926. Tourism barely existed. There was only one major hotel on the beach. There was no marine industry, no manufacturing plants. In fact, there was little business of any kind. That which existed clustered near the intersection of East Las Olas Boulevard and Andrews Avenue.

But Landmark's founders had faith in the city's future and they were confident that better times were ahead in South Florida. Fortunately, they

were right.

The new First National Bank was capitalized at only $125,000—a relatively small figure in today's financial market. Less than half of that amount was raised locally. Local directors included city attorney George W. English, a civic activist whose name would list among those most important in Broward County's future; realtor Arthur H. Ogle; and N.B. Cheaney, board chairman of Broward County Title Company. George Haskins, another Fort Lauderdale realtor, became president in 1938.

Despite beginning at an inauspicious time, the new bank saw its assets increase steadily, reflecting the area's spectacular population growth and economic expansion. On Memorial Day, 1948, a local group,

headed by English, assumed control and the First National Bank moved to larger quarters in a new building, three blocks to the east, at Las Olas and Third Avenue.

During the '50s the bank financed the development of Harbor Beach, a luxury development in east Fort Lauderdale on the Intracoastal Waterway, and other leading projects. By so doing it served as a primary source of financing at a time when northern sources were still uncertain about the new Florida boom.

Under the presidency of Charles L. Pierce, First National pursued aggressive lending policies designed to develop the area. Deposits soared from $16.2 million in 1950 to $70.1 million in 1960. That year, First National became the largest bank in Broward County. By 1970 deposits had reached $196.6 million and only 13 years later had risen to more than $664.8 million.

Also by 1970, First National had again outgrown its building. And in that year directors broke ground for the present 28-story structure, largest

---

This photo of George W. English, one of the original founders and directors of the First National Bank, was taken in 1936 when he was city attorney. Courtesy of the Fort Lauderdale Historical Society, Inc.

Fort Lauderdale High School, one of the city's earliest landmarks, on the site of the present Landmark First National Bank Building. Photo circa 1926. Courtesy of the Fort Lauderdale Historical Society, Inc.

in the county, on 12.7 acres in the heart of Fort Lauderdale's then-blighted downtown section. The huge facility rose on the site of one of the city's earliest landmarks, Fort Lauderdale High School. When the school's old cornerstone was opened, the clock was turned back to 1915, when Fort Lauderdale was a small farming community. The cornerstone contained copies of two weekly newspapers from March 19, 1915, and other artifacts. Among those participating in the groundbreaking ceremony and the opening of the cornerstone was Mrs. Frank Stranahan, widow of the city's founder, the town's first schoolteacher and a donor of part of the land on which the high school stood. The bank was renamed Landmark First National Bank and designated lead bank in an affiliated five-county system.

Landmark's new headquarters at One Financial Plaza became the centerpiece of a revitalized downtown. A new skyline emerged, including, besides an impressive array of new office facilities, a city parking garage for 2,200 cars and a new federal building. Then would come Broward County's main library building, a new Fort Lauderdale Museum of Art, and a four-year state university located on the former site of the First National Bank.

Meanwhile, Landmark's personnel and operating philosophy were also changing. In 1973 Lucius Weeks, a South Carolinian with impressive banking credentials, became president of Landmark First National. Under the leadership of Weeks and board chairman L.C. Judd, Landmark expanded countywide, following Broward's growth pattern north and west. By the end of 1983 it included 14 branches. Similar growth occurred in Pinellas, Hillsborough, Orange, and Brevard counties.

A major stock sale to a group of Tennessee investors financed further expansion into additional developing markets. Federal deregulation created opportunities for diversification into a broad range of financial services. Landmark subsidiaries include a mortgage banking corporation, a data service corporation to promote computerization and automation, two capital equipment leasing companies, and discount brokerage services.

Landmark is one of 10 major underwriters of a statewide electronic funds transfer network.

"We've come a long way since 1937," Weeks said in 1983. "Over the years, we've been closely identified with Broward's phenomenal growth into Florida's second largest population center. As we offer more financial services to more and more people, we're confident that Landmark has a bright future."

The 28-story Landmark Bank Building became the cornerstone of a revitalized downtown Fort Lauderdale.

STEEL FABRICATORS, INC.

Steel Fabricators, Inc., is entering its third decade as a member of the greater Fort Lauderdale corporate community. It was founded in 1962 when H.J. Langsenkamp, a salesman for Bethlehem Steel Corporation, recognized the growth potential of this area and the need for a structural steel facility in Fort Lauderdale.

The original site was at Sunrise and Northwest Ninth Avenue, but was moved to undeveloped land in northeast Fort Lauderdale, its current site, so room for expansion was available.

Business relationships established in 1962 remain to this date. Many of the original customers who believed in Steel Fabricators in 1962 are its customers today, attesting to the firm's professionalism, flexibility, and performance.

The corporation fabricates and erects structural steel members for use in high- or low-rise commercial and industrial complexes. It purchases raw steel beams, bars, and plates from steel mills, has them shipped to Fort Lauderdale, and then cuts, fits, and welds the steel into structural assemblies that are shipped to construction sites for erection as the steel framework of the building. All connections and bracing are engineered and fabricated from drawings, so once they arrive on site, they can be erected to meet the

The firm fabricates and erects structural steel members for use in high- or low-rise commercial and industrial complexes.

standards set by the engineers, industry, and local government authority.

Many of the firm's original employees are still with Steel Fabricators, and labor turnover is less than 5 percent. This is truly an outstanding statistic for the industry and today's market.

Subsidiaries of Steel Fabricators in Fort Lauderdale include Steel Contractors, Inc., the operation that erects the steel beams and columns once they are fabricated; Door Masters, Inc., a fabricator of pre-hung steel doors for residential and commercial applications; and Steel Structures, Inc., a distributor of pre-engineered steel buildings. A western Caribbean operations office, Overseas Steel Fabricators, is maintained in Puerto Rico.

Local real estate projects that have been successfully completed include Spectrum office complex, Fort Lauderdale commerce center, Atlantis-The Water Kingdom, the Yankee Clipper bridge across A1A, Cypress Plaza, and many more. The company currently employs 130 individuals in Fort Lauderdale and has completed projects in Texas, Georgia, Colorado, Puerto Rico, Saudi Arabia, and most of the Caribbean Islands. Its engineering department has worked with professional engineers worldwide.

H.J. Langsenkamp, the founder, was raised in Fort Lauderdale, graduating from St. Anthony's High School and attending the University of Miami.

One of Steel Fabricators' many construction projects.

HURON MACHINE PRODUCTS, INC.

Ask someone at Huron Machine Products, Inc., to describe the company in one word and the reply will be: "family." Such corporate intimacy is not, in truth, just a product of Huron's promotional literature. The firm has been "family" from the beginning.

That beginning was in 1946 in the basement of Harold and Iva Lindemann's home in Dearborn, Michigan. Harold, a tool and die maker for Ford Motor Company, wanted to establish his own business. After the war, he discovered and bought a defunct machining company, which produced gage blanks and handles for quality-assurance uses in industry. It also provided Lindemann with a customer base for the products.

During the early years he worked at Ford and then pulled another shift in his basement workshop. Iva took care of administration and the books and, in the mid-1950s David and Nancy, their two children, joined the organization. By then Lindemann had resigned his job. He never looked back.

In the early '50s Huron grew rapidly and Lindemann, the manufacturing expert, discovered he had a flair for marketing as well. He opened sales and warehouse facilities in Newington, Connecticut, in 1952, and in Burbank, California, three years later. By the late '50s he had introduced a new product line: jaws that bolt on chucks. Chucks, in turn, are clamping devices that hold parts to be machined.

The Lindemanns began a profit-sharing program for their employees in 1953, establishing in practice a philosophy that would become the cornerstone of their company's success.

With their eastern, western, and midwestern operations functioning, the Lindemanns began to look south and, in 1968, they opened a manufacturing plant in Fort Lauderdale at 228 Southwest 21st Terrace.

Iva Lindemann, secretary/treasurer, and Harold Lindemann, chairman of the board, are the husband and wife team that co-founded Huron Machine Products, Inc.

Nancy moved to Fort Lauderdale to assume responsibility for the administration of the new corporate offices in 1969. A year later David arrived to take command of marketing and manufacturing. Meanwhile, the business kept growing, but David had the feeling that something was missing, that the employees and management were not working together as well as they might.

In the late '60s David and Nancy had been impressed by the work of industrial human resource academicians and theorists who were proponents of "quality circle," or group employee, participation to help increase productivity.

They began their own "team" program in the late '70s and with astonishing results. In one year productivity at Huron increased 57 percent as the team concept opened new and productive lines of communication between management and worker and created interaction between fellow employees. By the early '80s Huron was a recognized national leader in the team concept, and David Lindemann and Nancy Lindemann Mikaelian were in demand as speakers for industrial and academic seminars, conventions, and management-training sessions.

In an industrial world largely indifferent to the opinions of its workers, Huron's success was due largely because its employees participated so closely in the family.

Dr. Michael J. Hart (left), an advisor in the "People in Productivity" program at Huron, talks to employees Peter Samai, Eugene Salvatore, engineering manager Jim Jaggers, Bruce Tustin, and Florida operations manager Eric Riegler.

FLORIDA COAST BANKS, INC.

In the early 1920s William Kester and his brother Clay decided to retire to Pompano Beach, Florida, a tiny retirement and agricultural community a few miles north of Fort Lauderdale. That decision and their arrival might well have gone without notice except for one thing: Kester was only 38 years old.

He had made a fortune as a sales representative for an American manufacturer in Europe and, as is the case with most young financial wizards, "retirement" was short-lived.

The Kesters quickly became involved in Pompano's business, cultural, and civic affairs. In fact, they attained celebrity status when they installed the city's first telephone. They invited the entire town to come listen while they dialed home to their mother in New York City.

But it was the time of the Depression and banks throughout the country were sinking. The town's only bank—the Bank of Pompano—was no

exception. In 1929 it closed and not long afterward, William Kester bought the building, furnishings, and land from federal liquidators.

In the early '30s, though, local citizens persuaded Kester to establish a new bank and in 1934 the doors opened once more. The bank was called Farmers Bank of Pompano Beach and it was an entirely new operation at Northeast First Avenue and Northeast First Street, a location occupied in the second half of the century by the Pompano Office Supply store.

Besides Kester as president, the bank had three employees: a teller, cashier, and bookkeeper. The bank's earnings for its first year were $1,900. Still, it was enough to provide a solid base for growth. And grow is what Farmers Bank did.

By 1950 it was one of the area's major financial institutions and, once again, too big for its old facilities. The bank moved to Northeast First Street

and Fourth Avenue in 1952. Two years later, after 25 years of "retirement" in his adopted home, William L. Kester died and his brother Clay became president.

It was apparent, however, that Farmers Bank would need some youth in its management. And so, by 1956, Robert L. Kester, the nephew of the founder and a businessman with Union Carbide, was asked to move to Pompano Beach and become president of Farmers Bank. His brother Stewart, then working for Procter and Gamble, was asked to participate as a director. Together they formed the nucleus of a new senior management staff that was ambitious and aggressive.

Farmers Bank gave the city of Pompano Beach two more firsts in 1958. The bank became the first to stay open until 7 p.m. on Friday night. And it became the first bank to stay open

Farmers Bank opened at this location in 1934. It is now occupied by Pompano Office Supply.

until 7 p.m. on Friday night that was robbed the first Friday night it did so. Alerted by the bank's promotions, the robber lurked by the front door until the late closing time, robbed the bank, and then was quickly apprehended by local police.

By 1960 growth once again had taken over the bank's space and Farmers Bank built a new corporate headquarters and bank at 1101 East Atlantic Boulevard. It was also in 1960 that the board changed the bank's name to Pompano Beach Bank. With the addition of trust services in 1963, the bank was renamed Pompano Beach Bank and Trust Company.

At the time, state law did not allow for branch banking, so in the 1960s Pompano Beach Bank and Trust opened its "branch" offices as separately chartered banks. The Lighthouse Point Bank opened in Lighthouse Point in 1963 and eventually came to house the installment loan and personnel departments, the bank's in-house teller school, and the Florida Coast

Midlantic Trust Company, N.A., formed in 1982. Oceanside Bank, with Stewart Kester as president, opened in 1969. By 1972 the board had formed a multi-bank holding company— Florida Bancorp, Inc.—with four members: Florida Coast Bank Oceanside, Margate, Pompano Beach, and Lighthouse Point. The next year the holding company changed its name to Florida Coast Banks, Inc.

When branch banking was legalized in Florida in 1977, Florida Coast blossomed throughout Broward County. It opened branches on Oakland Park Boulevard (later moved to Commercial Boulevard and Route 441), Palm Aire, Boca Raton, Coral Springs, and, by 1983, was planning additional branches in Delray Beach and Coconut Creek.

Florida Coast acquired controlling interest in First Bank and Trust of Palm Beach County in February 1981. It was the bank's most ambitious project and accounted for a 50-percent increase in assets and five new banking offices.

The assimilation of First Bank was made easier by Florida Coast's massive, 28,000-square-foot operations and computer center, which opened in 1981 in the Gateway Industrial Center west of Pompano Beach. Operations centralized all data-processing, mail, supply, accounting, and finance departments and its sophisticated mainframe computer could handle in seconds Florida Coast's thousands of daily transactions.

Since 1934 the small, conservative Farmers Bank has grown into a regional, computerized corporation with 20 offices in Broward and Palm Beach counties and more on the way. Its annual earnings have gone from $1,900 that first year to close to $4 million in 1982. For a company begun on a whim by a young retiree, it has proved to be a vigorous and dynamic bank and an integral part of the community it serves.

Florida Coast Bank's main branch in Pompano Beach, 1983.

CORAL RIDGE HOSPITAL

Coral Ridge Hospital began as a nursing home in 1963, started by a family from Chicago that had no experience at all in nursing homes—or hospitals either.

But Robert T. Held, Sr., was a businessman and when he retired from his construction and real estate business and came to Florida he quickly saw the need for private nursing homes in Broward and Palm Beach counties.

And so, in 1963, he broke ground in Fort Lauderdale for a new facility. It was called the Darcy Hall Nursing Home, but its name and purpose would not stay the same for long. Indeed, in 1964, Held was approached by members of Broward County's medical community and urged to open the county's first private psychiatric hospital. At the time only Broward General Hospital had psychiatric beds as part of its service, and local doctors saw a need for a private hospital targeted to an affluent market willing—and able—to pay for the best treatment.

Held dedicated 15 beds to psychiatric patients in 1964 and by 1966 the hospital was devoted totally to the treatment of mental disorders. That year it changed its name to Coral Ridge Hospital and was accredited by the Joint Commission on Accreditation of Hospitals.

Part of the Helds' early success was, of course, marketing. Theirs was the only hospital of its kind in Broward County. But it also was a result of the family's determination to make Coral Ridge a pleasant place with effective treatment and a first-rate medical staff. Its quiet, comfortable rooms were augmented by a complete recreational complex as well, with swimming, volleyball, and more.

It developed an adolescent unit in 1974 to treat illness in young people such as depression or schizophrenia, but did not treat violent behavorial problems. Its biochemical (or orthomolecular) program is the only one of its kind in the Southeast. A combination of conventional and "new" psychiatry, the orthomolecular approach emphasizes the impact of diet and other external factors on a patient's internal chemical balance, theorizing that chemical imbalances can relate to mental disorders. Coral Ridge has a major alcoholic treatment unit of 15 beds and a 28-day program for inpatients that is based on the pioneering research done by Alcoholics Anonymous. In addition, there is a drug program, begun in 1966, that detoxifies and then guides patients into a Narcotics Anonymous rehabilitation program.

The facilities and programs have created a system of referrals from around the world, sometimes making the hospital a victim of its own success. In 1976 a federal judge ordered Coral Ridge to evaluate a young man who had threatened Ronald Reagan with what turned out to be a toy pistol. The media attention caused a furor and prompted executive director Michael Held, one of three Held sons working in the family business, to call the judge and refuse.

"He said he wanted to send him here because it was the best," Held recalls. "I thanked him for the compliment. Then I told him the privacy and confidentiality of our other patients comes first. He withdrew the order."

Coral Ridge Hospital, located on North Federal Highway in Fort Lauderdale, is a complete psychiatric facility.

HOLLYWOOD, INC.

Some men, like leaves before a strong wind, tend to be swept along by the indifferent power of history. But not Samuel A. Horvitz, an aggressive paving contractor from Cleveland, Ohio, who came to South Florida in 1920 to forge new markets for his business.

Certainly young Horvitz had dreams, but not even his wildest could have conjured the actual occurrences of the next three decades, a period in which he and the company he founded—Hollywood, Inc.—would become an integral part in the development of Broward County's second largest city and, more than any other person, business, or agency, would help shape its destiny.

In the early 1920s Horvitz met Joseph W. Young, the redoubtable entrepreneur, promoter, and land developer who founded the small south Broward city of Hollywood. Young contracted with Horvitz to pave the new city's streets. At the time Hollywood's growth was robust, but the 1926 hurricane destroyed the city and the subsequent Depression ruined the economy. By year's end the city's population had fallen from 9,000 to 2,500 and Young's empire was in ruins. Horvitz's role in shaping Hollywood, however, was just beginning.

Risking everything to own land in Florida, Horvitz held Young to his contract. In 1926 Florida courts gave him Young's approximately 25,000 lots to settle their debts. Hollywood, Inc., was formed to manage the vast properties and it dug in for the long haul.

It would not be until after the war that Horvitz' decision to hold the land would prove a good one.

Even during the postwar boom, entreaties by local governments to build quickly to meet demand were resisted. The company, as might be expected, was criticized for this stand, but Horvitz had a plan of high-quality

Samuel A. Horvitz, founder and moving force behind Hollywood, Inc.

development in Hollywood which did not include hasty planning or shoddy workmanship.

In 1954 Hollywood, Inc., developed its first residential community adjacent to the Orange Brook Municipal Golf Course. Golf Estates, as it was called, became successful and inspired the

company to embark on an aggressive building program over the next two decades.

Samuel Horvitz died soon after Golf Estates opened and so it fell to his son William to carry on his father's careful and conservative tradition. Hollywood, Inc., developed the city's finest residential development, Emerald Hills, in 1969. It built the city's first enclosed shopping mall, office and industrial parks, and constructed residential, commercial, and industrial property throughout South Florida. In 1967, Mack Industries was acquired. It has become one of the leading building materials supply companies in South Florida.

In 50 years the company that had come to Samuel Horvitz on the crest of a hurricane became one of the most successful conglomerates of land development, construction, and building supply companies in the state, all centered in Hollywood, one of the state's most successful cities.

The award-winning Venture Corporate Center, Hollywood, Florida.

WASTE MANAGEMENT, INC.

To the content, yet weary, platitude about the inevitability of death and taxes in a consumer society of more than two billion people worldwide, we might easily add a third component.

That, of course, is the abundance of society's wastes and the issue of how logically and effectively to manage or dispose of them. In a contemporary world concerned with the preservation of our health, air, water, and land resources, it is one of the knottier questions. And most important.

The solutions to those questions are the corporate aspiration—and inspiration—of Waste Management, Inc., one of the world's most successful waste management companies, with a demonstrated ability to provide efficient, reliable, and cost-effective collection, transportation, treatment, and disposal of residential, commercial, and industrial waste services to more than 2.7 million households and businesses in North America and over 14 million people worldwide.

The company's services embrace the industry's gamut. In fact, they define it as the collection, transportation, processing, and disposal of solid waste, chemical waste, and low-level nuclear waste, and including resource recovery, energy conservation, and street sweeping.

Waste Management, Inc., is now the largest company in the waste industry with over 15,000 employees and thousands of collection, street-sweeping, and support vehicles in North and South America and the Middle East. In North America alone the company owns and operates a fleet of over 800 chemical and low level radioactive waste transport vehicles and more than 3,300 solid waste collection and transfer trucks, and employs 8,000 people.

By 1983 Waste Management, Inc., would be a $1.2-billion corporation, a statistic made even more astonishing because by then it was only 13 years

The Solid Waste Reduction Center in Pompano Beach.

old. More interesting, perhaps, is that the Florida arm of this mega-company was begun in Broward County in 1962 by an indefatigable Pine Crest School graduate with one truck and a big dream.

His name is H. Wayne Huizenga and he had lived in Fort Lauderdale since 1953. He wanted his own business and one day, in 1962, he saw an ad in the local newspaper which announced the sale of a $500-a-month refuse route.

He bought the route and began a career that in 20 years would help create a billion-dollar business with holdings worldwide. At the time, however, he was labor and management, rising at 3 a.m., running the route, finishing at 5 p.m., and then showering and donning coat and tie so he could solicit more business. In six years Southern Sanitation, as it was and still is called, had more than 40 trucks, many commercial customers, and had spread south to the city of Key West under contract.

Meanwhile, in Chicago, Huizenga's cousin by marriage, Dean L. Buntrock, had expanded a family-owned waste business from a $750,000-a-year,

12-truck venture in 1956 to one with business in Milwaukee and Madison, Wisconsin, as well. In 1970 the two men sat down to discuss the possibility of merger, making a public stock offering and expanding on a regional basis. Buntrock would operate the new company in the Midwest and Huizenga would operate in the Sun Belt.

The companies merged on January 1, 1971, and went public with 320,000 shares in June of that year. The stock opened at $16 a share, sold out, and closed that day at $21. In less than six months its value climbed to $60 and Waste Management, Inc., was on its way.

Using stock rather than cash, the firm began acquiring companies throughout the United States. In June 1972 it made a second stock offering and raised an additional $40 million to continue expansion. In less than two years Waste Management acquired 110.

A bear market slowed corporate growth in 1974, but only temporarily.

In 1975 it bid a job in Riyadh, Saudi Arabia, and won it. Waste Management mobilized an operation involving more than 3,000 employees that won the firm worldwide recognition as the premier company in international city cleaning. Soon it was awarded a similar contract for the port city of Jeddah, Saudi Arabia, plus contracts in Buenos Aires and Cordoba, Argentina, and part of Caracas, Venezuela.

From the beginning, Waste Management wanted to create a complete system for the management of wastes, from collection through disposal. That included everything from a Department of Energy-sponsored experimental methane conversion plant in Pompano Beach, Florida, to its own landfills, creative land-use reclamation projects, and resource recovery, to nuclear waste disposal capabilities and the $22-million chemical waste incinerator ships *Vulcanis I* and *II*, as well as hazardous chemical waste processing and disposal facilities throughout the United States.

Waste Management sanitary landfills are conceded to be models for the industry, and, indeed, the firm has pioneered techniques for recreational amenities at completed sites in several of the communities it serves.

Waste Management, Inc., is dedicated to the preservation and maintenance of a high quality of life and protection of the environment not only throughout North America, but the world. It is this corporate premise—and promise—that means the preservation and maintenance of our most precious resources. It was upon this premise that Waste Management was founded, and because of it that the venture grew in such a spectacular fashion during the 1970s.

It is upon this premise that the corporation will endure as a leader in the industry in the 1980s and beyond.

Top: A front loader at the Breakers Hotel in West Palm Beach.

Bottom: Waste Management's newest incinerator ship, Vulcanus II, *en route to Rotterdam, Holland.*

LEONARD L. FARBER INCORPORATED

Leonard L. Farber Incorporated, developer of the Galleria at Fort Lauderdale and Pompano Fashion Square, is one of the world's leading shopping center development companies. Founded by Leonard L. Farber, the company has developed 34 shopping centers from California to New York and Puerto Rico. Farber presently serves as chairman of the board and Eric W. Deckinger is president.

The firm's history closely parallels that of shopping centers, an industry that was born and nurtured in America's suburbs after World War II. Beginning in the late 1940s, Farber launched its first shopping centers, called "strip" centers because the stores were lined up with a grocery store at one end and a drugstore on the other.

As suburban growth intensified, shopping centers became more sophisticated and the industry became aware of its impact on society. The International Council of Shopping Centers was formed and Leonard L. Farber named founding president. He continues today as the only life member of its prestigious worldwide board of trustees.

Farber was among the first development companies to recognize the importance of enclosed regional malls. In 1968 the firm launched Pompano Fashion Square, one of a number of regional malls developed by Farber throughout the United States. Pompano Fashion Square combined Burdines, Jordan Marsh, Sears, JCPenney, and more than 100 other stores in a state-of-the-art shopping center that continues to be a major center of retailing in Broward County.

Two years later Farber intensified its commitment to Broward County by moving its corporate headquarters from New York to Pompano Beach. Then, in 1977, the company launched what is considered to be one of the most unique and exciting shopping

Leonard L. Farber, chairman of the board of Leonard L. Farber Incorporated.

centers in the world: the Galleria at Fort Lauderdale.

The Galleria has added immeasurably to the sophistication of the city. Developed on the site of the old Sunrise Shopping Center, the Galleria includes Neiman-Marcus, Saks Fifth Avenue, Lord & Taylor, Burdines, and Jordan Marsh, along with stores such as Brooks Brothers, Ann Taylor, FAO Schwarz, Sara Fredericks, Les Must de

Cartier, and more.

The corporate commitment to Broward County is matched by Leonard Farber's personal commitment to organizations such as the Fort Lauderdale Symphony Orchestra Association, the Boys' Clubs of Broward County, the Museum of Art, Holy Cross Hospital, the Jewish Community Center, the Broward Workshop, and the United Way of Broward County. In addition, Farber is a member of the board of trustees of Brandeis University, site of the Leonard L. Farber Library. He is a former member of the National Council on the Arts.

Yet with all his civic leadership, Leonard L. Farber is quick to say that it is the company's shopping centers that have had the greatest impact on life in Broward County. They are the focal points of the community, much like latter-day village squares.

A bronze-colored medallion marks the main entrance to Fort Lauderdale's Galleria shopping center, the largest and most spectacular of the 34 centers developed by Leonard L. Farber Incorporated.

SUN BANK/SOUTH FLORIDA, N.A.

On February 16, 1928, the *Fort Lauderdale News* announced the concurrent closing of the last bank in town and an effort by a group of local businessmen to organize a new bank. The front-page story stressed the quality of the organizers stating that the board would be comprised of those in whom the public had confidence. The paper went on to mention the bank organizers' desire to be of service to the community as the reason they agreed to become a part of the new bank.

A new bank charter was issued a week later. The paper's lead article said, "The personnel of the board of directors . . . is to include names . . . which will give it as strong a backing as any banking institution in South Florida." On February 28, the newspaper reported that J.D. Camp, J.S. Powell, C.N. McCune, and John Lochrie would be among the key officers and editorially stated, ". . . they are men who know conditions in Broward County perfectly and the very fact that their names are connected with the enterprise will give the community confidence in its success."

Though the newspaper was trying to bolster public confidence at a time of great economic hardship, it is significant that the cornerstone for the bank was recognized as its board of directors. Others who joined the board

during its formulative early years were Hugh Taylor Birch, Robert B. Lochrie, E.N. Sperry, Leigh R. Robinson, W.E. Nevling, Jr., D.D. Oliver, and Logan T. Brown.

The Fort Lauderdale National Bank was organized in 1947 by the same group and to this bank soon were added second-generation members James D. Camp, Jr., and J.S. Powell, Jr., of the founding families, and other business leaders including M.R. McTigue and William H. Maus.

The Wilton Manors National Bank was organized in 1954 by a group of similarly dedicated men, including J. Morgan McJunkin, Dwight L. Rogers, Jr., Edward W. Smith, Jr., Claybourne D. Dyal, and John E. Morris.

These banking groups also organized other banks in Lauderdale By-the-Sea, Coral Ridge, Lauderdale Lakes, Tamarac, and Plantation. By December 2, 1982, all of these institutions became one—Sun Bank/South Florida, N.A.

As Fort Lauderdale's oldest banking group, Sun follows the philosophy of its founders: that by building the community you will build the bank. According to Sun Bank/South Florida Chairman R.B. Lochrie, Jr., a director

---

Sun Bank/South Florida, N.A., had its beginning in this building on Andrews Avenue in downtown Fort Lauderdale.

has an obligation to serve the community. Sun's present board members have carried on that tradition by assuming leadership roles on the boards of hospitals and educational institutions, the YMCA, health organizations, the United Fund, chambers of commerce, and numerous charitable organizations, and by actively participating in the arts and state and local bar activities. Banker/ directors have included three presidents of the Florida Bankers' Association: J.D. Camp, R.H. Makemson, and Daniel S. Goodrum.

Over the years many community and business leaders have served on the boards of the banks that have become Sun Bank/South Florida, N.A. They include J. Dewey Hawkins, longtime mayor of Oakland Park; Dave Turner, mayor of Wilton Manors; C.C. Kittredge; John Tidball, Joe N. Morris, and N.B. Cheaney, mayors of Fort Lauderdale; city commissioners M.A. Hortt and Charles Knight; real estate pioneers H.C. Jelks, M.R. McTigue, and Tom Bryan; Port Everglades developers C.C. Freeman and Warren Eller; marine contractor J.S. Powell; citrus grower R.B. Lochrie; construction suppliers D.D. Oliver, Sr., and Jr.; well-known physicians Leigh F. Robinson and Milton N. Camp; and many others who, through their businesses and association with the bank, helped to build Fort Lauderdale and Broward County and, thus, participated in developing a great community bank.

Seven second-generation directors— R.E. McTigue, W.H. Maus, Jr., J.S. Powell, Jr., R.O. Powell, William E. Nevling III, D.D. Oliver, Jr., John E. Morris, Jr.—and R.B. Lochrie, Jr., a third-generation officer and director, have served the community and the bank. This record of management continuity and contribution to the community is a heritage of which Sun Bank is extremely proud.

FORT LAUDERDALE NEWS/SUN-SENTINEL

Eventually they would call him "The Governor," and he would become a leading figure in the maturation of Fort Lauderdale and Broward County, but in 1928 R.H. Gore, Sr., was just a successful insurance man selling an insurance plan under which newspapers sold insurance to subscribers.

Searching for a newspaper in South Florida, he found one in Fort Lauderdale. It belonged to Horace and Tom Stilwell, two pioneer entrepreneurs whose venture into the newspaper business had turned sour along with the local economy. A few years before, the Stilwells had bought *The News* for more than $450,000. The paper already had accumulated a long history. It began as a weekly in the spring of 1911. Then called *The Sentinel*, its competition was *The Herald*. The paper was begun by a grandson of the governor of Georgia named George G. Matthews, who had come to Fort Lauderdale in 1907 as part of a gubernatorial legislative committee investigating Everglades drainage.

Leroy and W.J. Galvin, owners of an Ohio newspaper chain, bought *The*

The News building in the 1960s.

Sentinel from Matthews in 1925 for $140,000. The Galvins also bought out *The Herald* and consolidated the operations into *The Daily News and Evening Sentinel*. During the 1926

Situated on Fort Lauderdale's picturesque New River Drive East, News and Sun-Sentinel Company's headquarters is pictured just after completion in early 1977.

boom, the Galvins sold the paper to the Stilwells who were left holding a rather substantial white elephant when the bubble burst the next year. They were happy to part with it to Gore for $75,000.

Gore traded stock he owned to buy the paper. When the market collapsed so did the price of his stock, but he already had bought *The News*.

Located on the north bank of the beautiful New River, the afternoon daily *Fort Lauderdale News* and, later, its sister, the morning *Sun-Sentinel*, grew into the most powerful publication in the county's history and the Gore family into one of the most influential. In the beginning power flowed from Gore, a politically active man at local and national levels. President Roosevelt, in fact, appointed him governor of Puerto Rico. But later "The Governor" became less involved in the newspapers' operations and his sons Jack and Theodore took over as editor and president of Gore Publishing, carrying on the family's influence in the community.

The paper's growth was steady, reaching 60,000 in circulation by the late '50s. In 1960 Gore Publishing bought the weekly *Pompano Beach Sun* and began the *Sun-Sentinel*.

Not long after, in 1963, the huge Tribune Company of Chicago bought Gore Publishing. Tribune Company owned newspapers throughout the country, not to mention television and radio stations, cable television systems, newsprint mills, and other support subsidiaries. Ted Gore became chairman of the board of directors in 1978 and was replaced as president and chief executive officer by Byron Campbell of Tribune Company. Jack, editor for 28 years, died in 1982.

By the early '80s the enterprise was named News and Sun-Sentinel Company, had 1,500 employees, a circulation exceeding 200,000, and was one of Tribune Company's most successful subsidiaries.

NORTH BROWARD HOSPITAL DISTRICT

The renovated Granada Apartments were the first home for Broward General Hospital back in 1938.

Broward General Medical Center.

Local "hospitals" opened and closed with startling and unsettling rapidity in Broward County during the Depression years. The reasons were simple: They were private hospitals and their patients had no money.

And so it was that in June 1937, James D. Camp of Broward National Bank joined a group of concerned citizens to form a Broward Hospital Association charged with the mission of creating a publicly financed and operated hospital.

It seemed on January 2, 1938, the committee had succeeded. They had bought the old Granada Apartments at 17th Street and Southeast First Avenue in Fort Lauderdale for $26,000 cash and for another $31,500 converted it into a hospital that could accommodate 45 patients, had

operating rooms, and, on that day, admitted its first patients.

Several expansions and 10 years later, though, the hospital still was not large enough to meet the demands of Broward's escalating population. Yet the Fort Lauderdale City Commission, which held title to the hospital, refused to authorize the building of a new wing, a decision that prompted Camp and most of the board to resign.

In 1952, with the total number of beds at Broward General up to 142, the legislature (and the people in a district referendum) approved the creation of a North Broward Hospital District, a taxing authority that would be responsible for the maintenance and operation of public health facilities in the northern two-thirds of the county (from the Dania Canal on the south to the Palm Beach County Line on the north). The legislation called for the District to be governed by a seven-member board of commissioners, each to serve a four-year term. The governor appoints members of the board from the community, and they serve voluntarily and receive no compensation.

The city turned Broward General over to the District the following year and an expansion program began.

Within 45 years Broward General Medical Center, as it is now called, had grown from 45 beds to 744 and is now capable of doing everything from stitching a cut finger in emergency to repairing a heart valve in its sophisticated operating rooms.

Joining Broward General under the administrative and taxing authority of the North Broward Hospital District was North Broward Hospital, a five-story structure in 1961 which, in 20 years, grew to a nine-story, 347-bed major medical and surgical hospital now called North Broward Medical Center and is in the process of expanding to 419 beds.

In 1972 the District's newest member, Imperial Point Hospital,

opened. Imperial Point Medical Center is a 204-bed full-service, medical-surgical hospital with a specialized mental health unit, a cardiac rehabilitation program, and a pulmonary rehabilitation program for patients suffering from lung disease.

The North Broward Hospital District is today the health care leader in the area and represents 30 percent of the total acute care beds in Broward County. In the first quarter of 1984 the District will begin building a 200-bed acute care hospital in the center of the city of Coral Springs to meet the needs of a growing population in the western sector of the District. The District is constantly seeking to provide the finest facilities and state-of-the-art equipment for patients at the lowest possible cost.

North Broward Medical Center.

Imperial Point Medical Center.

LES BYRON ASSOCIATES

Lester A. Byron, Sr., grew up in Dayton, Tennessee, a tiny valley town not far from Chattanooga. It was the kind of start one might choose for a pioneer. And certainly, Byron became just that in Broward County.

After World War II, in 1945, Byron gravitated toward the warm Florida climate and stopped when he arrived in Fort Lauderdale. "Fort Lauderdale was small, about 18,000 people I think," Byron recalls. He signed on with a construction firm, W.A. Hart & Company, then W.L. Kroetz, Inc., as estimator, expeditor, and manager. During his early years in Fort Lauderdale, Byron was involved in the construction of stores, houses, and apartments along fashionable Las Olas, the city's unique shopping street.

In 1952 he began to buy industrial and commercial land in northwest Broward which, up to then, had been used only for vegetable and dairy farming. "I felt the move was on for people to come to Florida—and that industry would follow people."

And so, in 1952, Byron formed his own company, originally named Enterprise Developers, Inc., now Les Byron Associates, and began building small warehouses and manufacturing plants. Many of those, and about half of his real estate holdings, would be in the 800-acre Gateway Industrial Center on Powerline Road northwest of Fort Lauderdale. When Byron first began putting together land there it cost $5,000 an acre. Twenty years later the value had risen to more than $150,000 an acre.

The company's large inventory of industrially zoned property was only one reason for its ultimate success. In addition, Byron had a design and engineering staff geared to produce data and renderings in 48 hours and construction crews that could produce quality products with amazing speed.

Sunbeam Electronics, for example, decided to move to Fort Lauderdale in the early 1950s and had an immediate need for a 10,000-square-foot building. Byron got a lease signed and finished the entire building, ready for occupancy, in 26 days.

In addition, Byron provided one-stop turnkey service for prospective industries. A manufacturer or investor could either go to a realtor, then to an engineer, then to a contractor, and then to a bank for financing, or he could go to Byron for all of it, from start to finish.

By the early 1980s Byron had developed several industrial parks and built plants for some of the county's oldest industrial names: Modular Computer Systems, Computer Products, Airpax Electronics, Glendale Federal, NCNB (a North Carolina-based bank holding company), Westinghouse, Burroughs, Pier 66, Racal-Milgo, Southern Bell, CitiBank, Hewlett-Packard, Eckerds, Levitz, Wells Fargo, Bendix, and many more.

In the 1980s Byron began building the 1.1-million-square-foot, 60-acre office Hi-Tech Park called Spectrum in a joint venture. Two other projects are on the boards. Spectrum would be the county's largest such park, and an exclamation mark to a career that brought Broward from infancy to international prominence as a center for clean, light industry and corporate headquarters.

Lester A. Byron, Sr.

CHARLES F. McKIRAHAN, JR., A.I.A.—ARCHITECT

From the earliest years of his childhood, Charles F. McKirahan, Jr., knew that he wanted to be an architect. And little wonder. He was the progeny of two skilled architects, his father Charles Foster McKirahan, Sr., and his mother Lucille.

The senior McKirahan came to Fort Lauderdale in 1947 as an associate for a local firm. Within a year he had begun to do work for developers James S. Hunt and Joseph Taravella, two of the principals in the huge Coral Ridge Properties, Inc., which would become one of the county's major builders. That association made it possible for him to open his own firm, and in the 1950s work was coming quickly.

Coral Ridge, the rapidly growing residential development in north Fort Lauderdale, was only one of the projects in which the firm was involved. McKirahan also designed buildings for the Mai Kai restaurant, the Nassau Beach Hotel, helped plan Coral Springs, an entire city built by Coral Ridge Properties, and designed Seaquarium, one of the first buildings to employ the geodesic dome made famous by scientist/philosopher Buckminster Fuller.

Tragically, Charles F. McKirahan, Sr., died in 1963 in an automobile accident. But in time, the tradition he started as an architectural pioneer in Broward County would be carried on by his son.

The junior McKirahan was graduated from Tulane School of Architecture in 1975 and joined the successor to his father's firm as an associate. In 1979 he started his own firm and hired his favorite architect to head the design department: his mother Lucille.

Soon he was able to move into a building designed, constructed, and used by his father in 1954, and one of his most memorable early jobs was the restoration of a house on Southeast 10th Street in which the McKirahans had lived nearly 30 years before.

One of the early buildings designed by Charles F. McKirahan, Sr., was for the Mai Kai restaurant in Fort Lauderdale.

Charles McKirahan, Jr., believed in community service and so became a member of the Fort Lauderdale Planning and Zoning Board and the Metropolitan Planning Organization for Broward County, and was a chairman of the Community Appearance Board as well.

His early work included residential and commercial buildings in Broward County and contracts to do housing for the City of Fort Lauderdale. Predictably, many of his clients were the children of clients of his father and, perhaps also predictably, Charles Jr. was not satisfied with just local work.

His goal was to become an architectural firm of national and international reputation and, like his father, he sought and won contracts for jobs throughout the southern United States; the Caribbean; Jeddah, Saudi Arabia; and Rio Chico, Venezuela.

McKirahan was a founder and past president of Second Century Broward, a group of second-generation Broward County residents dedicated to promoting the cultural and political interests of the county, a visible sign of the community commitment that has been a trademark of Charles F. McKirahan, Jr., A.I.A.—Architect, since its beginning.

A proposed McKirahan project is this office building in downtown Fort Lauderdale for Thomas J. Owen & Son.

ENGLISH, McCAUGHAN & O'BRYAN

George Washington English, a Harvard lawyer destined to become one of the most influential pioneers in Fort Lauderdale history, arrived in Broward County in 1924, determined to make his fortune.

In time he would do just that, and, in the process, become one of the city's most charismatic financiers, philanthropists, civic leaders, and educators, not to mention the senior partner in one of the largest and most successful law firms.

From 1928 to 1939 he served as city attorney for Fort Lauderdale and it was during this period that he began a professional association with J.B. Patterson, a brilliant, if flamboyant, local attorney. It was Patterson who, in 1940, discovered a hungry, young Miami attorney who seemed both capable and willing to share the firm's increasing work load. His name was Samuel O'Bryan.

By the war, English had already helped form First Federal Savings & Loan and was a principal figure in what would become the Landmark Bank group holding company. But Germany and Japan intervened and all three men left for the service. Hugh Lester, an experienced lawyer beyond draft age, was asked to help maintain the practice in their absences.

When they returned Patterson went into practice on his own and English, Lester, and O'Bryan established a partnership in 1946. English was an office lawyer and, as O'Bryan would call him, a rainmaker, the man who brought in the work. O'Bryan became skilled, then, in performing it: real property law, corporate law, litigation, divorces, and closings, but no tort work. The firm became proficient in providing advice and counsel to some of the area's largest financial and corporate offices, first as legal advisors and then as chairmen of the board and as members of the boards of directors.

Lester retired in 1952 and O'Bryan persuaded Russell McCaughan, a

First Fort Lauderdale Place will be the new home of English, McCaughan & O'Bryan in June 1984.

meticulous, methodical, and extremely competent attorney with a superior accounting and tax background to join the firm. On July 1, 1952, Russell McCaughan became a partner and later was instrumental in bringing the condominium form of ownership to Florida.

English used to tell both O'Bryan and McCaughan that a law firm that failed to grow, failed. The firm adopted his observation as something of a credo. Within the next 30 years it would grow to more than 100 employees, including 20 partners and 20 associates with offices in both Coral Gables and Fort Lauderdale.

The age of legal specialization and high-tech applications to law practice, something unheard of during the early

years of the firm's existence, descended with a fervor in the late 1970s. To maintain a competitive position in an environment that seemed to explode with litigation and lawyers, English, McCaughan & O'Bryan added to the firm an office administrator and comptroller, a communications manager, a personnel manager, a professional librarian, bookkeeping personnel, para-legals, clerks, and messengers. The office is now completely computerized, and the magic of word processing and telecommunications machines now speed documents to clients all over the world.

The premise—and the promise— was to allow the firm to concentrate on its strongest asset: a reputation for sophisticated, quality work supported by state-of-the-art technology that can meet a client's needs, whatever they are.

UNIVERSITY COMMUNITY HOSPITAL

Health care in the fast-growing regions of west Broward County entered a new era in 1974 when its newest and most modern community hospital opened for business.

University Community Hospital opened in August and immediately provided medical, surgical, and pediatric services, 24-hour emergency room, diagnostic radiology, nuclear medicine, pulmonary and cardiovascular testing, an automated clinical laboratory, and more.

The hospital was the progeny of Dr. Thomas Frist, Sr., one of the founders of Hospital Corporation of America, the nation's largest organization of investor-owned hospitals. It was Dr. Frist who encouraged HCA to buy University Community from a local land developer. The acquisition was consummated in July and the first patients treated less than a month later.

Its association with HCA enabled University Community Hospital to employ the sound management techniques common to other

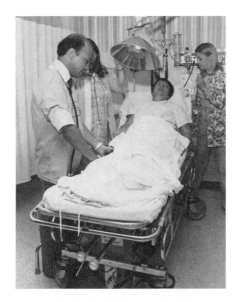

When University Community Hospital opened in 1974, its 132 employees treated 1,333 patients. In 1983 there were 797 employees caring for nearly 10,000 admissions.

industries with the benefits to the patients of improved services, modern technology, and the latest in equipment and room accommodations without sacrificing the warm and friendly atmosphere associated with a community hospital.

When the hospital opened in 1974, it was to serve northwest Broward County which, then, contained nine cities and 129,529 residents. In less than 10 years that population had grown to more than 230,000 and University Community had expanded to meet the demand.

In their first year the 132 employees at the hospital treated 1,333 patients. In contrast, by 1983 there were 797 employees caring for the needs of nearly 10,000 admissions. By 1982 the hospital had outgrown itself and a construction program began for a new emergency room, intensive care unit, kitchen/cafeteria, and environmental services. The program was completed in 1982, and a second phase of the plan to house new office space, storage, outpatient surgery, CAT scan equipment, and medical records was under way by mid-1983.

In its first few years the hospital grew dramatically in services both to patients and to the community. There were also problems. An isolated fire destroyed the environmental service area in 1974 and in 1977 severe storms and roof problems led to leaks and flooding. But despite minor difficulties, by 1980 University Community Hospital had become the largest employer in the city of Tamarac.

By the end of 1982 the hospital admissions had surpassed 10,000 and emergency room visits had risen to 20,000. Demand created a bed shortage and the hospital applied to local and state agencies for permission to add an additional 73 beds. Inexplicably, from the hospital's point of view, the agencies denied their requests, and so hospital administrators were forced to fight the denial with appeals to the State of Florida. By late 1983 that appeal was still being considered and the issue was far from solved.

Nevertheless, in 1983 University Community Hospital was facing, with anticipation, the exciting new challenges of the coming decade.

University Community Hospital is located at 7201 North University Drive, Tamarac.

WATERWAY RESTAURANTS, INC.

Architect Dan Dunkham, with owners Al Kocab and Leonce Picot, discussing initial plans for The Down Under in 1968.

When restaurateurs Leonce Picot and Al Kocab began stalking the community in search of investors for a new venture in 1966, their idea was not to start a fine dining restaurant at all. What they had in mind was a waterfront tavern with a pub menu and atmosphere, something with a fascinating decor and impertinent accoutrements, something unique in a bibulous city already numbed by vinyl lounges and beer joints.

Instead, the pair and their company, Waterway Restaurants, Inc., became pioneers in high-quality cuisine and service, setting standards for excellence that would be envied and emulated throughout the Eastern Seaboard.

Picot had learned the business as an employee of a fine, local theme restaurant and he had lived in Fort Lauderdale since 1940. Kocab, a designer and illustrator, was on retainer to the same restaurant. The two met, became friends, and embarked on a collaboration to write and illustrate guides and cookbooks focused on the nation's finest restaurants.

Their travels resulted not only in books, but in ideas as well and, in 1966, armed with these ideas, they decided to try it on their own. Picot sought investors among his many friends in the community and, with $186,000 in capital, the new corporation built The Down Under on the Intracoastal in the shadow of the Oakland Park Boulevard Bridge.

Two things changed the original concept. First, the design and decor of The Down Under was much more dramatic than they anticipated. It seemed a sacrilege to feature a hamburger and spinach salad menu. Second, chef Christian Planchon joined the business.

They opened on December 12, 1968, and, as it became clear that Planchon was there to stay, Picot recalls that they "went in an entirely different direction. I never in my wildest dreams believed we'd be doing what we're doing now."

At the time Fort Lauderdale was growing, but there still was no place for businessmen to meet and dine well at lunch. The Down Under changed all that. It became the first place in the city with sophisticated lunches.

The restaurant's success was extraordinary. Within eight years Picot and Kocab opened another, completely different type of restaurant named La Vieille Maison in Boca Raton. Owned under a separate corporate banner than The Down Under (but with some of the same principal investors) La Vieille Maison's French cuisine and fine service made it one of the few five star restaurants in the United States.

In January 1979 Waterway Restaurants, Inc., opened Casa Vecchia, the first ultra-sophisticated, expensive Italian restaurant in Fort Lauderdale.

Without question these restaurants are three of the finest not just in Broward County, but in the country. But The Down Under, as the first, remains Picot's favorite.

"But it wouldn't have been any fun to just do another Down Under," says Picot. "The fun is in creating, producing. We wanted each restaurant to make a statement of its own. There are no ugly children in this family. We love them all."

Christian Planchon signed on as chef just prior to the 1968 opening and has since developed The Down Under's, La Vieille Maison's, and Casa Vecchia's cuisine into nationally acclaimed fare.

FRANK J. ROONEY, INC.

Frank J. Rooney, Inc., is high on the list of the top 100 general contractors in the United States. It began in 1933 in a one-room Miami building and has become a multimillion-dollar corporation operating throughout Florida and the Southeast.

Now its offices are in Fort Lauderdale in the heart of one of the world's most active and booming construction areas, to which Rooney, a Fort Lauderdale pioneer company, has made significant contributions. It demanded great versatility, new techniques, and the ability to adapt to changing designs and construction methods through the years.

From its national headquarters on East Oakland Park Boulevard in Fort Lauderdale, Rooney has directed the construction of more than 5,000 dwelling units along Galt Ocean Mile. The firm has changed entire city skylines, building a variety of projects ranging from industrial plants, shopping malls, condominiums, bank and office facilities, hospitals, colleges, airports, penal institutions, and bulk mail centers, to the EPCOT Land Pavilion and Cinderella's Castle at Disney World.

That is an impressive record for a firm founded by a gasoline station owner who swapped gas for vacant lots during the Depression. Frank Rooney and his brother were on vacation in Miami when they called home to ask about returning to work in the family's general contracting firm. The answer was no. So the two bought a gas station in Miami and ran a barter trade. Frank Rooney built houses on two lots he bartered for and sold them at a profit.

Rooney bought more lots, built more houses, and expanded into commercial buildings and small apartment houses. During World War II he built the Naval base barracks at the Fort Lauderdale Airport, some of which still stands today.

James R. Tucker, the present chief

Frank J. Rooney, Inc., was the general contractor for the Edgewater Arms, the first high-rise apartment building on Galt Ocean Mile, in 1958. Note the unpaved Galt Mile roadway, undeveloped banks along the Intracoastal, Coral Ridge Golf Course sprawling in upper left, and Holy Cross Hospital standing a lone sentry in the background.

executive officer and chairman of the board, is a member of the Young Presidents' Organization, an international organization of select executives who became president of their companies before reaching the age of 40.

A Florida native, Tucker was brought up in the construction business. His father was a general contractor in Miami. He received his degree in civil engineering at the University of Miami and, after serving in the Marine Corps, joined Frank J. Rooney, Inc., as an estimator in 1953.

When the company opened its Fort Lauderdale office in 1957, he moved north to run it and constructed, among the first projects in Fort Lauderdale, the Burdines' parking garage, Sunrise Shopping Center, the major renovations and additions to the Broward County Courthouse, and the first high-rise on Galt Ocean Mile, the Edgewater Arms.

201

FORT LAUDERDALE AREA BOARD OF REALTORS®, INC.

Retired Fort Lauderdale Area Board of REALTORS® executive vice-president Norman Chappell (1959-1979) wrote that the city was so small in 1922 it had no sanitation department. Instead, "It had a woman come in twice a week." To control traffic there were two signs: "Slow down, entering Fort Lauderdale" and "Resume speed, leaving Fort Lauderdale." The signs, Chappell claimed, were on the same pole.

Chappell's tongue-in-cheek hyperbole contained much truth. Fort Lauderdale was indeed painfully small; it was nothing more, really, than a tiny village of about 2,000 people surrounded by mangrove swamps. Still, in 1922, six men, possessed with vision and energy sat down to form the Fort Lauderdale REALTORS® Association. The group included C.C. Ausherman, the first president; R.W. Whelan, secretary; and members W.G. Austin, M.A. Hortt, W.F. Sunkel, and C.P. Weidling.

Few records exist detailing board activities in the first years. Quite possibly they were destroyed along with most of the county's real estate by the hurricane of 1926. There is evidence, however, that the group changed its name to the Broward County Realty Board in 1924 (then with 26 members), and then changed the name again three years later to the Fort Lauderdale Realty Board.

Formal documentation of the board's workings began in 1934 with the minutes of a meeting in Fort Lauderdale City Commission chambers. Six members attended and voted to assess active members dues of $20 a year (payable semiannually and in advance) and associate members $4 annually (also payable semiannually and in advance).

Despite what would, by today's standards, seem a reasonable rate, fellow REALTORS® found it rather easy to resist its allure. During the next few years participation in board activities was quiet, as was real estate activity.

But the decade of the '40s was an active one. The future seeds for real estate growth and development were being planted. The board worked hard with the Navy to find housing for military personnel and their families, an activity that had long-range implications for the community and the real estate industry. Many of the military people stationed in Fort Lauderdale during World War II returned to become some of its most important and respected citizens and leaders.

In 1946 the board achieved several milestones that would have an impact on its influence on the profession and on the community. That year it established a system of property records to itemize all real estate sales on cards. Arranged lot by lot, parcel by parcel, and subdivision by subdivision, the cards detailed every transaction in 55 subdivisions and 10,000 lots.

In addition, a central listing bureau (now called the Multiple Listing Service) was started that year, enabling sellers to list their property with the board and, therefore, with all of the board's members. In 1946 there were

The Fort Lauderdale Area Board of REALTORS® was located at 424 Federal Highway in 1958.

The home of the Fort Lauderdale Area Board of REALTORS® has been at 1765 Northeast 26th Street since 1971.

80 homes and 82 vacant lots listed for sale.

Such additional services required not only additional space (up to then the board's paperwork was kept in a file drawer of the volunteer president), but a permanent staff. So, in 1946, the board rented its first office space, a room at the Brickell Hotel on Southwest First Avenue. It cost $75 a month. In 1948 the board bought what was known as "The Service Bulletin," a record of every instrument recorded in the courthouse including all the deed transfers in the county.

The board incorporated as a nonprofit corporation (a title it would lose in a battle with the Internal Revenue Service some years later) in

1949 and continued to grow. In the 1950s it moved its offices to larger quarters at 613 East Broward and 424 North Federal Highway in 1958 and finally, in 1961, moved to 2301 North Federal Highway. There the board had an auditorium for orientation and education courses for members.

By the 1960s multiple listings had increased so dramatically that it was difficult to keep members up to date. In 1970, after years of study and debate,

the board adopted a computerized multiple-listing book, a system that produced weekly listings in book form and updated the contents weekly as well. Since then listings have been totally computerized as well as all the rest of the board's records, making the Fort Lauderdale Area Board of REALTORS® a computerized model for similar organizations, not only throughout the state, but throughout the nation.

The board was, of course, involved in scores of civic, political, and charitable enterprises throughout its long history, including contributing donations to drug abuse programs, involvement in young people's activities such as Boys' Clubs and Junior Achievement's Project Business, an educational program to teach the community's youth about the free enterprise system; art shows; and a week-long observance called Private Property Week, which recognizes one's right to own real property.

In the summer of 1981 the board became directly involved with the Fort Lauderdale Historical Society in a project to save and restore the house of Frank and Ivy Stranahan, two pioneers of the city.

By 1981 the board was one of the largest in the state of Florida, with 4,500 members representing 600 real estate offices in the county's 18 of 29 municipalities. It opened a branch office in Plantation in the summer of 1981 to service western Broward.

In 1971 the board moved to its present location, a stately, American colonial building at 1765 Northeast 26th Street. With the addition of more administrative office space in 1979, the facility now has more than 10,600 square feet.

The Fort Lauderdale Area Board of REALTORS® has come a long way from that day in 1922, has grown with its community and, it would be remembered, has helped its community grow as well.

NORTH RIDGE GENERAL HOSPITAL

North Ridge General Hospital was the dream of Dr. M. Lee Pearce, a Pompano Beach physician and attorney who, in the early 1970s, perceived that Broward County needed a private, sophisticated medical complex that could meet the burgeoning health needs of the community.

At the time there were few hospitals in the county that had a total cardiovascular capability as part of its initial design, and Pearce, chairman of the board of American Hospital Management Corporation, believed that North Ridge's success would depend upon just such a capability. He also believed that such a center of medical excellence, to be successful, needed to maintain an intimate and positive relationship with the community it served.

With these objectives in mind, plans were made to begin construction in 1972 and, in 1975, the 400-bed hospital opened. From the beginning the emphasis was on quality care, equipment, and personnel. Its cardiovascular laboratory became a model for the industry in South Florida and, indeed, was the foundation for the hospital's reputation as a superior cardiovascular and full-service facility.

In 1978, under the supervision of Dr. William O. Russell, former chief pathologist at the M.D. Anderson Cancer Institute in Houston, Texas, North Ridge opened the North Ridge Tissue Culture Laboratory, a cancer research facility, one of the first of its kind in South Florida. Its capabilities included the Stem Cell Assay, a sophisticated process that helps determine which drugs are most suitable in the treatment of different cancers. The clinical research facility works in conjunction with the Goodwin Institute for cancer research in Broward County.

The hospital also began a program of bimonthly community education

lectures on health-related topics for the public and, in addition, began winning a reputation for excellence in continuing medical education programs for medical professionals and physicians.

Another unique service was the North Ridge Senior Physicians' Association in which the hospital provided retired doctors space to meet, special hospital privileges, and continuing education programs to keep them part of the profession to which they have dedicated their lives.

By the late 1970s Broward County had grown so much that it was authorized, under federal law, to establish a Veterans' Administration outpatient facility. The government chose to build that facility on North Ridge property adjacent to its medical complex, a decision that testified to North Ridge's demonstrated ability to interact and cooperate with the local community and to serve veterans' needs.

In the early 1980s North Ridge had

North Ridge General Hospital, Fort Lauderdale.

established two research foundations, the Cardiovascular and Pulmonary Research Foundation and the North Ridge Cancer Foundation. Today the hospital is well on its way to accomplishing the tasks assigned to it less than a decade before by Dr. M. Lee Pearce.

North Ridge physicians confer on a recent stem cell study in the pathology laboratory.

CURCIE BROTHERS, INC.

One of Broward County's oldest contracting and construction companies, Curcie Brothers, Inc., began in 1934 with a used Ford one-and-a-half-ton Model A truck and a staff of one.

The staff was Theodore E. Curcie, the son of a Key West musician and one of 11 children. Curcie was born in Hallandale in 1915, the year Broward became a county. At the time, South Broward and most of Dade County, from Homestead to Port Everglades, was farmland. Primarily, tomato farmland.

Curcie borrowed $75 from his mother, financed another $75, and bought the truck which he used to haul produce, fence posts, or any other commodity for which he would be paid the going rate of 20 cents an hour. At the same time he helped farm the family's 100-acre tomato field each winter.

After two years, however, Curcie decided to expand his one-truck operation and move gradually into the construction business. By 1937 his inventory included two dump trucks and a stake-body truck for hauling

produce. But the war interrupted progress and Curcie spent three and a half years in the Pacific. While he was gone, his older brother John ran both the farm and the trucks.

Farming was declining when Curcie returned from the service, but construction opportunities were soaring. By 1951 Ted had been joined by brothers John and Frank and the company had acquired its first dragline. All they needed now was one big break.

That break came in 1955, the same year the company incorporated as Curcie Brothers, Inc. It was then the brothers won a contract to prepare more than 400 acres of swampland that would become the Diplomat Country Club in south Broward County. Curcie's bid was two cents per yard better than the nearest competition and, using 80 trucks, it hauled 7,000 yards of fill a day, more than 1.6 million yards in all, to finish the job under budget and ahead of schedule. It was the first million-dollar job for Curcie and it would establish the company's reputation for diligence, innovation, and reliability.

From there Curcie was able to bid and help build 20 golf courses

throughout the state, including the Presidential, the Blue Monster at Doral, Hollybrook, Hillcrest, and Royal Palm Beach. The firm did the paving work at Calder Racetrack, all of the roads in the cities of Pembroke Pines and Miramar, 18 federal aid projects, Interstate 75 near Lake City, and a multitude of other municipal and state projects.

Curcie's rapid growth (by the mid-1960s the company had 250 employees and more than $5 million a year in business) required acquisition of its own rock quarries for fill and then its own sand and gravel plants. The vertical integration of the company had an added bonus when land surrounding the rock pits could later be sold for residential development. The pits made excellent lakes.

By the 1970s the second generation of Curcies, Ted's son, Joseph E., and John's son, John P., were executives in the firm, carrying on a tradition begun by their fathers and one as old as Broward County itself.

In 1968 Theodore "Ted" Curcie, president (right), looks over a Curcie Brothers project—the Calder Race Track—with Roy Barth, superintendent.

This was Curcie Brothers' fleet of trucks in 1954.

BAHIA MAR

Ages ago, when Europe still considered the world flat, Bahia Mar was already a mariner's mecca.

Excavated artifacts offer evidence that prehistoric Indians took their canoes from New River Sound into the Atlantic and enjoyed a shellfish feast on this site.

The area's first settler, a Bahamian adventurer named Charles Lewis, landed here and settled a mile inland during the 1780s. In the 1830s, during the Seminole Indian War, a Tennessee volunteer named Major William Lauderdale came to build a stronghold against Indian attacks. The fort he built bore his name, as did the city that followed.

In 1875 Bahia Mar became the site for one in a chain of houses of refuge to provide shelter for survivors of the area's frequent shipwrecks.

The Coast Guard took over the house during Prohibition as a base for chasing rum-runners who brought illegal whiskey in from the Bahamas. In one such case, in 1927, rum-runner Jimmy Alderman opened fire on the pursuit boat and killed two Coast Guardsmen. Alderman was hanged in the Coast Guard base in one of the last public hangings in U.S. history. The base stayed in active service until the end of World War II.

After the war, the city bought the base and local residents rejoiced when the 350-slip marina was completed here in 1949. But after several abortive attempts by private owners to create a resort on the site, the city reclaimed the property.

Patricia Murphy of Westchester, New York, Candlelight Restaurant fame, opened her Florida Candlelight Restaurant here in the late 1950s. The rest of the basin was later leased to MCD Holdings of Seabrook, Maryland, which has since turned it into one of the finest water-resort complexes in the world.

Bahia Mar South, with its 115 rooms, was completed in 1966. The pedestrian walkway to the ocean beach followed in 1970. And the 15-story, 185-room Bahia Mar North Tower was completed in 1975.

As a convention center, it comfortably accommodates groups of 20 to 750. As a resort, it provides excellent restaurants, lounges, rooms, pool deck, ocean swimming, fishing, boating, and a proximity to Fort Lauderdale's other major attractions.

As a marina, it ranks as one of the biggest and best in the world, greatly enhanced by a marina control tower, fuel dock, and marine store. As a major Fort Lauderdale landmark, it continues to make history with each additional achievement.

The Bahia Mar Hotel and Yachting Center is located at 801 Seabreeze Boulevard in Fort Lauderdale.

PINE CREST

The stories of enterprises and businesses often orbit the energy, the persuasiveness, the power of a single person. But seldom are those qualities found in as pure a form or as great a quantity as possessed by Mae McMillan.

She was born Mae Horn on a farm near Corning, Iowa, but grew up in South Dakota and attended Yankton College. She married attorney Albert L. McMillan in 1922 after a five-week courtship and in 1925, with their son Stephen and infant daughter Patricia, the family moved to Fort Lauderdale.

They came to be part of the Florida land boom, and were until the multiple disasters of the late '20s. The 1926 hurricane hurled their tiny cottage into a neighbor's yard. The 1929 stock market crash virtually destroyed the local economy.

"We ate a lot of green beans," she recalls. "Only 20 cents a hamper."

By 1931 Fort Lauderdale was trying to come back. The McMillans had two more children (twin sons) and Mae

was able to tutor tourists' children for one dollar an hour in season. In the fall of 1933 she began to administer a small tutoring school at the Colonial Hotel but the principal lost the lease.

Her husband "Mac" was secretary of the Elks Club and leased the first floor of their building on South Andrews in the fall of 1933. There Pine Crest school began.

In 1939, with fewer than 100 students, they moved the site to the Pine Crest Sanitarium on East Broward Boulevard where it remained for 26 years.

In 1943 Mrs. McMillan returned to the University of Chicago to complete a master's degree. In November of that year her husband died suddenly at the age of 46, leaving her with a family and a school still rapidly growing in size and reputation.

As time went on her children also became involved in Pine Crest. Son Bill began teaching there in 1950, becoming headmaster in 1966. Son George served for many years as a school director and daughter Patty and son-in-law Leon Vincenti have made long careers at Pine Crest as well as

Bill's wife Dorais.

In her book *My Life Plus 100 Years,* published on her 80th birthday, Mae McMillan says that "a school . . . started to provide food for a family became a source of loyalty and pride for which four members [of that family] have given more than 100 years of devoted service."

The school was incorporated as a nonprofit institution in 1959 and moved to its present Imperial Point location in 1965. By then it had 550 students and a reputation as the finest private educational institution in Broward County. In the next two decades, it would grow to 1,363 students in grades kindergarten through 12 on the 47-acre campus.

Before his death, Mr. and Mrs. McMillan would take long walks in the neighborhood near Broward Boulevard and plan for Pine Crest, a school he predicted "would become the great private school of the South." And so it has.

Founder Dr. Mae McMillan reflects on the 50-year growth of Pine Crest.

The Alumni Bell Tower is a well-known Fort Lauderdale landmark.

McCUNE, HIAASEN, CRUM, FERRIS & GARDNER

Although they served as machine gun officers in the same unit in World War I, Charles Nathaniel McCune and Carl Andreas Hiaasen would not meet until 1919 when both were at law school at the University of North Dakota.

It was a providential encounter for McCune, the teacher, and Hiaasen, 10 years his junior, the student. Yet they became friends and less than two years later, when McCune wrote Hiaasen urging him to leave the North's silent cold and join him in the promised land, Hiaasen packed his bags. It was July 1921.

The promised land was Fort Lauderdale, then a tiny village of 2,000 set in a mangrove swamp in the new county of Broward. One of the city's few attorneys, Carl Weidling, had persuaded McCune to stay. "It was a new country," Hiaasen recalled more than 60 years later. "It was growing and he thought it might be well to try it out."

McCune and Hiaasen formed their law firm in September 1921, during the Warren G. Harding Presidency. It was boom in Broward and their practice flourished. Joseph W. Young, the founder of Hollywood, was one of their biggest clients. They set up a branch office in Hollywood and worked around the clock. There were 26 attorneys in McCune, Hiaasen then, easily making it the largest firm in Broward County.

Then came the real estate bust and the September 1926 hurricane, which laid waste to Hollywood and Miami. Economic collapse caused McCune and Hiaasen to demobilize and in the early '30s the size of their firm dwindled to three: McCune, Hiaasen, and Thomas Fleming.

They practiced all law except criminal law. McCune was the banking and business expert, the office lawyer. Hiaasen was the trial attorney, who handled cases not just in Broward County or South Florida, but from

Carl A. Hiaasen. ©1983 News and Sun-Sentinel Company.

New York to Los Angeles, Minneapolis to New Orleans. In 1928 they helped found and form what was, at the time, Fort Lauderdale's only bank: Broward National Bank. That relationship would outlast McCune. He died in 1964 and Hiaasen, then 70 years old, became the senior partner.

The late '40s and early '50s marked a time of dramatic growth at McCune, Hiaasen. Partners James M. Crum, a midwesterner who served in the Secret Service during the war, joined the firm not long after the armistice. So did Robert E. Ferris, another veteran who had served in the Philippines. Russell Gardner, a Duke law school graduate, was hired by McCune to help with probate, trusts, and wills in 1948. K. Odel Hiaasen, Carl's son and only child, now deceased, joined his father's firm in 1951.

More followed, of course, until by the 1980s the firm had 15 members in its professional association and 10 associates. Its modern offices in the

Sun Bank Building in downtown Fort Lauderdale took up space on the fifth and sixth floors, were totally computerized, and possessed, according to Hiaasen, the finest private legal library in Florida. Broward County has come a long way since 1921. And, as the oldest and one of the most successful and respected law firms not only in Broward but in Florida, so has McCune, Hiaasen.

Charles N. McCune (1885-1964).

FLEMING, O'BRYAN AND FLEMING

In 1950 John and Foy Fleming joined their father in a family law practice that would become, in the next decade, one of Fort Lauderdale's and Broward County's premier defense litigation firms.

At the time, however, there were few signs the firm's future would be in any way so auspicious.

John and Foy were young and, as attorneys, inexperienced. Their father, Thomas F. Fleming, was, on the other hand, already 65 years old, one of Broward's most distinguished lawyers, and prepared to retire, the sons discovered to their dismay, with alarming alacrity.

It quickly became clear to the Fleming brothers that they would need additional help, preferably a lawyer who was both capable and experienced. They found such a man in a 37-year-old defense attorney with 10 years of experience named William O'Bryan.

And so, in December 1950, the four began what they remember as the

William M. O'Bryan

John W. Fleming

Golden Era of the '50s. At that time, for example, there was one circuit judge (by 1983 there were 61), 80 lawyers, and 80,000 people in Broward. With four members, Fleming, O'Bryan and Fleming was already one of the county's largest firms. And with Thomas Fleming as its senior partner, it was also one of the county's most skilled.

They started their new practice in the old Sweet Building at Las Olas and Andrews; then, in 1953, Thomas Fleming organized the American National Bank and the firm moved from the Sweet Building to the Sunrise Center on Sunrise Boulevard. Later they moved again to the Sunrise Professional Building and finally to the American Bank Building on Sunrise, now known as the NCNB Building.

During this time the firm built a diverse civil practice, including banking, probate, real estate, and more, with defense litigation as its backbone. When in the 1950s the county population tripled, Fleming, O'Bryan

and Fleming rode the crest of the boom.

Thomas Fleming died in 1958, but by then the firm was prepared to carry on. The elder Fleming had sold his interests in the American National Bank not long after organizing it, but in 1961 Foy, whose practice included banking law, organized his own group of investors and bought the bank again. Fleming, O'Bryan and Fleming was an integral part of the bank's leadership from that time on.

By 1963 the firm had 12 lawyers and the entire sixth floor of the American Bank Building. Twenty years later there were 38 attorneys in the firm, including five in Boca Raton and two in the West Palm Beach office.

In addition, Fleming, O'Bryan and Fleming had expanded to include the sixth, seventh, and half of the fifth floor in the NCNB Building—a far cry indeed fom the tiny, family-run enterprise that first leased quarters in the Sweet Building more than 30 years ago.

Foy B. Fleming

ARVIDA CORPORATION

At 81, an age when most people are slowing down, Arthur Vining Davis developed a strong interest in South Florida real estate. As chairman and one of the principal founders of Aluminum Company of America (Alcoa), he had money to spend and by the mid-1950s he had spent $70 million on more than 100,000 acres, 23,000 of them in southwest Broward County. At an average outlay of $330 an acre, his Broward County holdings had cost him a little over $4 million.

The land, purchased from the R.L. Clark family, originally had been platted under several subdivision names by the Florida Fruit Lands Company, formed by Richard J. Bolles. He had bought 500,000 acres from the State of Florida in 1908, when it was just beginning to drain the Everglades.

In 1958 Arthur Vining Davis, then 91, put the first two letters of his three names and 100,000 acres of Florida real estate into a company he called the Arvida Corporation. The southwest Broward land he bought in the 1950s is now being developed into Arvida's largest community—Weston.

Weston lies less than 15 miles west of the Fort Lauderdale-Hollywood airport, which has been picked by Chase Econometrics as the nation's second-highest growth rate area in the 1980s and less than 30 miles north of Miami. The community is bounded roughly by State Road 84 on the north, U.S. 27 on the west, Griffin Road on the south, and the new Interstate, I-75, on the east.

Ten years in the planning, Weston will be home for 60,000 people when it is completed in the early 21st century. The 10,000-acre property will contain championship tennis, swimming, and golf facilities, an equestrian facility with bridle paths, fresh-water boating, fishing, and canoeing, bicycling, jogging and walking paths, and park areas. As a self-contained community, Weston will have its own shopping

The Boca Raton Hotel and Club is a landmark in the city of Boca Raton and the foundation upon which the Arvida Corporation was built. The Cloister section was designed by legendary architect Addison Mizner in 1926. It is one of a dozen hotels in the world to receive the Mobil five-star award.

and business areas as well as its own water management and water and sewer services.

An unusual feature of the new town will be the Arvida International Business Center, a 1,000-acre commercial and industrial

development reflecting the growing South Florida involvement in international trade and business. Foreign trade zones already are in operation at Port Everglades and the Port of Miami.

Engineering studies for Weston, begun in 1972, stressed the need for an effective drainage and water management design. By 1974 the overall plan for the community, first designated as Indian Trace, was ready for submission to the regulatory agencies for Broward and South Florida. The plan, submitted as Broward County was beginning to evolve its long-range use plan, developed along with the county's emerging land use policies. Approval to move ahead with Weston was received on August 17, 1979.

Arvida Corporation is a subsidiary of the Penn Central Corporation. Its Arvida Weston Communities office is headquartered at 901 East Las Olas Boulevard, Fort Lauderdale.

An aerial view of a portion of the tennis complex, aquatics center, and one of four championship golf courses at Boca West, a 1,436-acre resort/residential community developed by Arvida Corporation in south Palm Beach County.

BROWARD COMMUNITY COLLEGE

In the late 1950s Leroy Collins, then governor of Florida, proposed that the state strengthen its educational capabilities by developing a viable system of two-year community colleges. During his tenure 28 community colleges were formed, including what came to be named Broward Community College.

The legislature authorized the school in 1959 and a local advisory committee was formed that would answer to the State Board of Education Regulations.

In the fall of 1960 the college opened with Dr. Joe B. Rushing as president and 701 students. The campus was a dismal, abandoned Naval Air Station at the Fort Lauderdale-Hollywood International Airport. The insects and dust were pervasive. Students attended class armed with a can of bug repellent and dust cloths.

Dr. Rushing resigned in 1965 and was succeeded by Dr. Myron Blee

The Naval Air Station barracks where Broward Community College first began classes in 1960.

who, in turn, resigned in 1967 and was succeeded by Dr. A. Hugh Adams. Dr. Adams began his term as president in 1968, the same year the college separated from the supervision of the Broward County School Board and went under the auspices of its own District Board of Trustees. In addition, the school was renamed in 1968, from the Junior College of Broward County

to Broward Junior College. It would be renamed again in 1970 to Broward Community College.

Name changes, meanwhile, don't a college make. But comprehensive 10-year plans and a commitment to development do, and that is exactly what Dr. Adams had in mind.

The plan was a blueprint for three campuses, Central, North, and South, with other centers in high-population areas and many off-campus courses offered throughout the county.

The college's administration offices were centralized at 225 East Las Olas Boulevard in Fort Lauderdale. The Central Campus was built on a 152-acre site on Davie Road and includes the beautiful Ralph R. Bailey Concert Hall, Buehler Planetarium and Observatory, and the Criminal Justice Institute.

The North Campus, opened in 1970, is west of Pompano Beach in Coconut Creek. Buildings on the 113-acre tract include the OMNI, a multipurpose building used for teaching, an auditorium, and a gymnasium.

The South Campus (also known as the Judson A. Samuels Campus) began in a First Methodist Church in Hollywood in 1978. From there it expanded rapidly, and eventually was located on the North Perry Airport site at 7200 Hollywood Boulevard.

The college has expanded its programs until it has a comprehensive curriculum that offers work in various technical areas as well. Plans require continual reevaluation and adjustment to serve the educational needs of all facets of the Broward County community, the state, and the nation consonant with the college's purposes and resources.

In less than three decades Broward Community College has grown from the dust-swept campus for 701 students at an abandoned Naval Air Station, to a massive educational institution with three campuses and more than 52,000 students.

The new Broward Community College administration building on East Las Olas Boulevard in downtown Fort Lauderdale.

DIPLOMAT RESORT AND COUNTRY CLUBS

The Diplomat Resort and Country Clubs, in Hollywood, Florida, is one of Broward County's premier resort/convention complexes.

In the late 1940s Philadelphian Samuel Friedland, founder of the Food Fair supermarket chain, moved to Miami and began to scour the region for a good land investment.

The population growth, he perceived, would push north into Broward County, a place that was, at the time, barely developed. He bought more than 900 acres in Broward in Hollywood, some of it farmland (where one day he hoped to build a golf course and hotel) and part on the ocean. In 1956 Friedland began to build a hotel there and, as an adjunct to what he envisioned as a top-quality resort destination, a golf course.

It was a massive and risky project. Except for a few small motels and apartments sprinkled along the shore, the Hollywood Beach Hotel, and millions of land crabs, there was very little between Miami and Fort Lauderdale in the late 1950s.

Despite the obstacles, Friedland pushed ahead and, by the winter of 1957-1958, had finished the course, clubhouse, and a 150-room hotel on the west side of AIA near the sea. A year later the 370-room hotel opened on the beach and, setting a trend for top-name entertainment that would become one of the Diplomat Hotel's trademarks over the years, singer Tony Martin performed the hotel's first show.

Despite top-name entertainment and a first-class facility, however, the Diplomat still had problems. Set as it was there in the "boondocks," convention business was hard to sell and the management group Friedland had hired to run the hotel was making very little progress.

It was in 1960 that he asked his son-in-law, Irving Cowan, for help. Cowan was in the meat wholesale business in Bartow, Florida, and had no hotel-restaurant experience. But he was a determined and capable young man, and, it would be proved, an adroit hotelier.

Cowan fired the management group and began aggressively to make improvements. In 1963 they finished the first part of a new convention hall.

The following year they built a 150-room racquet club on Hallandale Beach Boulevard. In 1967 they completed a four-story addition with 150 rooms and more meeting space, and, in 1969, they added a tower with an additional 330 rooms.

From a 150-room motel in 1957, the Diplomat had grown, in less than 20 years, into a massive resort complex with 1,170 rooms, two golf courses, 19 tennis courts, and, at one point, 2,000 employees, more at the time than the cities of Hallandale and Hollywood combined.

Irving and his wife, Marjorie Cowan, meanwhile, had become fixtures in the Broward County tourism and entertainment milieu, host to Presidents and would-be Presidents, dignitaries, and the finest entertainers in the world. And the Diplomat had become a fixture as one of the county's premier resort/convention destinations, and would remain so for decades to come.

Irving Cowan, president, and his wife, Marjorie, are co-owners of the Diplomat Resort and Country Clubs.

FRED. S. JAMES & CO. OF FLORIDA, INC.

Fifty years before Fort Lauderdale was incorporated, Fred. S. James & Co., Inc., was already one of Chicago's largest insurance brokerage firms.

A hundred years later, in the late 1960s and early 1970s, it was one of the largest insurance brokerage firms in the world and planning to enter the brimming Florida market by opening an office in South Florida.

The company did so in 1971 by acquiring Walker Insurance Associates, an insurance agency owned by Thomas J. Walker, a successful Fort Lauderdale insurance entrepreneur and prominent citizen whose business was already one of the area's largest commercial insurance agencies. Walker's firm specialized in bonds, marine, aviation, and commercial insurance, a direction James continued after the acquisition.

Walker became the first president of Fred. S. James & Co. of Florida, Inc., with headquarters in Fort Lauderdale, and during the next decade it would expand its staff and departments to include personal lines, employee benefits, technical services, self-insurance, mass marketing, and captives, a new field in which the Fort Lauderdale office became a specialist.

In 1980 the firm named Edward A. Prater, executive vice-president and head of office, and Thomas N. Tight, Sr., senior vice-president and sales manager, to help direct the office's dramatic growth and to continue to add prestigious local and national clients.

In November 1982 Fred. S. James became a wholly owned subsidiary of Transamerica Corporation, a major, publicly held conglomerate, and the Fort Lauderdale office continued to grow despite a nationwide economic decline in the industry. By 1983 its offices occupied the entire 24th floor of the city's Landmark Bank Building and had more than 55 employees.

A hundred years and a decade after Fred. S. James began his agency in Chicago, the company had 5,000 employees worldwide, $242 million in revenues, $20 million in earnings, and was one of the top five insurance brokers and consultants in the world.

And in Fort Lauderdale its office had become one of the firm's largest and most successful.

The officers of Fred. S. James & Co. of Florida, Inc., are (seated) Thomas J. Walker, president; and (standing, left to right) Thomas N. Tight, Sr., senior vice-president; and Edward A. Prater, executive vice-president. © 1983 Bill Groendyke.

ROGERS, MORRIS AND ZIEGLER, ATTORNEYS-AT-LAW

Rogers, Morris and Ziegler was founded by John E. Morris, Sr., and Dwight L. Rogers, Sr., in Fort Lauderdale in 1925. Both men, drawn to Broward County by the Florida land boom, remained here after the 1926 hurricane and the subsequent economic collapse because of their vision of the area's immense potential.

They stayed and raised families through Broward's best and worst of times and, following their deaths, their sons carried on in the tradition they had begun.

Their firm's first office was in the Marshall Building on Northwest New River Drive downtown. In 1927 the firm moved into the Sweet Building on Andrews Avenue where, during those early days, virtually every Broward attorney seemed to have an office.

In 1928 they supported George W. Tedder, Sr., in an election for Broward's only circuit judgeship. Tedder won, but the incumbent, Vincent C. Giblin, refused to vacate the office. Eventually Giblin surrendered

his place on the bench and Tedder occupied the office. Later Rogers and Morris could joke that had Giblin remained on the bench, they would have had to leave town.

In 1931 Rogers was elected to the Florida State House of Representatives, where he served until 1938. In 1944 he was elected to his first of five terms as U.S. congressman. In December 1954, after being reelected in November to his sixth term, Dwight Rogers died of a heart attack. He was succeeded by his son, Paul, who served 12 terms in Congress.

Sons Dwight Jr. and John Jr. joined the firm after service in World War II. They were lifelong friends, schoolmates, and even served as president of the same fraternity at the University of Florida. From 1947 to 1952 John served as Fort Lauderdale

municipal judge and, in the early 1950s, as attorney for the Broward County School Board.

Rogers, meanwhile, was an assistant state attorney from 1948 to 1952 during which time he was responsible for shutting down the infamous illegal gambling casino, the Colonial Inn.

John Morris, Sr., died in 1955, just months after the death of his law partner, Dwight Rogers, Sr. The sons continued the firm, adding, in 1955, partner Robert E. Ziegler, born in Miami and educated at the Universities of Florida and Miami. In addition to his active practice, he is the firm's managing partner. J. Patrick Dyal, from the University of Georgia, became a partner in 1969. Then came Dwight's son, Romney Rogers, from Rutgers and Mercer University where the senior Rogers and Morris had earned their law degrees; he was followed by William C. Davell, from Ohio but educated at Stetson University.

The law firm, through the years, maintained a general practice in order to retain the close personal relationship with clients that Rogers and Morris felt was the cornerstone of their success. To meet their clients' changing legal needs, partners have acquired expertise in special areas of the law, including wills and estate planning, trial practice, corporate law, and real estate law.

For over 25 years Rogers, Morris and Ziegler's clients have included banks in Broward County. Presently it represents Sun Banks, the largest bank in the county. Rogers is on the board of Sun Banks, Inc., and is vice-chairman of the Sun Bank in Broward County. Morris also serves as a director of the bank.

Through three generations the law firm of Rogers, Morris and Ziegler has maintained the pioneer spirit and community consciousness that has been an integral part of the firm's success.

The partners in the law firm of Rogers, Morris and Ziegler are (seated, left to right) Dwight L. Rogers, Jr., John E. Morris, Jr., and (standing, left to right) Romney C. Rogers, Robert E. Ziegler, J. Patrick Dyal, and William C. Davell.

MADSEN, SAPP, MENA, RODRIGUEZ & CO., PA

As many had been before him, Joseph E. Phillips was lured to Fort Lauderdale's palm-studded coast by the 1920s boom and then marooned there by the dreadful hurricane of 1926 and the even more dreadful Depression which followed.

Unlike some of his friends who moved out during these hard times, Phillips, his wife, and six children stayed and became part of the community's early—if somewhat reluctant—pioneers.

Phillips, an IRS man, had come to Fort Lauderdale from Washington, D.C., and, in the 1930s, was one of two certified public accountants in the county. He was young, impeccably honest, implacably fair, and would, during the coming years, be the motivating personality in one of the county's most enduring and respected public accounting firms. But not, of course, without help from his friends.

Phillips became auditor for the City of Fort Lauderdale, a duty he performed for 24 years. He also met and worked with virtually everyone in town. His business grew and by the early '40s it was clear that he would have to expand. And so, during the war, he hired a young bookkeeper whose poor eyesight had kept him from the military.

Arthur F. Madsen signed on with Phillips and stayed with the firm for 40 years, specializing in estate planning and trust work, tax planning, and tax-return preparation.

Less than three years later, in January 1946, Phillips hired A. Edwin Sapp. As a Fort Lauderdale High School senior, Sapp had worked part time for Phillips before World War II. When he returned from the service he signed on for a career during which he would not only become the firm's managing partner, but also an expert in business information management, individual, estate, and trust tax matters.

Phillips began his practice on the

Arthur F. Madsen

A. Edwin Sapp

Edwin G. Mena

Ramon A. Rodriguez

second floor of the old Bryan Building in downtown Fort Lauderdale, later moving to the Hector Building on New River, then as the firm grew, moved it to the Radio Building on Las Olas Boulevard. He turned the firm over to his longtime friends and partners, Madsen and Sapp, in 1968 and he died two years later. But what he had begun, 42 years earlier, went on.

Madsen and Sapp moved to 727 Northeast Third Avenue in 1974, not long after they had taken in Ramon A. Rodriguez, and shortly after moving, Edwin G. Mena joined the firm. Rodriguez, a Florida Atlantic University graduate, became an expert in auditing, cost accounting, taxation

for business, manufacturing management, and more. Mena, who had 21 years in public accounting, excelled in estate and gift tax planning, individual, corporate, and foreign income taxes, and tax management.

In 1980 Rodriguez became the concern's managing partner and, two years later, was elected chairman of the Florida Board of Accountancy.

By the 1980s the firm was Madsen, Sapp, Mena, Rodriguez & Co., PA, with corporate offices on East Oakland Park Boulevard, clients throughout the world, and a proud heritage. This CPA firm with experience in commerce, industry, community affairs, and business practices in Broward County is rivaled by few others.

LANGSTROTH MORTGAGE COMPANY

In 1969, only 14 years ago, State Road 7 was considered the boondocks of Western Broward with "doggies" and MacArthur Dairy the major landmarks. Oakland Park Boulevard west of the turnpike was a vast undeveloped wetland; Inverrary was a dream, so was Welleby; and Coral Springs was just being chartered as a model community. "Condominium" was a new word, as were "subordination," "esculpultory," and "encumbrance" to Russell H. Langstroth, who was just beginning to cut his teeth in the mortgage business. Langstroth's career began with D.R. Mead and Company.

Langstroth's early training and full mortgage banking exposure provided a solid basis. "We had to report to work at 8:30 each morning and did not leave until the project we were working on was ready for submission to a lender. This work ethic and striving to provide the best possible service for the client has been the key to my company's success," he says.

Starting from a den in a Coral Ridge residence, Langstroth Mortgage Company was formed in January 1972. "It was an exciting time," Langstroth remembers. The real estate investment trusts and banks were competing for multimillion-dollar construction loans. "I was fortunate enough to place over $30 million in mortgages my first year."

In September 1973 Langstroth Mortgage Company moved to a new corporate headquarters at 2880 West Oakland Park Boulevard. The firm has operated from there ever since in a building Langstroth developed with other partners. "That experience gave me important insight from a developer's point of view," Langstroth says.

Not only has Broward County grown and changed by leaps and bounds, but so has the mortgage lending business. The emergence of the savings and loan institutions in the '60s nudged the life insurance companies from residential to commercial lending. Inflation during the '70s pushed the life insurance companies into the equity sector and left a serious void in the long-term marketplace, especially during the recent high-rate cycles.

After surviving the 1974 to 1977 real estate crunch, Langstroth decided to expand his operation into a multi-dimensional company. Flexibility and diversification are the cornerstone to Langstroth Mortage Company today. "First, we formed two separate divisions: residential and commercial. Residentially, we arrange first- and second-mortgage financing on homes, condominiums, townhouses, duplexes, triplexes, and quadplexes. Loans range from $10,000 to one million dollars on first mortgages and no dollar limits on second mortgages. Commercially, we place mortgages on apartments, shopping centers, office buildings, warehouses, hotels, motels, hospitals, and condominiums," Langstroth explains.

Langstroth Mortgage Company prides itself in being able to accommodate any real estate financing request that makes economic sense in a professional and timely manner. "I am pleased to have been in a position where the financing I have arranged on various projects has provided others with the opportunity to live and work in a community I am proud to call home."

The Langstroth Mortgage Company's financing covers a diverse range from commercial to residential properties.

AUTOHAUS

Between Fort Lauderdale, the "Venice of America" with its ocean-access canals, meandering river, huge yachts, and multimillion-dollar homes, and Palm Beach, with its legendary wealth, is the city of Pompano Beach, hardly an impoverished enclave in its own right.

And to Rudy Kraft in the mid-1970s, it seemed a very likely place to fulfill his lifelong dream. As a child, Kraft had known he wanted to own his own automobile dealership. In high school his spare time was spent overhauling engines. His first job, at 13, was in a used car lot. His BA degree in business administration was from the General Motors Institute of Technology in Flint, Michigan. In fact, everything he had done seemed to point the way to Pompano Beach.

As zone manager for the southeastern United States for Mercedes-Benz of North America, Kraft traveled often to South Florida and so, when he heard a Mercedes franchise in Pompano Beach was up for sale, the idea was too tempting to pass up. And for many reasons.

R.A. Kraft, president of Autohaus.

He knew the dealership. It began in 1968 as the ancillary operation of a Volkswagen dealership next door to its 744 North Federal Highway location. The owner was Jan Brundage; it was called "Brumos" (short for Brundage Motors), and it sold both Mercedes-

Benz and Porsche sports cars. Brumos had 16 employees, including a sales staff of two who one day, it was planned, would be able to sell 10 Mercedes a month.

Brundage made the first addition to the dealership in 1971 when he added six bays, but the next year, eager to join the infant cable-television industry, he sold Brumos to Henry and Marie Martens, a retired couple who had been successful industrialists in Wisconsin.

From 1972 until 1977 Henry Martens operated the Volkswagen franchise and Marie the Mercedes dealership. When they decided to sell, it was Kraft who stepped up to bid. He knew the Martens and Brundage well. And he also knew that their operation had a good reputation, good employees, outstanding department heads, and, from a marketing standpoint, a spectacular location. So, in November 1977, Kraft bought Autohaus, as it would be called.

In the beginning he operated on a shoestring and wondered if he had done the right thing. When he began, there were 35 employees and $9 million in annual sales. He sold the Volkswagen dealership in order to concentrate company efforts on the Mercedes. The emphasis, he decided, would be on service and parts. What kept customers coming back to a luxury auto dealer, he knew, was superior service and maintenance.

Autohaus built a body shop that was completed in 1980, an 8,000-square-foot building that it outgrew in less than two years. By the end of 1983 Kraft was planning two more expansions, one for additional body repair space and service bays, and one for additional parts and general office space. By the end of Kraft's first five years, Autohaus sales were up to 40 new Mercedes-Benz a month and $25 million a year, there were 72 employees, and for Rudy Kraft, a boyhood dream had come true.

The Pompano Beach Mercedes-Benz dealership, Autohaus, is located at 744 North Federal Highway.

CORAL RIDGE INTERIORS, INC.

Josephine Robinson, founder of Coral Ridge Interiors, Inc.

James Robinson, manager of Coral Ridge Interiors since 1964.

The fact is, Josephine Robinson was bored. Her husband Harry was traveling as a sales representative for a major cement company and she was in Fort Lauderdale with nothing to do. She had, of course, a degree from the University of Wisconsin-Stout, and had studied interior design at the Academy of Fine Arts in Chicago. But she had never thought, really, about putting that training to commercial use.

At least, not until 1955.

That year she took $3,000 and bought the Drapery Plaza, a small storefront at Federal Highway and Oakland Park Boulevard. She began to retail draperies and answer customers' questions about their interior design problems. Her new shop quickly evolved into an interior design firm, helping northern newcomers develop their homes into the airy, lighter "Florida look" they so wanted.

Within four months she had formed a partnership with two New York designers, Joseph Spencer and Charles

Marks, and renamed the firm "Robinson, Spencer and Marks."

The firm's early growth paralleled that of Fort Lauderdale, which is to say, it was phenomenal. By 1960 Jo Robinson had dissolved her partnership with Spencer and Marks and created Coral Ridge Interiors, Inc. In addition, she had moved the store to a 5,000-square-foot space on 34th Street near the beach. She knew something big was about to happen in the area, something that would make her company's growth even more dramatic.

And dramatic it was. Across the street, along the beach dunes, rose one of the county's most astonishing construction projects, a forest of high-rise hotels and apartment buildings dubbed the Galt Ocean Mile. It was built by Coral Ridge Properties, one of Jo Robinson's customers, and it would provide her firm with creative and business challenges for years to come. There were lobbies and homes and apartments by the score, and with each job and each success the reputation of Coral Ridge Interiors grew.

Business had become so brisk by

1964 that Jo Robinson needed help; so she asked her son James to join her and manage the company. Jim Robinson was a career Naval officer, a fighter pilot, and a Naval Academy graduate who had some experience in - real estate and general construction but none in interior design. It was a drawback he quickly would overcome.

As the Galt Ocean Mile neared completion, Coral Ridge Interiors' customers began to come from farther north along the beach as well as from new single-family markets in Coral Ridge Properties developments in other parts of Broward County.

In July 1977 Jim located a 15,000-square-foot building on North Federal Highway near Commercial Boulevard. It would provide enough space not only for the company's growing inventory of furniture and accessories, but for its five full-time designers and 20 employees as well. What had started in 1955 as a tiny drapery store had grown into one of Broward's largest interior design firms.

WFTL RADIO

The last time ownership of WFTL, the oldest radio station (FCC-approved 1946) in Broward County, changed hands was in 1958. Its location? On Southeast Fifteenth Street, just west of the Intracoastal Waterway. Offices and studios? What now is the Marine Building near the public small boat launch area. The seller? R.H. Gore, Sr., who also owned the *Fort Lauderdale News*. The new president? Joseph C. Amaturo, a diminutive, energetic, newly married, Harvard Business School graduate. The purpose? A new start, this time with radio people in a market that was just beginning to be appreciated as one of most dynamic growth areas in America.

Despite its previous consistent record of losses, within months WFTL became profitable and has stayed profitable ever since.

Just ask Joe, and he will tell you that the station's prosperity was due as much to the area's growth as to any efforts his group might have introduced. Perhaps. But what was the success formula? Complete immersion into the community with local news, local service, plus an intricate blend of adult appeal music, topped off by using locally oriented "personality" announcers. In the news area, then as now, no other broadcast facility has more on-the-street reporters. The result? For 25 years WFTL has achieved a consistency with a seasoned, loyal listener base large enough to make the station a viable advertising and public service medium.

But it was during hurricane season that WFTL became the hurricane station serving Broward County. Its commitment to quality news coverage gave it a reputation separate from its competitors—and that includes its hurricane service.

But WFTL also has had its share of fun. Each April 1st, the station pulls an April Fool's joke on its listeners. One year it was a fake strike; another year it

Top: Broadcast Boat, 1946.

Bottom: Broadcast House, 1983.

was an on-the-air argument and resignation by its most popular announcer.

Beginning in 1963 the company began experimenting with a sister FM station to complement WFTL-AM. The experiment enjoyed mixed results, until finally "JOY 107 FM" (WWJF) hit the air.

Today Amaturo Group, Inc., consists of a group of leading stations located in markets such as Houston, Detroit, and St. Louis, and also includes the Nebraska Television Network, which is the ABC affiliate voice that covers over 100,000 square

miles.

But even now in Florida, Amaturo and WFTL have passed 25 years on the air in Broward and, in his words, nothing would stop them now. "We believed the prognostications about Broward being a growth area in 1958 and we believe it has the same growth potential in 1983. It is still going to grow like crazy and, in AM and FM, we plan to grow with South Florida."

219

McLAUGHLIN ENGINEERING COMPANY

The Minnesota winters held a deadly grip on J.W. (Jim) McLaughlin's father during the early 1900s. His bouts with pneumonia were chronic and the prognosis was clear: move to a more temperate climate or face the consequences.

And so it was that the McLaughlin family came to Fort Lauderdale in 1925. At the time it was the land of promise. The city and Broward County were locked in the throes of a vigorous land boom. Real estate speculators flourished, fortunes were made overnight, and the local economy looked so spectacularly strong it would last forever.

In fact, it barely lasted for two more years.

The 1926 hurricane (and subsequent, although less severe, storms over the next three years) made the rest of America's economic collapse in 1929 almost unnoticeable. When Jim McLaughlin graduated from Fort Lauderdale High School in 1929 there was not much of anything around, least of all jobs.

But through a friend the miraculous happened: McLaughlin signed on as a chainman with Fort Lauderdale's oldest civil engineering and land surveying firm, Charlton and Davis, later named Charlton and Associates, Engineer Surveyors.

In land surveying the chainman holds the surveying rod so that others can make appropriate measurements. At 20 cents an hour McLaughlin welcomed the work, but it was not going to be his career choice.

Charlton and Davis, who were resident engineers for the Florida Inland Navigation District, designed and surveyed the Intracoastal Waterway from Jupiter Inlet to Biscayne Bay in the early 1930s.

McLaughlin began night school to improve his chances for professional advancement, gained his engineering license, and in 1937 he became a partner. Within two years he began his

McLaughlin Engineering Company began at 400 Northeast Third Avenue in 1938. The McLaughlin home is in the background.

own firm and, with his wife Frances, and Alice Jones (Forum), opened an office over Hardy's Drug Store in the Bryan Arcade at South Andrews Avenue and Southeast Second Street in Fort Lauderdale. The family resided at 400 Northeast Third Avenue, and decided to move the business there also. It was a location that would serve McLaughlin Engineering well. Forty-five years later the corporate and administrative headquarters remain at the same spot.

During the first three years, the only full-time employees were the McLaughlins and three hourly workers (including Willis Fail who, in 1983, was still with the firm). They worked out of Jim's garage and jobs came slowly. Then, in the early '40s,

they were awarded significant jobs at the Boca Raton Naval Air Station and the Port Everglades complex and the future, promised to McLaughlin's father by Florida nearly 20 years before, seemed fulfilled.

Then came the war. The Navy called McLaughlin into the Seabees and from 1943 until the armistice he was in the Pacific. Although the business was closed, Frances maintained the records and subcontracted work to other firms,

J.W. (Jim) McLaughlin (left) directs survey crew on the initial survey of Galt Ocean Mile in 1953. Son James is kneeling in the foreground.

especially that of Walter McElfresh, an early local surveyor and engineer.

In August 1945 McLaughlin returned and, on his first day back, was commissioned to do a surveying job on the beach. McLaughlin Engineering quickly went back to work and began a growth cycle that would make it one of the county's most prominent engineering and surveying firms.

In the late '40s Coral Ridge Properties gave McLaughlin a major opportunity by developing the county's first and largest upper-income residential neighborhood, Coral Ridge. In addition, another development, this one for working class families, began in Chateau Park. Both projects sold rapidly and the demand for housing in Broward grew dramatically.

McLaughlin grew with it and the increased demand meant long hours and back-breaking work. Coral Ridge, for example, was partly a mangrove swamp, and when it was first being surveyed for development, McLaughlin crews had to hack their way through the vegetation to make proper surveys.

In the 1950s the company grew rapidly. Besides Coral Ridge, projects included Bahia Mar, Galt Ocean Mile, the cities of Lauderdale Lakes, Margate, and, later in the '60s, Plantation Acres and virtually all of Coral Springs.

The firm has worked not only throughout the state but in the Caribbean as well, from the Kennedy Space Center to Curaçao, from the Everglades to Eleuthera Island in the Bahamas. McLaughlin Engineering has done major projects for the Department of Transportation, country clubs, developments, and shopping malls. Jim McLaughlin maintained a high profile in the community, serving as an appointee on the Fort Lauderdale Planning and Zoning Board, the Board of

Adjustment, and the Contractors' Examining Board of Broward County.

In time McLaughlin's sons—James, the eldest, and Robert—would become involved in company management. As children they had worked in the business after school and evenings running blueprints and doing errands. On weekends the boys would work in the field with surveying crews and later they chose a career with their father.

For over 20 years James Jr. has managed various company operations; he became president in 1979. Robert became involved in management in the early 1970s, and was named vice-president in 1974. In addition, a third generation of

Still located at the same Northeast Third Avenue location, McLaughlin Engineering spans three generations and now has 35 employees.

McLaughlins was already busy working in the company.

By the early 1980s there were more than 35 employees at McLaughlin Engineering, including computer specialists, draftsmen, and field crews. Jim McLaughlin, now in his seventies, could look at the company he founded nearly 40 years before with certainty it would endure for generations to come.

The founder of the firm, Jim McLaughlin (seated), poses with his sons (standing, left to right), James and Robert.

FEDERAL MILLWORK CORPORATION

It is one of the curious ironies in Broward County that you might pass by Federal Millwork Corporation on your way to the airport hundreds of times without realizing the company is even there. And yet, it is a huge, 50,000-plus-square-foot factory for the creation of custom millwork and cabinetry, one of the leading suppliers of such products in the Southeast.

Located east of U.S. 1 at 3300 South Federal Highway since it began in 1945, Federal Millwork is one of Broward's oldest businesses, built by a young, energetic custom woodworking specialist, Paul Ziebart.

The company started as a partnership between Ziebart, a former Broward Marine employee, and then-sheriff Robert Clark. Ziebart built the plant from the foundation up. On Thanksgiving Day, 1945, Ziebart and his five-year-old son, Paul Jr., began digging the foundation for the building that would house not only the business but the family as well.

The original structure was 32 feet wide by 64 feet long, 500 square feet of which became the Ziebarts' home for two years.

In February 1946, prior to completing the structure, the business opened due to the pressing demand for building supplies. Finding it difficult to work around the construction debris, Paul hired his first employee, Lou Freeman, still dressed in his Navy uniform.

In 1947 the first addition to the facility was built, and a two-story concrete structure with a mezzanine was later added. By 1955 expansion was again necessary and so a corporation was formed, $125,000 was borrowed, a permanent structure was built around the lumber, and a department for finishing was created with the addition of a new mezzanine.

Ziebart had outgrown his zeal for millwork by 1964 and sold the firm to his cabinet hardware suppliers from Miami, Top Products Supply

This aerial view shows Federal Millwork Corporation shortly after the first addition was completed in 1947.

Company, along with an established cabinetmaker, George Yeoman. While Yeoman was familiar with kitchen cabinets, his new partners, Robert Boulter and Russell Watt, were factory representatives with a mutual resume which included several years with General Electric.

Just 19 years and one month from the day the foundation was dug, the new owners were about to contribute to the end of a flourishing business. Mortgaging all within their grasp, Boulter and Watt, along with help from family and friends such as Ed Gray, bought Yeoman's interest and began to turn the tide. They promoted 12-year employee Lyle Mathison to shop superintendent and a talented Welsh craftsman, Dennis Counsell, to shop foreman.

Richard Ungerbuehler joined the firm in 1970 to help bolster the sales

and estimating force. He maintained his relationship as a director of Christian education in the Church of the Nazarene and in 1978 returned to the ministry.

Robert Boulter was stricken with a massive heart attack and died in 1979. His partner, then 64 years of age, brought Ungerbuehler back as his general manager, a post he held until Watt's death in 1981. At that time he became president and part owner with his two partners, Lyle Mathison and Dennis Counsell.

With an enviable reputation for quality and service, Federal Millwork, the "Home of Wonders In Wood," holds the world as its marketplace where its fine-quality products may be found in churches, hospitals, restaurants, hotels, and schools, as well as exquisite apartments and homes.

Although taken in 1956, this photograph depicts much the way Federal Millwork looks today. Only the surrounding landscape has changed.

MEMORIAL HOSPITAL

In 1947 the Florida Legislature acceded to the requests of a committee of dedicated south Broward citizens and passed the South Broward Hospital District Act, a bill that would, given the approval of local voters, establish a taxing authority with the ability to build, operate, and maintain a public hospital for the region.

At the time there was no public, nonprofit health facility in south Broward. In fact, only two hospitals with 71 beds existed to serve a population of 29,000. A hurricane in 1950 added impetus to the idea of a large public hospital in Hollywood, where the hurricane's impact was most severe. The injured in West Hollywood had to travel over debris-strewn roads to hospitals as far away as Fort Lauderdale or Miami.

In 1950 the act creating the South Broward Hospital District was ratified by the region's voters and a million-dollar construction bond issue was approved by voters a year later.

On February 16, 1953, the hospital first opened its doors. It had a nursing department staff of 28, with 32 doctors on staff and 100 beds. Its tiny two-

story building at 35th Avenue and Johnson Street was practically in the wilderness. The caseload on its first day: 12 patients.

By contrast, in 1982 Memorial was a 728-bed acute care general hospital with a medical staff of more than 380 doctors and dentists and 2,450 employees. The nursing staff exceeded 800. In one year Memorial and its medical staff have experienced 25,000 admissions, 54,000 emergency cases, and performed 8,700 operations.

The hospital's growth during the first 30 years was dramatic. By the late '50s the original two-story facility had added an autopsy building, an east annex for medical units, and an obstetrical care area, and there were plans for a $4-million expansion program.

An eight-story expansion was finished by August 1963, dominating the Hollywood skyline, and more expansion followed with the Ester L. Rosenthal Pavilion in 1967 and the S.S. Holland Wing in 1974.

Memorial now offers a full program of diagnostic and therapeutic procedures in radiology, including

radiation therapy, cardiac catheterization, and CAT scan; comprehensive obstetrical services, including a neonatal intensive care unit; a pediatrics unit; alcoholism treatment unit; and psychiatric unit. Its medical staff represents all clinical specialties.

It is administered by a governor-appointed, seven-member board of commissioners and in 1975 opened a 24-hour, walk-in Medical Center in neighboring Pembroke Pines. The walk-in center offers a modern treatment, observation, and holding area; a laboratory; and radiology services.

By the early '80s Memorial was one of Florida's five largest hospitals and the most sophisticated and largest health care facility serving the South Broward Hospital District communities. The hospital is currently in the first stage of a multi-phased program of modernization that will extend through the 1980s and cost $50 to $60 million.

Memorial Hospital is located at 3501 Johnson Street in Hollywood.

BARNETT BANK OF SOUTH FLORIDA, N.A.

William B. Barnett founded a bank in Jacksonville, Florida, in March 1877. And, more than one hundred years later, events occurred that created one of the largest banking institutions in the state—Barnett Banks of Florida, Inc.

By 1983 Barnett Banks of Florida, Inc., was an $8-billion holding company serving 118 cities with 240 locations, 16 of which were in Broward County.

The Barnett system in South Florida

Barnett Bank Plaza, Fort Lauderdale.

truly began on January 1, 1977, when the state legislature approved branch banking within a county. As a result, seven individual Barnett Banks became the Barnett Bank of Broward County headed by its chairman, J. Edward Houston, a lifelong resident of Broward County, past U.S. Bankruptcy Judge, attorney, and civic activist. The original seven banks included the Barnett Bank of Plantation, which opened for business in January 1964 as the First Bank of Plantation.

Today's Fort Lauderdale office, known as the Fort Lauderdale Industrial and Savings Bank and the Central Bank, is a descendant of one of the oldest commercial banks in the Fort Lauderdale area. The Barnett Bank of Riverland opened its doors for business in September 1971. Barnett's first step into the southern end of the state started with the acquisition of the Bank of Hollywood, later known as the Hollywood Bank and Trust Company.

Originally formed in November 1950, it was one of the first state banks organized in the state of Florida and was ranked ninth in size at the time. The Barnett Bank of West Hollywood, the Barnett Bank of Port Everglades, and the Barnett Bank of Jacaranda became part of the Barnett Banks of Florida, Inc., between 1973 and 1975 to further meet the needs of an ever-growing community. By May 1978 Barnett's first de novo office located on East Commercial Boulevard in Fort Lauderdale had opened. In April 1977 Barnett Bank of Broward County's ninth office and Barnett Banks of Florida's 100th office in the state of Florida had opened in Miramar.

In 1979 the state legislature passed still another banking law allowing banks to branch across county lines. On July 1, 1981, offices in Broward County and Dade County, including the city of Homestead, were consolidated and officially became known as Barnett Bank of South Florida, N.A. The chairman of the Barnett Bank of Broward County, J. Edward Houston, assumed leadership of the newly formed bank as its president and chief executive officer.

Barnett Bank of South Florida has acquired two other banks since 1981 — the First State Bank of Miami and Great American Banks.

From 1977 to 1983, Barnett Bank of South Florida, N.A., grew from seven offices to 45 and its assets rose from $200 million to $2.2 billion, making it the 126th-largest commercial bank in the United States.

PATRONS

The following individuals, companies, and organizations have made a valuable commitment to the quality of this publication. Windsor Publications and the Fort Lauderdale Historical Society, Inc., gratefully acknowledge their participation in *Fort Lauderdale and Broward County: An Illustrated History*.

ACR Electronics, Inc.*
AIRPAX
   Ft. Lauderdale Division
Hollywood Commissioner Cathleen Anderson
Dr. & Mrs. Robert Andreae
Arvida Corporation*
Autohaus*
Bahia Mar*
Barnett Bank of South Florida, N.A.*
Broward Community College*
Broward Federal Savings and Loan Association*
Bruce Plywoods, Inc.
Les Byron Associates*
Causeway Lumber Company*
Chicago Title Insurance Company
Coral Ridge Hospital*
Coral Ridge Interiors, Inc.*
Coral Ridge Properties, Inc.*
Curcie Brothers, Inc.*
Dania Jai Alai*
Danish Furniture Center, Inc.
Diplomat Resort and Country Clubs*
English, McCaughan & O'Bryan*
Leonard L. Farber Incorporated*
Federal Millwork Corporation*
15th Street Fisheries
First American Title Insurance Company
Fleming, O'Bryan and Fleming*
Florida Coast Banks, Inc.*
Fort Lauderdale Area Board of REALTORS®, Inc.*
Fort Lauderdale High School—Class 1943
Fort Lauderdale News/Sun-Sentinel*
FPA Corporation*
Gould Inc., S.E.L. Computer Systems Division*
Gulfstream Land & Development Corp.*
Hardrives Company*

Mr. & Mrs. Paul D. Himmelrich
Hollywood, Inc.*
Hollywood Federal Savings and Loan Association*
Holy Cross Hospital*
Huron Machine Products, Inc.*
Fred S. James & Co. of Florida, Inc.*
Jungle Queen*
LaBonte Diversified Holdings, Inc.*
Lago Mar*
Landmark First National Bank*
Langstroth Mortgage Company*
McCune, Hiaasen, Crum, Ferris & Gardner*
Charles F. McKirahan, Jr., A.I.A.—Architect*
McLaughlin Engineering Company*
Madsen, Sapp, Mena, Rodriguez & Co., PA*
Mai Kai*
Mayhue's*
Memorial Hospital*
MODCOMP: Modular Computer Systems, Inc.*
North Broward Hospital District*
North Ridge General Hospital*
Novatronics, Inc.*
Nova University*
Pine Crest*
Rauch, Weaver, Millsaps & Co.
Regency Square Properties, Inc.
Law Offices of Dewey A.F. Ries, P.A.
Rogers, Morris and Zeigler, Attorneys-at-Law*
Frank J. Rooney, Inc.*
Wallace and Nell Setliff
Steel Fabricators, Inc.*
Sun Bank/South Florida, N.A.*
John & Leah Thomason
University Community Hospital*
Waste Management, Inc.*
Waterway Restaurants, Inc.*
WFTL Radio*
Virginia S. Young

* Partners in Progress of *Fort Lauderdale and Broward County: An Illustrated History*. The histories of these companies and organizations appear in Chapter 8, beginning on page 158.

ACKNOWLEDGMENTS

In writing a book one must draw on the help of many people. Special thanks must go to Dr. Cooper Kirk, county historian and editor, *Broward Legacy,* Broward County Historical Commission, who read the entire manuscript and offered many helpful observations that made this a better and more accurate book. Thanks are due to Dr. Harry Kersey, Florida Atlantic University, our resident authority on the Seminoles, who reviewed the early chapters in which Florida's Indians played so prominent a role.

A list of people who helped by sharing their scrapbooks, their memories, and their expert knowledge of Broward County's history must include:

Maynard Abrams, George Allen, Bobbie Amo, Kathleen Anderson, Robert Anderson, Vicki Askew, Maxine Banash, Steve Bourie, Lois Brickhouse, Lucille Gillespie Brown, August Burghard, Bob Carr, Russell Carson, M.D., Eugene Chamberlain, M.D., Philip Cheaney, Harriet Colucci, Mary Copeland, Sherman Crise, Betty Alexander Davis, James Dean, Emily Dietrich, Burns A. Dobbins, M.D., Allen Finkelson, Foy B. Fleming, Charles Forman, Hamilton C. Forman, Becky Gerren, Gypsy Graves, Ronnie Grossfeld, Phyllis Guy, Talle Hasis, Carl Hiassen, Helen Hoffman, Gordon Ickes, Norman Johnson, Betty Mae Jumper, Carolyn Kayne, Marlyn Kemper, Stewart Kester, Eddie King, Kenneth King, Joe Knetsch, Edmond Markel, C. Gray Mullon, James Naugle, George T.F. Rahilly, M.D., Bill Raymond, Ethel Rosen, Joanne Runkel, L.B. Slater, Veronika Stalcup, Neil Sterling, Bill Stewart, Hully Stirling, Midge Turpen, Hewitt Wagner, Phil Weidling, Bernard Welsh, Lee Wentworth, Patsy West, and Virginia Young.

BIBLIOGRAPHY

Books

Blake, Nelson M. *Land into Water— Water into Land.* Tallahassee: University Presses of Florida, 1980.

Buker, George E. *Swamp Sailors.* Gainesville: University Presses of Florida, 1975.

Burghard, August. *Alligator Alley.* Fort Lauderdale: Lanman Company, 1969

———. *From $2,519 to a Billion Plus— the Story of First Federal Savings and Loan Association of Broward.* Fort Lauderdale: Wake-Brook House, 1977.

———. *Half a Century in Florida.* Fort Lauderdale: Manatee Books, 1982.

———. *The Story of Frederick C. Peters.* Fort Lauderdale: Tropical Press, Inc., 1972.

———. *Watchie-Esta/Hutrie (The Little White Mother).* Fort Lauderdale: The Historical Society of Fort Lauderdale, 1968.

——— and Philip Weidling. *Checkered Sunshine—The History of Fort Lauderdale, 1793-1955.* Gainesville: University of Florida Press, 1966.

Carter, Luther J. *The Florida Experience—Land and Water Policy in a Growth State.* Baltimore and London: The John Hopkins University Press, 1974.

Caudle, Hal. *The Hanging at Bahia Mar.* Fort Lauderdale: Wake-Brook House, 1976.

Cory, Charles B. *Hunting and Fishing in Florida.* Boston: Estes and Lauriat, 1896.

Cuddy, Don. *Tales of Old Hollywood.* Decatur, Ill.: Spectator Books, 1977.

DeCroix, F.W. *An Historical and Progressive Review of Miami, Fort Lauderdale and other Sections in Dade County, Florida.* St. Augustine: The Record Company, 1911.

Douglas, Marjory Stoneman. *The Everglades.* New York: Rinehart & Company, 1947.

Eller, Warren T. *Port Everglades, Florida.* Privately printed, 1971.

Erkins, Albert W. and August Burghard. *My Early Days in Florida.* Fort Lauderdale: Wake-Brook House, 1975.

Glenn, James Lafayette. *My Work Among the Florida Seminoles.* Orlando: University Presses of Florida, 1982.

Hanna, Alfred Jackson and Kathryn Abbey. *Lake Okeechobee, Wellspring of the Everglades.* Indianapolis: The Bobbs-Merrill Company, 1948.

———. *Florida's Golden Sands.* Indianapolis: The Bobbs-Merrill Company, 1950.

Henshall, James A., M.D. *Camping and Cruising in Florida.* Cincinnati: Robert Clarke and Co., 1884

Hortt, M.A. *Gold Coast Pioneer.* New York: Exposition Press, 1953.

Johnson, Lamar. *Beyond the Fourth Generation.* Gainesville: University Presses of Florida, 1974.

Kefauver, Estes. *Crime in America.* New

York: Greenwood Press, 1968.

Kersey, Harry A., Jr. *Pelts, Plumes and Hides*. Gainesville: University Presses of Florida, 1975.

Kirk, Cooper. *William Lauderdale*. Fort Lauderdale: Manatee Books, 1982.

Linehan, Mary Collar. *Early Lantana*. St. Petersburg: Byron Kennedy & Co., no date.

Links, Inc. *Black Pioneers in Broward County*. Fort Lauderdale: Fort Lauderdale Chapter, The Links Incorporated, 1976.

MacCauley, Clay. *The Seminole Indians of Florida*. Washington: Bureau of American Ethnology, 1887.

McGoun, William. *A Biographic History of Broward County*. Miami: The Miami Herald, 1972.

_____. *Hallandale*. Boynton Beach: Star Publishing Company, 1976.

Mahon, John D. *History of the Second Seminole War*. Gainesville: University of Florida Press. 1967

Martin, Sidney Walter. *Florida's Flagler*. Athens, Ga.: University of Georgia Press. 1949.

Meddick, Hank. *Syndicate in the Sun*. London: The MacMillan Company, 1968.

_____. *Lansky*. New York: Putnam, 1971.

Motte, Jacob. *Journey Into Wilderness*. Gainesville: University of Florida Press, 1953.

Munros, Ralph Middleton and Vincent Gilpin. *The Commodore's Story*. Ives Washburn, 1930.

Nurmi, Victor, and August Burghard. *The Fabulous Finn*. Fort Lauderdale: Wake-Brook House, 1979.

Parks, Arva Moore. *Miami, the Magic City*. Tulsa, Okla.: Continental Heritage Press, Inc. 1981.

Peters, Thelma. *Lemon City*. Miami: Banyan Press, 1976.

Pierce, Charles W. *Pioneer Life in Southeast Florida*. Miami: University of Miami Press, 1970.

Proctor, Samuel. *Napoleon Bonaparte Broward*. Gainesville: University of Florida Press, 1950.

Smith, Horace. *A Captain Unafraid, the Strange Adventures of Dynamite Johnny O'Brien*. New York-London: Harper Bros., 1912.

Stuart, Hix C. *The Notorious Ashley Gang*. Stuart: St. Lucie Printing Co., 1928.

Swarthout, Glendon. *Where the Boys Are*. New York: Random House, 1960.

Ten Eyck, Virginia. *The History of Hollywood*. Hollywood: City of Hollywood, 1966.

Wagner, Victoria. *The History of Davie and Its Dilemma*. Davie: Nova University/New York Institute of Technology Press. 1982.

Will, Lawrence. *A Cracker History of Okeechobee*. St. Petersburg: Great Outdoors Publishing Co., 1964.

_____. *Okeechobee Boats & Skippers*, St. Petersburg: Great Outdoors Publishing Co., 1965.

_____. *Okeechobee Hurricane*. St. Petersburg: Great Outdoors Publishing Co., 1961.

Winer, Dick. *The Devil's Triangle*. New York: Bantam Books.

Young, Virginia. *Mangrove Roots of Fort Lauderdale*. Fort Lauderdale: Poinsettia Press, 1976.

Periodicals

Broward Legacy
The Florida Historical Quarterly
Fort Lauderdale News
Fort Lauderdale Sentinel
The Fort Lauderdale Weekly Herald
Miami Herald
Miami Metropolis
New River News
Sun-Sentinel
Tequesta
The Tropical Sun

Unpublished Manuscripts

Akin, Edward Nelson, "Southern Reflections of the Gilded Age: Henry M. Flagler's System, 1885-1913." Dissertation, University of Florida, 1975.

Kemper, Marlyn, "Pompano Beach in Perspective: A Comprehensive Documented History of the City of Pompano Beach." Survey sponsored by Historic Broward County Preservation Board, 1982.

Knetsch, Joe, "A Brief History of Broward County." 1982.

Megma, Ralph, and Patrick R. Currie, "New River Chronicle, A Documentary History of Life in the Fort Lauderdale Region, 1765 to 1911." Produced by the *Look Back, Fort Lauderdale!* project team, supported by a grant from the National Endowment for the Humanities, 1978.

Other Sources

Government documents from Dade and Broward County courthouses, U.S. District Court, South Florida Water Management District, and Florida Department of Transportation.

Historical collections at Fort Lauderdale Historical Society, Broward County Historical Commission, Historical Association of Southern Florida, Historical Society of Palm Beach County, the Flagler Archives, Broward County Public Library, as well as a number of city historical societies in the county.

Manuscript collections, principally the Stranahan and Wesley Stout Collections at the Fort Lauderdale Historical Society and the Flagler Collection at the Flagler Archives, Palm Beach.

INDEX